GINETTA
ROAD AND TRACK CARS

TITLES IN THE CROWOOD AUTOCLASSICS SERIES

Alfa Romeo 916 GTV and Spider
Alfa Romeo Spider
Aston Martin DB4, DB5 & DB6
Aston Martin DB7
Aston Martin V8
Audi quattro
Austin Healey 100 & 3000 Series
BMW M3
BMW M5
BMW Classic Coupés 1965-1989
BMW Z3 and Z4
Citroen DS Series
Classic Jaguar XK: The 6-Cylinder Cars 1948-1970
Classic Mini Specials and Moke
Ferrari 308, 328 & 348
Ford Consul, Zephyr and Zodiac
Ford Escort RS
Ford Transit: Fifty Years
Frogeye Sprite
Ginetta Road and Track Cars
Jaguar E-Type
Jaguar Mks 1 and 2, S-Type and 420
Jaguar XK8
Jensen V8
Jowett Javelin and Jupiter
Lamborghini Countach
Land Rover Defender
Land Rover Discovery: 25 Years of the Family 4×4
Land Rover Freelander
Lotus Elan
MGA
MGB
MGF and TF
MG T-Series
Mazda MX-5
Mercedes-Benz Cars of the 1990s
Mercedes-Benz 'Fintail' Models
Mercedes-Benz S-Class
Mercedes-Benz W124
Mercedes SL Series
Mercedes SL & SLC 107 Series 1971-2013
Mercedes-Benz W113
Morgan 4/4: The First 75 Years
Morgan Three-wheeler
Peugeot 205
Porsche 924/928/944/968
Porsche Boxster and Cayman
Porsche Carrera: The Air-Cooled Era
Range Rover: The First Generation
Reliant Three-Wheelers
Riley: The Legendary RMs
Rover 75 and MG ZT
Rover 800
Rover P4
Rover P5 & P5B
Rover SD1
Saab 99 & 900
Shelby and AC Cobra
Subaru Impreza WRX and WRX STI
Sunbeam Alpine & Tiger
Toyota MR2
Triumph Spitfire & GT6
Triumph TR: From Beginning to End
Triumph TR6
Triumph TR7
TVR: Cars of the Peter Wheeler Era
TVR 1946-1982
VW Karmann Ghias and Cabriolets
Volvo 1800
Volvo Amazon

GINETTA
ROAD AND TRACK CARS

TREVOR PYMAN

THE CROWOOD PRESS

First published in 2018 by
The Crowood Press Ltd
Ramsbury, Marlborough
Wiltshire SN8 2HR

www.crowood.com

British Library Cataloguing-in-Publication Data
A catalogue record for this book is available from the British Library.

ISBN 978 1 78500 415 5

Typeset by Jean Cussons Typesetting, Diss, Norfolk

Printed and bound in India by Parksons Graphics Ltd

CONTENTS

DEDICATION

To my family

ACKNOWLEDGEMENTS

It is not possible to write a book such as this without a great deal of assistance from those who have been associated with the marque either past or present. I am so grateful to those who have given their valuable time to pass their memories and experiences on to me.

I set out to include as much period material as possible and to achieve this I have been hugely grateful to those who have been kind enough to assist in supplying old photographs, many of which are previously unpublished; these are individually acknowledged.

I would particularly like to thank Ivor Walklett, his son Tom and members of the extended Walklett family for their enthusiasm and support towards this book; my fellow committee members at the Ginetta Owners' Club and to John Rose of Bookmarque Publishing, all of whom encouraged this venture and supported me in a wide variety of ways. Special thanks also to my wife, Hilary.

The following people have also assisted me and I would like to acknowledge their help: Don Armstrong, Scott Baillie, Clive Berry, Alex Brown, Geoff Butcher, Duncan Campbell, Mary Carden, Bill Cowing, Alison Davis, David and Caroline Doolan, Millie Farrance, Lester Goody, Joe Gowland, Stephen Greensword, Colin Hards, Per Gunnar Johansson, Dan Lekander, Ian Logan, Nick Luard, Bruce Lyon, Stephen Lyon, Luigino Maserati, Bruno Meier, Jurg Meier, Richard Petit, Dean Petley, Michael Pinner, David Pleasance, Richard Robarts, Neil Sayer, Mark Smith, Maurice Steel, Paul Summerville, Jim Swansborough, Leigh Trevail, David Wallace, Tim Wallace, Steve Wyatt and members of the Ginetta Owners' Club past and present.

My thanks go out to all the above and to anyone I have inadvertently omitted from the list.

Trevor Pyman

TIMELINE

February 1958	The first production Ginetta, the G2, announced by Walklett Bros.
November 1958	Fairlite glass-fibre body announced
March 1960	Ginetta G3 offered as an improved version of the Fairlite with Ginetta chassis
September 1960	Series 1 G4 launched
January 1963	First Ginetta G5 built
March 1963	Series 2 G4 made available
April 1963	First DKW-powered Ginetta G6 built
September 1963	DKW-engined G7 project abandoned
June 1964	First Ginetta single-seater racing car, the G8, announced
September 1964	G4R, with independent rear suspension, is made available to customers
January 1965	G10 with Ford V8 engine is launched at the Racing Car Show
Autumn 1965	G9 Formula 2 car is not making progress and is abandoned
January 1966	G11 MGB-powered version of the G10 launched at the Racing Car Show
July 1966	Completion of the G12, with the first car delivered to a customer
January 1967	Series 3 G4 announced at Racing Car Show
Spring 1967	Prototype G14 chassis built but not progressed with
October 1967	Imp-powered G15 launched at the London Motor Show
May 1968	First G16 delivered to a customer
December 1968	G17 and G18 single-seater cars are announced
Summer 1969	G19 Formula 1 car abandoned
Autumn 1969	Possibility of building the Petit-designed version of the G12 to be branded as G20 abandoned
October 1970	New G21 1600 and 3-litre cars launched at the Motor Show, together with a revised version of the G15 featuring larger side windows
March 1971	First G15R (Racing) delivered to a customer

October 1971	G21, now with Sunbeam Rapier engine, announced
August 1972	Further revisions to the G15, including recessed door handles, stand-forward front indicators and steel fuel tank, introduced
April 1973	Final factory-built Type 4 G15 version with Exaction road wheels and other refinements introduced
January 1978	G22 Sports 2000 car announced
March 1980	G23 and G24 models announced
February 1981	G4 Series 4 announced
October 1982	GRS Tora Mark I announced at the Motor Show
June 1983	First public showing of the G25
October 1983	GRS Pick Up announced
July 1984	G26 sports saloon announced at the Newark Kit Car Show
August 1984	First GRS Mark 2 delivered to a customer
March 1985	G27 introduced
March 1986	G29 Thundersports car announced and first raced
October 1986	Grand announcement of the G28, G30 and G31 sports saloons alongside the G32 mid-engine sports car at the Motor Show
July 1989	GRS Mark 3 announced at the Newark Kit Car Show
Autumn 1989	G4 Series 5 announced but the model not progressed and only one car made
November 1989	Ginetta Cars sold to Martin Phaff.
October 1990	G32 convertible and G33 announced at the Motor Show
October 1992	G33 SC launched at the Motor Show but the model not proceeded with
January 1993	G27 relaunch commenced with the Series 2, also known as the G27 GRS
Autumn 1994	G27 Series 3 gradually introduced
Autumn 1994	G34 announced although full production will not commence for some time
Winter 1995	G27 race series car introduced for the 1996 race season
January 1998	G27 Series 4 introduced
October 2000	G20 introduced
Winter 2001	G20 Cup cars announced for the 2002 race season
Winter 2002	G20 Junior car introduced for the 2003 season with closed coupé bodywork
December 2005	Ginetta Cars purchased by Lawrence Tomlinson of LNT Group.

INTRODUCTION

Rather surprisingly I can remember exactly where I was when I first heard of Ginetta cars: I was ten years old and we were on a family holiday in Austria. Friends of my parents holidaying with us lived in Witham and, knowing my interest in unusual sports cars, mentioned that a little company were making cars at the end of the High Street. A trip to the Racing Car Show with my father when I was seven had awakened my interest in this 'underworld' of car makers. Today I would define these makes as those that did not appear in my 1961 edition of *The Observer's Book of Automobiles*, which, until my trip to the Car Show, I naively thought contained every make of car in the world.

But, there at the show, I found makers like Rochdale, Falcon, Ashley and others I'd never heard of, and saw other makes like Tornado, Turner and TVR that I knew of from my book, but had never seen on the road. From that point on it was the British makes that you rarely, if ever, saw on the road that held my attention; the Morris, Austins and Triumphs of this world no longer had the same appeal. Adding Ginetta to my list of rare makes was particularly exciting as they were made just a few miles from my home.

A couple of years later I bravely ventured out on my bicycle over to Witham to see what interesting cars I could see and I wasn't disappointed! This very ordinary-looking building at the bottom end of Witham High Street had slightly grimy glass and the odd cobweb, but peering into the showroom revealed a G12 and a G4. Parked down the side of the building was another G4, and when I saw the stark interior, sports controls, tiny leather-rimmed steering wheel, I was completely hooked.

It wasn't just about Ginettas for me, though; the more I got around the more I became aware there were interesting cars all over the place. In my own small village I came to realize there were several of these unusual cars living

The author with his G21, which has been owned and enjoyed for the past thirty-eight years. AUTHOR

close by. I was able to see regularly an Elva Courier (an extremely rare Mark 4 T Type), a Falcon Caribbean and an AC Aceca.

The local estate agent was of particular interest. He seemed to change cars regularly and drove Marcoses and Jensens, but it was his brief spell with a Jensen C-V8 that had me spellbound: this brute had a road presence like nothing else I'd ever seen, and the rumble from its exhausts was music to my ears. From then on I noticed that rare cars were collectively all over the place: there was the Gilbern GT that overtook the school bus some evenings and the Rochdale Olympic that often parked over the road from my grandmother's house; the Berkeley seemingly abandoned in the shopping complex car park and the Lagonda Rapide for sale at the garage in the next village.

During the summer of 1967 a red Ginetta G4 was regularly flashing past our front gate. I soon traced it to a house in a nearby lane; later I found out it was the first Series 3 G4 delivered. I started making notes of these cars, and although I didn't know it at the time, this was really the start of what years later would become the Ginetta Owners' Club Register. During the late sixties in the hinterland around Chelmsford in Essex there were at least four G4s in regular use and they looked amazing as they moved among the traffic. My trips over to the Ginetta factory were now regular. The new G15 was under test and racing cars were everywhere in the yard at the back of the factory, as were the occasional G11 and then, much later, the new G21.

Together with friends I cycled all over the place always looking out for rare cars and visiting a few other specialist car factories, although none measured up to the range of cars you could regularly see at Ginetta.

Soon after leaving school I was in a position to buy my first Ginetta, and BTW10G, the sixth G15 built, came into my possession. Now I could discover what it was all about. Probably the biggest revelation was the road-holding. You could corner at great speed without any body roll: it literally felt like you were driving a racing car on the road – but then of course, in a sense, you were doing just that.

That first G15 began what has become a forty-five-year run of almost unbroken Ginetta ownership, during which time I've driven over half a million miles in these cars. Most were purchased as daily drivers, used for both business and pleasure; a couple of G15s in the early days were joined by a G21 and then, with small children to transport, a G26 kit was built. Along the way I found time to buy and rebuild a G2 that was in a dilapidated condition, but which was and indeed still is, the oldest known surviving Ginetta.

I've owned other specialist cars too. For a long time in the seventies and early eighties I ran a Gilbern Invader; a Rochdale Olympic proved a practical alternative for a while, as did a Reliant Scimitar GTE; then there is the Jensen C-V8 that I still have, but it's Ginettas that have dominated. Buying a G32 for my business travel in the nineties proved an inspired purchase and it mopped up a couple of hundred thousand miles; it's such a usable little car and so much fun to drive, yet another Ginetta design that is largely forgotten today outside the dedicated circle of Ginetta enthusiasts.

Closely following the Ginetta company over more than fifty years, coupled with holding the post of Ginetta Owners' Club Registrar since 1980, has given me a vast pool of knowledge, so when Crowood offered the opportunity to write this book it was, though daunting, an opportunity not to be missed. I'd written the history of the G4 model, which was published in 1990 with a second enlarged edition in 2004, but this was a wholly different experience. Detailing so many different models, describing their design and development, recounting the story behind them and the successes in racing – how could I do justice to this great marque?

My efforts will be judged by others, but if nothing else I hope this book will highlight just what Ginetta have achieved as a company, what the leading players had to go through to establish the marque and keep the name alive and why it is still a force sixty years later.

Trevor Pyman,
Maldon, Essex, October 2017

CHAPTER ONE

FAMILY MATTERS

On 18 October 1967, the fifty-second annual Motor Show opened at Earls Court in London, and for four brothers, directors of the Essex-based car maker Ginetta, this was a very proud day. In less than ten years since marketing their first special, they had grown a car-manufacturing business that was now rubbing shoulders with established makers to a worldwide audience on the grand exhibition floor of Britain's premier motor showcase.

By contrast to the many corporate makers surrounding them at the show, Ginetta was a family-run business that had developed out of sheer enthusiasm and the desire to succeed against all the odds.

The four Walklett brothers, Douglas, Trevers, Bob and Ivor, who together founded Ginetta cars, were born and grew up during the inter-war years. Typically of that period the family was large: parents John and Eva Walklett had seven children: five boys and two girls. John, a military man in the First World War, later moved around with his work before settling into farming after the Second World War. The young Walklett family lived a somewhat nomadic existence moving around the south of England, where the eldest four sons, Douglas, Trevers, Kenneth (known to all as Bob) and Brian arrived before they all moved to the London area, where the youngest three siblings were born at locations all around the capital, the last being Ivor.

The outbreak of the Second World War had a major impact on most families and the Walkletts were no exception, the three eldest boys all becoming eligible to join the forces at various stages during the war years. Douglas joined the Territorial Army just before the outbreak of war and his unit was deployed onto war duty at the start of hostilities. He was selected for training as a mechanical engineer and, following this intensive training, became a qualified artificer, serving in the Middle East at El Alamein and later in Italy. The knowledge gained from his training and experiences proved invaluable in later establishing a business with his brothers.

Trevers joined the Royal Armoured Corps at the age of eighteen but later transferred to the Parachute Regiment where he joined the 6th Airborne Division. He took part in the Normandy D-day landings on 5/6 June 1944, where he experienced hand-to-hand fighting with German forces. By 1945 Trevers was taking part in the battle for the Rhine Valley in the final stages of the war when, parachuting into action, he was hit in the right leg. Losing a lot of blood, he lay wounded for many hours before being picked up and hospitalized. Surgeons fought to save his gangrenous leg, which mercifully they managed to do, following which he spent many months in recovery. He had endured and witnessed some horrific moments during the war, experiences that would stay with him for the rest of his life. Above all, though, his training and experiences had left him with an attitude that everything was possible with determination and a focused mind.

In 1943 Bob Walklett turned eighteen and, like his brothers before him, volunteered for service. He followed

Trevers Walklett in his military uniform, his beret clearly showing the winged cap badge of the Parachute Regiment.
WALKLETT FAMILY

Bob Walklett smiles for the camera in uniform; a tough time lay ahead for him during the final days of the Second World War. WALKLETT FAMILY

Trevers into the Royal Armoured Corps, qualifying as a wireless operator and tank driver. He narrowly missed the D-Day landings, but having volunteered for the 6th Airborne Armoured Reconnaissance Regiment and been accepted, he trained on light tanks that could be dropped into action from the air. In the event he first saw action in the Ardennes in a Cromwell tank, before moving on to the Battle for the Rhine. Here, in a fierce clash with German forces, his tank was hit by anti-tank fire and, with burned hands and face and with shrapnel fragments close to his spine, he was picked up by German forces and hospitalized as a POW. However, with few medical supplies available, he received little or no treatment and was fortunate to be released by advancing Allied forces a few days later and to be treated by Royal Army Medical Corps personnel before being shipped back to England. In England, his brother Trevers was being treated for his severe wounds in Lichfield, Staffordshire, where through the good offices of the British Red Cross, Bob later came to be placed in the bed next to his brother. Their war was over. Both were very lucky to have survived and required a great deal of convalescence to make them fit and ready to return to civilian life.

When the war was over, siblings would typically go their separate ways due to employment or marriage but for the Walklett brothers the draw of family was strong. Immediately after the war, their father had taken on Little Napchester Farm in the Kent countryside just north of Dover and he set up J. F. Walklett & Sons, Dairy Farmers. This was the focus for the elder boys returning home, whilst some of the younger siblings were still attending school. The brothers busied themselves with duties on the farm and quickly discovered elements of the work they enjoyed and those they did not. Trevers, for one, was not keen on the animals but found he enjoyed the engineering side of farming, whilst on the personal side, during his time in Kent he met local girl Sherry, who he would later marry.

Their time in Kent was limited, however, as their father had plans for expansion and arranged to purchase a much larger farm at Bures in Suffolk. This move turned, through no fault of his own, into a nightmare, when the intended purchaser of the Kent farm died before the contracts were completed and the whole matter became part of his estate, meaning the farm could not be sold for a full year. With two farms on his hands, John Walklett was overstretched, and when the Kent farm was finally sold at a knockdown price the damage was done. The strain left him in bad health both mentally and physically, and he was forced to sell the Suffolk farm as well. During this period it was Bob, still only in his early twenties, who dealt with much of the fallout, both legal and financial, supporting his mother and siblings, and there can be little doubt that this experience shaped his future thinking on prudent business management.

It had been a tough lesson on just how easily things can go wrong in even the best-organized affairs, but by 1950 most

Enjoying the summer sunshine on the family farm in Kent in 1946. *GINETTA: THE INSIDE STORY* – BOOKMARQUE PUBLISHING

of the family, once again, were under one roof and living in the Old Rectory at Chillesford, a large and imposing building in its own grounds. Chillesford is a small hamlet nestling on the edge of the Tunstall forest and 6 miles (10km) east of Woodbridge; in the 1950s this was a remote location and sparsely populated. The area was totally dominated by agriculture and Doug, Trevers and Bob identified a business opportunity supplying engineering services to the agricultural community. In need of a source of income after the demise of the family farm, they launched into this business venture, setting up a new company known as Walklett Bros. Agricultural & Constructional Engineers.

At the time the three brothers were setting up their business, the youngest brother, Ivor, was still at grammar school, but at every opportunity he would be down with his brothers assisting in whatever way he could and absorbing engineering knowledge. As was the requirement for young men in the immediate post-war period, Ivor was called up to carry out a statutory two years' national service in one of the armed forces and Ivor chose the RAF. Cars were his passion, and in particular he enjoyed the challenge of car design: he sketched his own designs in great detail, including theories on the latest suspension layouts he had learnt from reading up on the subject.

WALKLETT BROS. AGRICULTURAL & CONSTRUCTIONAL ENGINEERS LTD

With some experience in farming and with a wartime service that gave them a grounding in engineering, it was perhaps inevitable that Doug, Trevers and Bob Walklett would combine the two. Doug's war experiences and training in particular were key in providing the knowledge required for such a venture.

The business was up and running by around 1950, with Bob looking after day-to-day management, administration and sales whilst Doug and Trevers dedicated their efforts to the incoming work and products offered by the business. In the early days in order to establish themselves they took on awkward work other businesses had turned away. With Suffolk's rural farming community offering a ready clientele, the business took off. Early on they operated from a tiny workshop premises in Orford down on a remote part of the east coast. As the business expanded during the early to mid-fifties they sought a larger site and settled at Hill Bridge Works, Campsea Ashe, near Wickham Market.

The Walklett Bros. Agricultural Engineers' first workshop in Orford, Suffolk. MILLIE FARRANCE

Not only did the Campsea Ashe site offer additional space for fabrication and storage, but crucially it was next to the railway station and therefore ideal for receipt of raw materials and despatch of finished goods at a time when road transport played a lesser role in movement of materials than today.

The business grew to a significant size, employing up to ten full-time staff with younger brother Ivor joining them after completion of his national service. Offering an increasingly large range of products, they started manufacturing a range of agricultural barns and enclosures. The brothers were able to develop and offer for sale one of the largest clear-span steel agricultural structures available at that time, drawing on customers from across Suffolk and further afield.

By the late 1950s, they were sufficiently established to exhibit their buildings at the Suffolk Show, offering farmers a one-stop shop of design, fabrication and erection of buildings. It had become a very successful business. To assist in the erecting of buildings, Trevers built a crane on the back of an old six-wheeler Dodge truck, the raising and lowering of which was taken care of by an old aircraft jack; such things were available as war surplus in those days, and it shows the ingenuity that the brothers brought to their work even in those early days.

Cars were important to all the brothers. Doug ran a Ford V8 and they also owned at different times classic Triumphs,

A Walklett Bros. barn built for the Campsea Ashe cattle auction business. Note the strong, slender framework supporting the roof and lightweight, strengthened purlins allowing increased length between steel support stanchions. AUTHOR

This garage building, still standing by the side of the A12 at Stratford St Andrew in Suffolk, was constructed by Walklett Bros. and features a huge 60ft (18m) clear span, one of the largest available in period. AUTHOR

including a Dolomite and Gloria. In particular, their attention was drawn by Sydney Allard, who had not only started manufacturing his own Allard cars, but had proved their ability by winning the 1952 Monte Carlo Rally, an unparalleled achievement. These cars were not for the faint-hearted: fitted with the flat-head Ford V8, the performance was more than impressive. Bob Walklett was keen to own an Allard and eventually purchased a used P1 Saloon, similar to the Monte Carlo-winning car, from Performance Cars in West London, a well-known supplier of used sports cars at the time. Bob recalls when picking the car up that the friendly salesman suggested to him that he take it easy at first and get to know the car. On the long run back through London and up to Suffolk, Bob quickly realized the wisdom of these words; it was extremely quick but could also be unpredictable, and was certainly a car for experienced hands.

Eventually, though, it was not the cars they drove but Ivor's passion for car engineering and design that would change everything.

During leave from his national service, Ivor planned to do more than just draw cars – he wanted to build one of his own design. All the brothers had been to Snetterton and witnessed motor racing first-hand and could not help but notice that small sports cars and specials made for exciting racing and offered the prospect of driving the cars to and from races. Inspired to make his drawings a reality, he turned to an old pre-war Wolseley Hornet that the family had at the house and decided that this would make the ideal basis for a special. The Hornet had a small 6-cylinder engine with an overhead camshaft and was advanced for its time. Brother Trevers was also interested in Ivor's ideas and offered some assistance, and so it was that the first Walklett brothers-engineered car started to take shape.

The powerful V8 Allard P1 Saloon. This example is similar to the one driven by Bob Walklett in the mid-fifties. AUTHOR

CHAPTER TWO

MAKING CARS

The 1950s was an exciting time for those interested in cars. There were many new models from major car makers who were determined to offer bright new products to help the public put the years of wartime austerity behind them. In motor racing, after a slow start immediately post-war, the grids were now full and the public flocked to circuits to spectate. Venues were often disused airfields with little or no safety measures for public or drivers.

On the road, cars were frequently patched up pre-war models; the latest new cars stood out, suggesting a certain level of affluence had been attained by their owners. Many young men wanted to join the car-owning fraternity but nice cars – and sports cars in particular – were expensive relative to wages, and this gave the hobby of special building a lot of momentum as the decade progressed. Fuelled by this interest, companies sprang up selling parts to assist in the building of specials, as they became known. The chassis frames from the Austin 7, and later Ford 10, were a particularly popular basis on which to build a special, but any chassis frame was fair game to the enthusiasts of the time. In the early years of this revolution, bodywork was usually created using aluminium in simple curves and chassis were modified or not depending on the skills and ambitions of the builder. For those looking to build an advanced special, companies like Buckler produced a tubular space-frame chassis to which components from standard models could be attached, whilst firms offering tuning equipment for Austin and Ford engines abounded.

It was however, Lotus, and the brilliance of its founder, Colin Chapman, that revolutionized the whole alternative sports car market, with a succession of models that simply blew away opposition from any source, leaving others to follow in his wake.

Ivor Walklett's sketch of the Ginetta G1. Sadly no known photographs survive of this car. IVOR WALKLETT

THE GINETTA G1

Having stripped off the body, Ivor found the chassis frame of his Wolseley lacking in some areas, so his first job was to improve this; after cutting and suitably modifying the chassis, he then tested his theories on the gravel drive of the Chillesford home. Satisfied with his improvements, he set about making the two-seater aluminium bodywork to clothe his new car. The finished product had more than a passing resemblance to the post-war Maserati 4CLT grand prix car and was a very competent effort for a first attempt at special building. Ivor was learning fast and he quickly developed the skill of making use of parts from the donor Wolseley in imaginative ways – a talent that would serve him very well in the years to follow.

It was now the mid-fifties. Happy with his completed special, Ivor took to the Suffolk roads with enthusiasm. He made full use of the car's potential, which, due to its lightweight body and modified chassis, was significantly quicker than the original Wolseley. The Walklett home at Chillesford had a long, winding driveway from the road through the trees and shrubs up to the house. It was here that Ivor pushed the special a little too hard, lost control and crashed through the bushes, coming to a very sudden stop on a large tree stump. The special was badly damaged and irreparable. Sadly no pictures of this car survive; only a sketch by Ivor gives us a feel for what he created. Although this was a one-off, this car was the spark that ignited the fire that would become Ginetta, and retrospectively this car would become known as the Ginetta G1. For now, however, Ivor was left without one of his own creations to drive but his mind and sketchbook full of ideas.

In fact Ivor and Trevers had already started work on a new project. As engineers, the brothers subscribed to several magazines targeted at the profession, and it was in one such publication that Ivor read about a new material pioneered in America that was now being traded in the United Kingdom by the Bakelite Company. Bakelite had made a big name for having developed resins that could be moulded to form many diverse objects. Due to its lack of conductivity, it had been widely adopted within the electrical industry for lamp holders, switches and sockets as well as by the motor industry for dash panels, switches and many other applications.

EXPERIMENTS WITH GRP

With this kind of track record, the new resin being marketed by Bakelite was of great interest. When the resin was mixed with a catalyst and impregnated into a glass-fibre matting, the resulting resin-bonded glass fibre would set hard into whatever shape it overlay and was both strong and very lightweight. Ivor immediately saw the potential for making car bodies: if a mould could be made, then replica bodies could be produced with relative ease. He wasn't the only one to take note of this material. In America, glass-reinforced plastic (GRP), as it became known, was used by Chevrolet for their new Corvette, while in the UK Jensen had just produced their 541 sports saloon with GRP bodywork. Simultaneously, other budding special makers were having similar ideas and quickly little companies sprung up selling GRP bodies for fitting to Ford 8 and 10hp or Austin 7 chassis.

After discussions with Bakelite, Ivor and Trevers set about putting together a full-size mock-up of the body they wished to make, from which a mould could be taken. The body was an open two-seater, all-enveloping in a modern style with a wheelbase to suit the Ford 8 and 10hp chassis. They chose to sculpt the 'plug' in the greenhouse at their Chillesford home, where the space was just large enough to work around the creation. They used various materials to form this structure, including wood, chicken wire and cement, and estimated the finished item weighed nearly two tons.

With the completed body plug looking just how they wanted it, the surface was made smooth and polished ready to take off moulds. The moulds were cast in GRP, and here their learning curve reached almost to the vertical. Neither Ivor nor Trevers had any experience of working with this material and they struggled to cope with it. To make matters worse, they had purchased the wrong type of glass-fibre matting, which was springy and kept pulling out of the resin during the lay-up process. The resin itself was unforgiving and it took time and much experimentation for them to find just the right amount of catalyst for it to stay workable for just long enough to wet out the glass fibre. They continued to struggle on, but when the Bakelite representative called by he was horrified to see them using the wrong matting and, worse still, the environmental conditions in which they were working. He deemed the extremes of temperature in the greenhouse to be totally unsuitable for any work with his resins. With the plug weighing two tons, however, it wasn't going anywhere so the Walkletts carried on anyway. Eventually, after a great deal of time and an equal amount of perseverance, they at last had moulds from which they could make glass-reinforced plastic bodyshells.

During this long process, Ivor had grown impatient and was keen to progress other ideas. His design sketches had many influences, and one particular idea drew on lines and details seen on the Jaguar D Type and the Lotus Eleven. Together with Trevers, he carried out initial work on the chassis and bespoke suspension before the complexity of the whole thing got the better of him and it was set aside. Later this development would be revived but for now he wanted a special he could drive, so decided to go back to first principles and make something relatively simple.

THE GINETTA G2

As 1957 dawned, Ivor began work on yet another idea. The Lotus 6 had impressed Ivor and he set off to design a special similar in appearance to the successful Lotus but with a chassis designed in such a way that most parts from a Ford 10 would bolt straight on without modification.

The Campsea Ashe factory in 1993. It had changed very little since Walklett Bros. built the first Ginettas here. AUTHOR

With the experience of the Wolseley special to draw on, he felt his latest idea could quickly become a reality. At the Campsea Ashe factory he fabricated a simple multi-tube space-frame with mounting points to accept the standard Ford front and rear axle assemblies complete with their transverse springs, steering components and wheels. To this he added mountings for the 1172cc sidevalve Ford engine and three-speed gearbox, whilst the Ford radiator and fuel tank could also be bolted straight in.

The only modifications needed were the lengthening of the steering column, the shortening of the torque tube-type propshaft and a realignment of the stabilizing arms of the front suspension. Ivor did, however, tweak the suspension in the interests of better handling by substituting the Ford lever-arm damper units for telescopic shock absorbers and removing some leaves from the springs due to the lighter weight of the car. With a fabricated remote gear linkage and cable brakes operated by a built-in pedal pivoted from the chassis, together with matching clutch pedal, the chassis could be driven.

The first G2 built, used extensively by the Walklett family. WALKLETT FAMILY

As part of the design, the chassis frame acted as a former for the aluminium bodywork. Flat sheets could be dressed and riveted over the tubing to clothe the car, complete with bulkheads, transmission tunnel, lift-off bonnet and riveted steel floor. The whole package was beautifully simple but the structure was very stiff and effective, and, importantly, it was easy to make. Cycle-type wings protected the wheels but there was one area of the body that needed special attention. The deep Ford radiator was angled back to reduce its effective height but in order to enclose this and give the front of the car an identity, they decided to call on their new skills in GRP moulding and produced a one-piece cowl in this material. To finish the car off, a flat aluminium-framed windscreen and fabric hood were fitted.

With this second special completed and ready for the road, the brothers wasted no time in getting out and about in it. Several locals and an ex-RAF acquaintance asked Ivor

The simple but effective G2 chassis frame. AUTHOR

With our **RIGID LIGHTWEIGHT MULTI-TUBE FRAME with STRESSED ALUMINIUM BODY PANELS** (*as illustrated*) complete with nose cowl, bonnet cover, front and rear wings. Price £156 ex-works. You can build this exciting **1958 GINETTA** sports car using FORD 8 h.p. and 10 h.p. COMPONENTS 1938-53 (Yes! even the radiator and fuel tank) or new components

Note these features ● Built-in brake pedal and linkage
Built-in clutch pedal and linkage ● Built-in accelerator pedal
Mountings built-in for engine, steering, headlamp, battery, shock absorbers, fuel tank, radiator, front and rear transverse springs

WALKLETT BROS., CAMPSEA ASHE, WOODBRIDGE, SUFFOLK
Telephone Wickham Market 477

The first advert for a Ginetta car appeared in *Autosport* in February 1958. GINETTA OWNERS' CLUB

to build them a copy. After discussion with his brothers, it was decided to purchase some steel tube and aluminium sheet, then Ivor and Trevers set about building another car. With the new chassis completed they were surprised to find it was an inch larger than the original – clearly if more cars were to be made, it was going to be necessary to make a jig to ensure uniformity.

With the first production body/chassis unit completed and ready for dispatch, the question of how much to charge arose. The material had cost relatively little to buy – the real cost was in the fabrication time. The bare chassis unit had been weighed on an old set of pig scales, and at just 156lb (71kg) it was commendably light. Eventually they decided to charge £156 in money for the body/chassis unit, including modifying the necessary Ford parts to be supplied by the customer. This was hardly a cutting-edge costing method, but at this price it was decided a good profit would result. Bob Walklett, always with an eye to new business opportunities, was sceptical, asking his brothers, 'Will people buy these?' Ivor and Trevers were confident that they would and so it was decided to test the market.

In January 1958 the motoring press were circulated details of the new car, together with a selection of photographs included in the hope of gaining useful publicity. The car now had a name, too – the Ginetta. The origin of the name was always kept secret. In his book *Ginetta: The Inside Story*, Bob Walklett stated it was taken from the name of a small, cat-like creature called a genetta (or genet); but there are still many who feel Bob was creating a smokescreen to maintain the brothers' agreement not to reveal the true reason for their choice.

Autosport magazine was first to break the news of this new car early in February in a short column accompanied by three photographs, and over the following weeks the brothers started to place small advertisements in magazines including *Autosport*, *The Motor* and *Practical Motorist*.

Ginetta's First Production Model

As a result, a few enquiries and some orders were received, and before long an area down one side of the workshop had been set aside for car production. Suddenly Walklett Brothers were no longer just agricultural and constructional engineers but Britain's newest car manufacturer as well. Their pricing structure was simple. Included within the £156 price

The works G2 with an unknown driver pictured close to the Campsea Ashe factory. GINETTA OWNERS' CLUB

The G2 engine bay with sidevalve engine, here mildly tuned with an Aquaplane twin SU carburettor set-up. AUTHOR

The G2 interior, showing simple controls and instrumentation mostly derived from the Ford E93A. AUTHOR

was everything necessary to build a car using salvaged parts from the Ford 8 or 10hp from the period 1938 to 1953. The hood, windscreen and front and rear lights were all provided.

That the Ginetta was fun to drive was in no doubt. Bob recalled how his sisters also loved driving the car, often taking it down to the golf club at nearby Aldeburgh, while Trevers recalled how he and Ivor raced a local farmer across Tunstall common. This particular gentleman drove a big Wolseley and was known never to be overtaken. One day, crossing the common, the Ginetta came up behind the farmer and pulled out to overtake. Immediately the Wolseley accelerated. The Ginetta came alongside and they remained side by side for half a mile or more on the empty Suffolk roads until, finally, the Ginetta pulled ahead – mission accomplished!

Most of the body/chassis kits were dispatched to their new owners boxed in returnable crates on the train from the adjoining station.

With the simple hood erected, the G2 was cosy but practical for everyday use. GINETTA OWNERS' CLUB

A typical G2 as driven by young enthusiasts in the 1950s and 60s – sports motoring on a budget. JIM SWANSBOROUGH

Even in 1970, when this photograph was taken, the occasional G2 could still be seen on the road. GINETTA OWNERS' CLUB

Michael Pinner presses on in his G2 in the 1960 Felixstowe Rally. EASTERN COUNTIES MOTOR CLUB

By mid-1958 some of the first cars supplied had been built up and were now on the road, but with such a sporting car it wasn't long before some owners used them in competitive events. One of the first sold was raced in Autocross events and used in Autotests by Mary Thompstone; the car built for her by her father was also driven at meetings by David Lomas and competed throughout Cheshire and Derbyshire. In York, Dr Stevenson entered similar events in his car, while local Suffolk-based Michael Pinner used his car in the 1960 Felixstowe Rally. Michael's car was also driven by Carl Giles, the famous cartoonist, after he had seen it parked one day in the Ipswich railway station car park and expressed an interest.

A later G2 development was independent swing-axle front suspension including coil spring damper units. JURG MEIER

Mary Thompstone with racing friends. She competed in her G2 in many Autocross and driving tests across northwest England in the late 1950s. MARY CARDEN

This G2 was exported to Switzerland in the early 1970s and beautifully restored there in recent years. JURG MEIER

Some of the last few Ginettas of this type built were fitted with a split-beam front axle with the Ford leaf spring substituted for coil spring damper units. This improved the handling but the extremely light weight and heavy axles made the Ginetta nervous in some conditions, particularly in the wet. The looks of the car, while echoing those of the Lotus 6 and 7, were nonetheless seen as a handicap to sales, being perceived even then as old-fashioned.

This was the first production Ginetta model, but at the time it was the only Ginetta; later, when other models were made, it became known retrospectively as the Ginetta G2.

Records no longer survive of the exact number of these cars built, but a figure of around twenty seems likely, with seven cars currently known to survive. After the initial interest and orders received, sales quickly tailed off and it is thought that few if any were made after the summer of 1959.

While the G2 was being put into production, Ivor and Trevers had laminated the first bodyshell to be taken from their moulds and were busily building up another car by mounting the body onto a Ford chassis frame. To top it off they made a split steel-framed windscreen with flat glass; the completed car looked extremely modern for its time when compared to the 'cycle-winged' style of the G2. The main issue with specials during this period was the standards achieved by the individual builder, but in the case of the Walklett-built car, the standard was very high.

But no matter how high the standard they had achieved, the new car was a disappointment to Ivor. Out on the road he realized the shortcomings of the Ford chassis underpinning this type of special were more than he could have imagined. In comparison with the bespoke chassis of the G2 it flexed and had little rigidity, while the steering was vague. When it came to the driving position, despite the lower seating, the driver was still perched up relatively high to the

GINETTA G2 (1958–60)

Layout and chassis	Two-seater sports car with space-frame chassis	*Suspension and Steering*	
		Front	Beam axle, transverse leaf spring (split beam optional)
Engine		Rear	Solid axle, transverse leaf spring, torque tube drive
Type	Ford E93A		
Block material	Cast iron	Steering	Steering box (worm and nut)
Head material	Cast iron	Tyres	4.50 × 17in
Cylinders	4	Wheels	Pressed-steel disc, bolt-on
Cooling	Water	Rim width	3.5 × 17in
Bore and stroke	63.5 × 92.5mm		
Capacity	1172cc	*Brakes*	
Valves	Sidevalve, 2 valves per cylinder	Type	Drum front and rear
Compression ratio	6.16:1	Brake size	10in (250mm)
Carburettor	Downdraught		
Max. power (DIN)	30bhp	*Dimensions*	
Max. torque	46lb ft at 2,400rpm	Track, front	45in (1,143 mm)
Fuel capacity	7gal (32ltr)	Track, rear	45in (1,143 mm)
		Wheelbase	90in (2,286 mm)
Transmission		Overall length	126in (3,200 mm), excluding spare wheel
Gearbox	Ford 3-speed and reverse		
Clutch	Single dry plate	Overall width	55.5in (1,410mm)
		Overall height	44in (1,117 mm) to top of hood
Internal Gearbox Ratios		Unladen weight	926lb (420kg)
First	3.07:1		
Second	1.76:1	*Performance*	
Third	1:1	Top speed	75mph (121km/h)
Reverse	4.01:1	0–60mph	not available
Final drive	5.5:1		

car body, and the Ford pedals were not suited to the seating arrangements and uncomfortable to use. The car may have looked the part but for Ivor and his brothers it really didn't deliver.

By now it was the summer of 1958 and their next move was far from clear. They had the G2, a good car whose sales were probably blunted by its older styling, and they had a modern-looking car whose performance they were unhappy with. The motoring magazines in which they advertised were quick to offer advice, telling Bob that body-shells for fitting to the Ford 10 chassis were the way forward: all their competitors were offering these and doing good business.

Typical of the Fairlite specials built by amateur constructors, this car featured a Standard 12 chassis. SCOTT BAILLIE

THE FAIRLITE

With so much work having gone into the production of the moulds, it was decided that they should go ahead and market the new shell but with one proviso – they would not call it a Ginetta.

The name they settled on was Fairlite, and in November 1958 the first advertisements appeared offering the Fairlite shell for just £49. They had decided on a competitive price that would attract customers. Although there were less expensive, very basic bodies on the market, the one-piece Fairlite shell was fitted with a steel internal frame and brackets for chassis mounting. For an additional £7 the shell would be supplied with the doors and bonnet openings cut out and rebated, something that was strongly recommended. The shells were supplied in a red gel coat finish and an additional £9 would provide a windscreen, while £13 10s would supply a 'duck' fabric hood or £16 a PVC hood, the latter available in a variety of colours. Purchasers also received a four-page information sheet entitled 'Useful Hints for Fitting the Fairlite Glass Fibre Bodyshell'.

Sales actually picked up quite quickly, and through 1959 a steady stream of orders were received. Delivery from receipt of order ranged from three to six weeks, depending on the number of pending orders and the speed at which bodies could be produced from the mould. The brothers were very concerned about the impact the sale of these bodyshells would have on their reputation. Most customers would use the Ford 10 chassis as a base for their own special – the quality of the finished car was down to the skill of

The "FAIRLITE" Glass Fibre Body Shell

for fitting to Ford 8 and 10 h.p. Chassis from 1932 onwards and other Chassis of similar dimensions.

Note these Features:–

★ CONTINENTAL BODY STYLING

★ BONDED IN STEEL TUBES WITH MOUNTING BRACKETS FOR FIXING TO CHASSIS

★ MANUFACTURED WITH HIGH IMPACT RESISTANT PLASTIC

★ BUILT-IN HEADLAMP MOUNTINGS

Price: Body Shell complete with mounting brackets, basic colour, Red: **£49 0s. 0d.** Cutting out doors and engine cover (optional): **£7 0s. 0d.** Carriage: **£4 0s. 0d.** Deposit on Crate (Returnable): **£7 0s. 0d.**

Terms: £10 0s. 0d. with order, balance on despatch.

Delivery: 2-3 weeks.

HIRE PURCHASE TERMS: One-third down. Balance over 9 months.

Spend Wisely by Choosing a

"FAIRLITE" BODY SHELL

It is UNEQUALLED in VALUE.

★

WALKLETT BROS.,

CAMPSEA ASHE

WOODBRIDGE - SUFFOLK

Telephone: Wickham Market 477.

The Fairlite brochure tempted many to purchase this new glass-fibre body to reach the market. SCOTT BAILLIE

the builder, and, while some made an excellent job that was a credit to them and reflected well on the bodyshell maker, others left much to be desired. Although the Ford chassis was predominant, builders used a variety of chassis with a suitable wheelbase. Fairlite bodies are known to have been fitted on Morris, Standard 12 and Wolseley chassis as well as specialist-built chassis frames including Buckler, Speedex and Halifax offerings. These specialist chassis would have been the choice of builders looking to make a high-end special with excellent handling and performance characteristics.

For Ivor the Fairlite was a stopgap. He wanted to build complete cars, and also realized that the fitting of plastic bodies to often pre-war chassis had no future.

However, with so much time invested in the Fairlite body and with their small sports car still under development, the brothers hit on the idea of turning the Fairlite into something more. Up until this point in time the Fairlite had seen no improvement aside from a better-looking windscreen arrangement, which saw the flat split-screen replaced by a slightly curved screen from a production car mounted in a reinforced GRP surround.

Now, taking a Fairlite shell, the first priority was to add more strength at the perimeters; this was achieved

This period photo shows the standard windscreen, a large split-screen flat glass unit; later cars would feature improvement in this area. SCOTT BAILLIE

THE END OF SPECIAL BUILDING

As we have seen this pastime started in the early 1950s with Austin 7-based specials, usually with aluminium bodies. As the decade progressed, the Ford 8 and 10hp chassis became the basis for most specials and GRP bodies of modern design were made available to clothe these creations. By the late fifties the bodies had become increasingly sophisticated.

The three leading players in the market by this time were Ashley, Falcon and Rochdale. These were quality bodies, well made with opening doors and fully hinged panels, glazing – some with wind-down door windows – internal bulkheads and wheel arches that were all bonded in.

All these companies sold bodies by the thousand, and all three also eventually offered a modern steel chassis as an alternative to the Ford item, but the relatively sudden end to the special building scene dealt a major blow, with orders drying up by 1962.

The availability of inexpensive, mass-produced cars such as the Mini and Austin Healey Sprite, together with the MOT roadworthiness test leading to many older cars being scrapped, spelled the end for special building: the way ahead for the small car makers was to build complete cars with brand new parts.

Of the big three, Ashley survived as a company by dropping car bodies and diversifying into supplying hardtops for sports cars. Falcon introduced their 515 model late in the day, which was a complete turn-key car but only survived until 1964. Only Rochdale really anticipated the collapse of the market with the introduction of their ground breaking GRP monocoque Olympic in 1960, and as a result were able to carry on making cars throughout the sixties.

It is clear that success in making special bodies did not smooth the transition to the emerging market for complete cars in component form that dominated the sixties only with forward thinking and planning could the management of the companies concerned steer a path to further success.

The Rochdale GT, just one example of the high-spec bodies that were on offer to special builders by 1960. AUTHOR

This rare photograph shows a Fairlite complete with a single-piece curved windscreen in fibreglass surround, an improvement on the early flat screens. This body is mounted to a Buckler space-frame chassis. GINETTA OWNERS' CLUB

by adding moulded 'bumpers' front and rear while shaped sills stiffened up the sides. By adding internal bulkheads and wheel arches the whole structure was much more rigid. Next they added an opening bootlid; and, turning to the bonnet, the whole front was made to lift in one piece, hinged at the bulkhead. This new front did away with the small opening 'hatch' used for engine access on the Fairlite. The windscreen also came in for attention. This time the Walkletts fitted a modern aluminium framed unit as used on the Austin Healey Sprite.

THE GINETTA G3

The skills the brothers had now acquired in glass-fibre laminating meant that the new body was vastly superior to the Fairlite and a match for the best the market had to offer. Pleased with the outcome, they decided to go further and produced a detachable hardtop, a feature of which was a raked-back rear window echoing the style of the recently announced new 105E Ford Anglia. In practice this angling of the window was necessary to give clearance for the bootlid.

The body would still bolt straight onto a Ford chassis and provide much-needed rigidity, but Ivor had also designed a tubular steel space-frame chassis to go with the new body. Just as he had done with the G2, it was laid out to accept running gear taken straight from a donor Ford 10. The chassis featured mountings for a split-beam front axle, sprung on coil spring damper units. As with the G2, the Ford fuel tank could also be used, but unlike on the G2, a crossflow radiator was needed, as the high Ford unit would not fit under the low bonnet line. New moulded seats were also available to give a comfortable driving position, together with the bespoke chassis-mounted pedals.

Already the brothers were thinking of ease and speed of fabrication to maximize profits, so the new chassis was fabricated in square tubing, making cutting and jointing much quicker. This new package performed well and the brothers were happy to announce its availability early in 1960, proudly naming it the Ginetta G3.

The price was considerably more than the Fairlite, but this was a far more advanced product. The body, including fitted doors, bonnet and bootlid complete with latches, was offered at £116, plus an additional £22 10s for the hardtop. The windscreen was an additional £13 10s and side screens with chrome-plated surrounds were £18 10s. In addition the chassis, including split-beam front axle, spring damper units, pedals and gearbox/propshaft cover, cost £95. For the enthusiast looking to build an advanced special, the G3 offered the potential of creating a smart modern sports car with excellent handling for between £350 and £400.

The Walklett brothers had moved to the top end of the special-building ladder, but the market was beginning to ebb

The G3 proved to be a good-looking, high-quality body chassis offering that stood out well in the crowded specials market. GINETTA CARS

The G3 chassis and running gear. This was the first Ginetta design to use square tubing. WALKLETT FAMILY

The purchaser of a G3 body would receive this kit of body components, in this case complete with both a hood and hardtop. GINETTA OWNERS' CLUB

The G3 body assembled. The hardtop is stylish and practical, and extremely rare today. GINETTA OWNERS' CLUB

as the demand for special-building products slowed. Nonetheless, the G3 found plenty of willing customers, although many purchased the body components only for fitting to the Ford chassis rather than taking the Ginetta chassis as well.

The works prototype G3, registered 361ERT, saw a lot of use in the hands of the brothers and remained in the company ownership for some years. Over many decades it has often been written that the G3 was supplied with the Ford 105E engine, but there is no evidence to suggest that this engine type was ever fitted. The chassis was designed for the sidevalve Ford engine, either E93A type or 100E, but it is possible the works car was at some point fitted with the 105E engine, perhaps for evaluation purposes.

Whether or not this ever happened, it certainly had a sidevalve engine when sold into private hands in the mid-sixties. However, later in the car's life, during the seventies, it was fitted with a Ford 1500cc pre-crossflow engine by its then owner.

One G3 was sold to Dave Sampter, an American medical officer stationed at the nearby US Air Force base of Bentwaters. Sampter raced his G3 at Snetterton on occasion and over time gradually developed the car; in its final form this car too was fitted with a 1500 Ford engine.

By 1962 sales had dwindled to nothing, but the last G3 was built in 1963. This car is worthy of special mention as, although the company had moved on, some time earlier Ivor had taken a body and chassis and modified the chassis in a number of areas. At the front, brackets and plates were added to facilitate the use of Morris Minor torsion bar suspension, while at the

G3 production at Campsea Ashe early in 1960. This is clearly a changeover period – while most of the bodies are G3s, a few are the earlier Fairlite type. *GINETTA: THE INSIDE STORY* – BOOKMARQUE PUBLISHING

The family home at Chillesford. The factory G3, 361ERT, is parked next to what was then a brand new Austin Mini, which shows just how small the G3 was. *GINETTA: THE INSIDE STORY* – BOOKMARQUE PUBLISHING

This G3 has wider wheels and slightly flared arches, typical of the modifications made to sports cars of this type in the 1960s. JOHN ROSE

rear, mountings were made for the installation of a Minor axle mounted on quarter elliptic springs with lateral location by Panhard rod. The engine was also from the Morris, a sidevalve 803cc unit coupled to its four-speed gearbox. Why this development was done is not completely clear; it may have been an idea to update the G3 concept by making it suitable for parts from the Morris, a far more modern base car than the Ford 10. It may also have been an exercise in evaluating the use of BMC parts for future models.

Whatever the thinking may have been, the car was never fully completed until a local Ginetta fan, David Pleasance, agreed to buy the car on the understanding that it would be completed and made ready for the road. Soon after getting the car he swapped the engine for a 948cc Austin Healey Sprite unit and enjoyed several years of happy motoring in

Here is the old factory G3, 361ERT, as restored in Italy, now sporting wire wheels and looking very smart. GINETTA OWNERS' CLUB

One of only two known photographs of the one-off G3 featuring Morris Minor running gear. The car is not known to survive. DAVID PLEASANCE

what turned out to be a very usable and capable sports car. Had the company followed a different path, maybe a model based around these components could have emerged, but as we will see in the next chapter, by 1963 they were involved in very different challenges.

As with the G2, no records exist of how many Fairlite or G3 cars were built. The company have stated that sixty G3s were made, but this would almost certainly include body-only sales as well as body/chassis units. The number of Fairlite shells made may well exceed this figure – known survivors of both types are roughly equal in number and include the original works car.

G3 (1960–62)

Layout and chassis	Two-seater sports car with space-frame chassis	*Suspension and Steering*	
		Front	Split-beam axle, coil spring damper units
Engine		Rear	Solid axle, transverse leaf spring, torque tube drive
Type	Ford 100E		
Block material	Cast iron	Steering	Steering box (worm and nut)
Head material	Cast iron	Tyres	5.20 × 15in
Cylinders	4	Wheels	Pressed-steel disc, bolt-on
Cooling	Water	Rim width	4 × 15in
Bore and stroke	63.5 × 92.5 mm		
Capacity	1172cc	*Brakes*	
Valves	Sidevalve, 2 valves per cylinder	Type	Drum front and rear
Compression ratio	7 :1	Brake size	10in (250mm)
Carburettor	Downdraught		
Max. power (DIN)	36bhp	*Dimensions*	
Max. torque	53lb ft at 2,500rpm	Track, front	45in (1,143mm)
Fuel capacity	7gal (32ltr)	Track, rear	45in (1,143 mm)
		Wheelbase	90in (2,286 mm)
Transmission		Overall length	148in (3,760 mm)
Gearbox	Ford 3-speed and reverse	Overall width	55.5in (1,410mm)
Clutch	Single dry plate	Overall height	43in (1,092 mm) to top of hood
		Unladen weight	985.5lb (447kg)
Internal Gearbox Ratios			
First	3.4:1	*Performance*	
Second	1.86:1	Top speed	80mph (129km/h)
Third	1:1	0–60mph	not available
Reverse	4.45:1		
Final drive	5.5:1		

CHAPTER THREE

ESTABLISHING THE MARQUE

With so much achieved over a short time, the Walklett brothers could have been forgiven for taking a break; after all, not only had they grown a car-making business but they had simultaneously developed the skill and knowledge to laminate glass fibre to very high standards. However, there was at least one ambition still to be attained – they had yet to build a complete car to their own design without the constraints of incorporating the mechanical parts of a donor car. This was important because in designing to include a collection of parts made for one specific vehicle there are inevitably compromises. They wanted to make a car where no such compromises were required, where they were free to design suspension and select an engine that would be right for their idea of the perfect sports car.

THE GINETTA G4 AND G5

The G4

As highlighted in earlier chapters, Ivor had designed a car that met this criteria as far back as 1957. He and Trevers had started to make the chassis and suspension but it had failed to make progress, partly because of their other projects but also because the complexity caused it to stall at certain key stages. The engine was one of the first hurdles to overcome. Ivor had in mind fitting a 750cc Coventry Climax engine, which was thought to be going into production following a successful debut at Le Mans in a Lotus.

When it became clear the engine wouldn't be built, the lack of a suitable engine was a problem, and they looked closely at the Standard 10 engine. They had already settled on Standard uprights for the front suspension and the idea of a complete package to include uprights, engine, gearbox and rear axle from this source had an appeal. They got as far as inviting a representative from Standard Triumph down to Campsea Ashe to discuss the idea and offer some costings. Based on a supply of 100 units, the offer was attractive at £138, but the brothers were still unsure: the Standard engine was no fireball, and few companies offered much in the way of tuning equipment for these engines.

When time allowed, Ivor and Trevers carried on with the prototype body and chassis. Then, at a key moment in the decision-making process, Ford announced the 105E ohv engine to be fitted to their new Anglia Saloon; coupled with its four-speed gearbox, this would surely be the way to go. The Walkletts knew their decision was right when tuning firms quickly started to give this unit their attention, and so by August 1960 they at last had their car completed – the now ubiquitous Ginetta G4.

Apart from the Ford engine, the car featured double-wishbone front suspension of their own design, making use of Standard uprights and inclined coil spring damper units and initially drum brakes, although after disc brakes appeared on the Triumph Herald these were fitted. At the rear a Ford 105E rear axle was sprung on coil spring dampers and located with twin upper radius arms and an A-frame under the axle, offering further restraint and arresting any

The prototype G4 pictured on Tunstall Common near the Campsea Ashe factory. GINETTA CARS

The G4 chassis complete with centre section bonded on; the bonnet and tail section were quickly detachable. STEVE WYATT/ QUILTER HOUSE

THE COMPONENT CAR

The component car was only really found in the United Kingdom and even then only associated with the makers of specialist cars.

It came about due to the taxation system in place following the war years, whereby all new cars were subject to a tax levied as a percentage of the basic manufacturers' price of a car. The percentage varied over the years but it was typically around 20 per cent, and therefore a substantial amount of money. Pioneering companies like Lotus started arguing that if the cars were supplied in component form for bolting together by the purchaser, purchase tax could not be levied as they were not actually selling a car, merely a collection of parts.

This argument was accepted by the exchequer on the understanding that if professional help was employed to build up the components into a car, tax would still need to be paid, and in addition the makers were not permitted to provide written assembly instructions. In the 1950s a small number of companies used this loophole, including Lotus, Turner, Fairthorpe and TVR, but during the sixties and early seventies a number of other makers joined the group, including Ginetta.

Unlike the slightly 'oily rag' image associated with the building of specials, the construction of component cars was considered a legitimate exercise by many in order to save a significant sum of money and at the same time have the opportunity to drive a new car that stood out from the crowd and usually performed better than the mass-produced alternatives.

This resulted in people from all walks of life building component cars, not just young sports car enthusiasts. In the case of well-finished four-seater sports coupés, such as the Gilbern and Tornado Talisman, people with families also built component cars.

Typically, component cars were supplied fully wired, trimmed and painted but with the engine, gearbox, brakes, suspension and axles supplied separately together with ancillary parts, and it usually took a few days' work to complete a brand-new car for the road. The saving in purchase tax was significant, often meaning that these hand-made specialist cars were no more expensive to buy than a comparable car from a major manufacturer.

The whole practice came to an abrupt end on 1 April 1973, when purchase tax was abolished in favour of value added tax (VAT), which taxed each part individually; as a result, the component car element of the British specialist car industry was shaken to its roots.

sideways movement. The crowning glory, though, was the two-seater open bodywork, now recognized as one of the prettiest of its era and still equally as desired over fifty years later. The front has strong similarities to the Jaguar E Type, although this was still a year from public unveiling, while at the rear, prominent, rounded wings complemented the smooth and aerodynamic shape.

The bodywork was made up of a number of smaller panels, making the process of producing moulds a little easier. The centre section of the car was fully bonded to the chassis frame, adding even more stiffness to the structure. A one-piece front-hinged bonnet gave easy access to the engine and front suspension, while at the rear the one-piece boot moulding was attached by just four bolts, making removal easy for access to the axle, fuel tank and other components. Double-skinned doors and bootlid completed the exterior, while numerous small panels clothed the interior.

Out on the road the G4 lived up to, and maybe even exceeded, their expectations. The handling and road-holding were of the highest order and, with its rack and pinion steering, the car was light and responsive to drive. Due to an overall weight just under 1,000lb the performance was exceptional, given the standard untuned 997cc engine. The brothers were full of confidence that they had a winner on their hands and immediately made plans to market the car as a complete brand-new car in component form.

Launch at the Racing Car Show

Announcing the G4 quietly at the end of 1960, the Walkletts made arrangements to take a stand at the Racing Car Show held at the Royal Horticultural Old Halls in London's Westminster during the first week in January 1961.

For the first time adverts appeared referring to Ginetta Cars Ltd instead of Walklett Bros., which had always been used up to that point. On their tiny stand they placed the white prototype car, now road registered 371GBJ, and another red body chassis unit they had made to enable visitors to view details of the car's inner structure. Priced at £697 in component form, the car achieved praise from many quarters, not just for its looks but also for its specification. They sold the red car pending its completion to a customer from Newcastle and other expressions of interest were recorded. A German DKW tuning specialist by the name of Albrecht Mantzel invited Bob to a meeting at his London hotel to discuss the supply of cars to Germany, less engine, for the fitting of his tuned DKW units. The talks seemed positive and, just two months later, pictures of the G4 were appearing in the German motoring press announcing the forthcoming DKW-powered car which they were calling the HM Jet 850. Mantzel had put together a group of backers, including Adrian Hoven, a well-known German film actor, and Wim Thoeke, at the time a radio personality and later a famous German television quiz master. The initials of Hoven and Mantzel inspired the HM in the project name.

The G4 slotted into the market in a similar place to the Lotus 7, very much a sports car equally at home for road or racing use. The brothers saw the G4 offering more, however, due to its modern styling and arguably less basic appointments for road use. The Lotus was also on display

The first public appearance of the G4, complete with body/chassis unit alongside, at the 1961 Racing Car Show. GINETTA CARS

This poor-quality photograph is all that is known to exist of the first G4s being built at Campsea Ashe. WALKLETT FAMILY

at the show and offered at a similar price to the G4, but halfway through the event Colin Chapman, the Lotus chief, announced a price cut of £100 for his car. The brothers were convinced this was a reaction to the threat he perceived the G4 might pose in the future and he wanted to deal with it straight away.

This was the brothers' first experience of just what a tough business they were now in, but they still felt the appeal of the G4 was strong and that it would sell well. After the show their mood was one of confidence. Trevers and Ivor felt that one of the things holding Ginetta back was their location in rural Suffolk. They were aware that when potential customers wanted to try the cars, the journey to their quiet backwater was often off-putting. In addition, once they did arrive, the premises didn't offer a particularly professional impression for a car-building concern and, from a production point of view, the facilities were small and restricting.

For the first time there was tension between the four brothers. While Trevers and Ivor wanted to move to better premises and build cars, Bob and Doug were less sure

G4 AND G5 (1960–8)

Layout and chassis	Two-seater sports car with space-frame chassis
Engine	
Type	Ford 105E, G5 122E
Block material	Cast iron
Head material	Cast iron
Cylinders	4
Cooling	Water
Bore and stroke	81 × 48.5 mm, G5 81 × 73mm
Capacity	997cc, G5 1498cc
Valves	Overhead valve operated by pushrods, 2 valves per cylinder
Compression ratio	8.9:1, G5 9:1
Carburettor	Downdraught
Max. power (DIN)	39bhp, G5 83bhp
Max. torque	53lb ft at 2,700rpm, G5 91lb ft at 3,600rpm
Fuel capacity	5gal (22.5ltr)
Transmission	
Gearbox	Ford 4-speed and reverse
Clutch	Single dry plate
Internal Gearbox Ratios	
First	4.12:1, G5 3.54:1
Second	2.40:1
Third	1.41:1
Fourth	1:1
Reverse	5.40:1, G5 3.96:1
Final drive	4.2:1, G5 3.7:1
Suspension and Steering	
Front	Twin wishbone, coil spring damper units, anti-roll bar
Rear	Solid axle, radius rod upper arms, A-bracket lower link, coil spring dampers
Steering	Rack and pinion
Tyres	5.20 × 13in
Wheels	Pressed-steel disc, bolt-on (alloy bolt-on or wire knock-on optional)
Rim width	4 × 13in (5.5J × 13 optional)
Brakes	
Type	Disc front and drum rear
Brake size	9in (225mm) front, 8in (200mm) rear
Dimensions	
Track, front	47in (1,203mm)
Track, rear	47in (1,203 mm)
Wheelbase	80in (2,027mm)
Overall length	Series 1 131.5in (3,344mm), Series 2 and 3 140in (3,547mm)
Overall width	56in (1,419mm)
Overall height	32.5in (823mm) to top of windscreen
Unladen weight	994lb (451kg)
Performance	
Top speed	92mph (148km/h), G5 120mph (193km/h)
0–60mph	13.5sec, G5 9.2sec

and were happy with the status quo. If they could all agree on one thing, however, it was that running the agricultural engineering business and the car-making business side by side wasn't a good long-term way forward and that they should concentrate on one or other. It is important to remember that the engineering side was already an established business with good prospects; car making, on the other hand, while it had done well for them so far, was a far more risky proposition.

Move to New Premises

It all came to a head when Ivor and Trevers spotted a disused garage in Witham, Essex and, going out on their own, made arrangements to purchase the premises. The West End Garage, as it was known, was situated at the extreme western end of Witham High Street, an established building that had been built in the early twentieth century. At this time the High Street was part of the A12 trunk road, linking London with Essex and east Suffolk, and indeed the brothers would pass this very building when driving from their Suffolk base to London. The A12 had become a very busy road and, in summer, with traffic heading for the east coast resorts, the build-up through the town caused long delays. By the mid-sixties a bypass had been built.

The West End Garage offered just what the growing business needed – a showroom and office at the front, a large workshop to the rear of the showroom and a long building to the side, ideal for laminating. At the rear, a large yard and a variety of sheds and outbuildings provided plenty of storage, while above the main building two large flats provided living accommodation.

The West End Works, Witham, Essex, where Ginetta moved in 1962. GINETTA OWNERS' CLUB

The new Witham showroom in April 1962. Ivor (left) and Trevers Walklett pose for the local newspaper. *BRAINTREE & WITHAM TIMES/* REPRODUCED BY COURTESY OF THE ESSEX RECORDS OFFICE

Ivor fills up the G4 with Trevers Walklett and his wife Sherry looking on. BRAINTREE & WITHAM TIMES/ REPRODUCED BY COURTESY OF THE ESSEX RECORDS OFFICE

Once the building was in their hands, the pair immediately set to work smartening up the showroom and preparing the workshop ready for production, which was transferred from Suffolk by April 1962. Trevers moved his family into one of the flats above. At this time G3 production had ceased and all efforts were focused on the G4. Both Trevers and Ivor were totally convinced they could make a go of it but in truth G4 sales were not what they had expected.

Well over a year after the excitement of the Racing Car Show debut, only around ten G4s had been sold. Something needed to be done, and Bob Walklett became involved once more with regular visits to Witham. In his view, the car was too expensive to be affordable to its target market and so he set about reducing costs. He wrote to all the suppliers requesting they review their pricing and offer further discounts. Engines and gearboxes had been purchased at trade price from the local Ford agent, Potters of Framlingham, when they were in Suffolk; now Bob arranged a special supply deal directly with Ford, thereby reducing their costs. In the end most suppliers offered to lower their prices and, with Ginetta also reducing their profits, the G4 was offered at the new lower price of £499. This wasn't actually a straight £200 saving as the hoodside screens and paintwork became extras at £22 12s 6d and £17 10s respectively, but the plan worked and sales started to take off. The Ford rear axle was now replaced with the BMC banjo type, which offered the advantage of a lower unsprung weight and the availability of a variety of ratios that were easily changed.

Eventually, Bob and Doug agreed to throw their weight behind the car-making business and the agricultural engineering business was wound down. They both moved down to Witham and all four brothers started working together again. Bob took up the reins of running the business and sales side of things, while Doug took on a role managing the factory and ensuring component supplies were to hand when needed; Doug's knowledge of auto electrics and wiring harnesses was another invaluable asset to the small firm. This left Ivor to design and develop new ideas, working closely with Trevers, who concentrated on turning those ideas into reality. There was also another member of the Walklett family on hand – their sister Dorothy, who supported Bob in the office, acting as his secretary and typist.

As well as increasing G4 sales, Bob brought in much-needed income by selling used cars (some taken in part exchange against new G4s) and a number of new Simca cars. At one point Simca offered Ginetta the opportunity of taking on an official dealership franchise, but Bob took the view that this would be a distraction from their objective of establishing the Ginetta marque and the offer was declined.

Nick Grace really put the G4 on the map, with many successes in 1963. Here we see him at Silverstone in May of that year. REVS INSTITUTE

As early as 1961, 'Fos' Wilson from Newcastle had started racing his G4, and the following year Malcolm Douglas also ventured out on the circuits. These two drivers, along with the occasional appearance of Ivor Walklett in the works car, gave a useful presence at meetings around the country; and in September 1962, Surrey-based Nick Grace took delivery of his G4. Nick, an engineer, was a remarkable man, turning his hand to many challenges, including finding fame in later life for single-handedly restoring a Spitfire aircraft from boxes of parts. He immediately started racing the G4, coming fourth in his first race. For 1963 he invested in a 997cc Martin-tuned engine and swept all before him in the class. At Goodwood he beat the Lotus of John Haynes, who was known to be particularly quick, lapping at 88.16mph (141.88km/h), and by the end of the season he had shown just what the G4 was capable of on tracks all over England.

A G5 seen here in picturesque Fowey in Cornwall. At the time this car was owned by Rod Leach, the famous AC Cobra specialist. GINETTA OWNERS' CLUB

The G5

The beginning of 1963 proved to be a watershed for several other reasons too. In January, for the first time, a 1500cc engine had been fitted into a car for a customer, and the brothers decided to call this version the G5. The performance with this engine was not far short of electrifying, and from then on this was a popular choice for buyers.

Around the same time, an American, Jack Walsh, a keen racer who ran a European car sales business in Haverhill, Massachusetts, ordered a car with a view to taking more if sufficient interest was shown. In addition, German Albrecht Mantzel had finally ordered two cars modified to accept his Mantzel-tuned 3-cylinder, two-stroke DKW engines and the complex exhaust system that they required to extract maximum performance from the power units. These cars were sufficiently different to be given the model name G6.

Finally the company had made an application to the RAC (who were acting on behalf of the FIA) for the G4 to be homologated in the 1000cc GT category; and in September the G4 was officially accepted.

In the USA, G4s were popular on the East Coast. Here the cars of Monty Wells and Gerry Rose are ready to sprint at Orange Airport, Massachusetts. GINETTA OWNERS' CLUB

The G4 Series 2

As well as making the G4 capable of accommodating these different engines, Ivor and Trevers had been working on body modifications. The first was a revised rear body section. Around 8in (200mm) longer, it gave a sleeker look to the rear as well as a larger boot capacity, and made it possible to accommodate a new hardtop which had also been designed.

The hardtop, although bolt-on, was not detachable in the recognized way, incorporating a curved laminated windscreen and 'bubble' Perspex rear screen. The top required the windscreen wipers to exit the body further forward than open-top versions. This version made the car look extremely sleek and also eligible for the GT class in racing events.

The new Series 2 bodywork proved a big success when introduced in 1963. GINETTA OWNERS' CLUB

Ivor Walklett's pencil sketch design for the G4 hardtop. IVOR WALKLETT

Cars equipped with the revised tail section were known as the G4 Series 2, and were offered at an additional £15, while the hardtop, complete with front and rear screens, was an extra £49 10s. Perspex sidescreens were priced at £9 10s a pair. The company offered a full range of tuning equipment for the engines in various stages but a fully tuned 1500 engine, complete with twin 40 DCOE Weber carburettors, was £110 extra.

THE GINETTA G6 AND G7

The first of the DKW-powered G6 cars was entered for the 1,000km sports car race at the Nürburgring, but by the time it was ready for dispatch at Witham, it was too late to send it to Mantzel's headquarters in Ingolstadt, Germany for fitment of the specially tuned DKW engine and ZF gearbox. To save time, the car was air freighted directly to Frankfurt from Heathrow and taken straight to the Nürburgring, where the engine and gearbox were fitted in the pits.

In the race it was driven by Mantzel's son Dieter and another German racer, Peter Ruby. Problems were encountered during practice, when the handling was found to be extremely bad. This mystified the Walkletts and Bob was flown out to investigate. He immediately saw the problem: the group had fitted a very heavy steel fuel tank in order

The G6 raced for the first time at the 1963 Nürburgring 1000km. The high screen in practice was to meet minimum height regulations, which were relaxed for the race itself. GINETTA OWNERS' CLUB

After the Nürburgring event, the Ginetta G6, complete with DKW engine, was sold to Swiss Alfred Junker, seen here at the St Ursanne Les Rangiers hill-climb. GINETTA OWNERS' CLUB

A G6 DKW road car was also built, seen here complete with hardtop in the late 1960s. GINETTA OWNERS' CLUB

to do the entire race without refuelling, but the weight had completely compressed the rear springs. With no time to remove the tank and fit the original, they were forced to carry on but with the tank only partly filled. Despite this compromise the car performed very well and was on for a good result, with the 850cc two-stroke clocking 117mph (188km/h) at one timing point, before a fuel blockage ended their challenge. The actual Nürburgring car is the only G6 known to have survived and sadly this car was stripped of its DKW parts in the 1960s and converted to Ford power.

Encouraged by this good showing, talks immediately started between Albrecht Mantzel and the brothers about an entry for the forthcoming 500km race to be held in September 1963. Mantzel wanted to try using the entire engine and transaxle assembly from the DKW F12. There were two options: one would be to use the whole package in a mid-engine configuration; or alternatively split the engine and transaxle, leaving the engine at the front and mounting the transaxle at the rear, thereby getting a better weight distribution and more weight over the driving wheels. As the first idea would have involved a new chassis, attention focused on mounting a transaxle at the rear.

Mantzel arranged for a five-speed transaxle to be delivered to Witham and work commenced on the new car, now dubbed the G7. Mounting the transaxle in the chassis proved straightforward, particularly as the package included inboard drum brakes, but it was necessary to develop an independent rear suspension arrangement. Ivor had been considering an independent layout for the G4/5 for some time; he was aware that since the 1500-engined G5 had been made, getting the power to the road at the rear of the ultra-light car was an issue. Time before the Nürburgring event was short and in Germany interest in DKWs was ebbing, Mantzel was losing enthusiasm and the brothers felt the whole project was losing momentum. Eventually the G7 prototype was shelved; the incomplete car was parked up at the rear of the factory and eventually broken up.

No photographs of the G7 remain but this DKW F12 transaxle was used in the prototype. GINETTA OWNERS' CLUB

THE G4R

Work on the independent rear suspension wasn't wasted, however, and before long a fully independent G4 with a cut-down axle, inboard drum brakes, short driveshafts and independently sprung hub-carriers was being put together in a car that was to be called the G4R. Confusion was beginning to reign over the models being produced, in particular the G4 and G5. Cars were now available with 997cc, 1200cc and 1500cc Ford engines at £499, £517 10s, and £525 respectively and, with these being built alongside one another in the workshop, they were all being referred to as G4. Customers were also calling cars G4 and eventually it was decided to call even the 1500cc cars G4 1500. This has led to the anomaly where 1500cc cars built between January and September 1963 carry a G5 chassis number while cars built thereafter have G4 numbers.

By the autumn of 1963 orders were being received at a rate that had the factory working at full capacity, and extra labour was taken on to cope with demand. One order

CHRIS MEEK

Born in 1932, Chris started his motor racing in the fifties, firstly on motorbikes but soon graduating to 500cc single-seater racing cars. He also raced sports cars, such as the rare Fairthorpe Atom Major, and built a strong relationship with Elva Cars in Hastings; he drove their Courier sports cars with some success, as well the Formula Junior Elva 300.

Chris Meek always kept a watchful eye on the latest developments in racing and he spotted the potential of the Ginetta G4. In October 1963 he made the journey down from his home town of Leeds to the Ginetta works at Witham to see for himself what the G4 was all about. This meeting proved a turning point for both Meek and Ginetta, and he ordered a new G4. The combination of the G4 and Meek was formidable. Following an unofficial works drive in 1964, he continued in a privately entered G4R with works support in 1965 and 1966 in similar vein. In between he assisted in development of other Ginetta models and forged a lifelong friendship with the Walklett family.

Chris continued to race in Formula 2 and Formula Ford and, during the seventies, was highly successful in production sports car racing, driving cars as diverse as a DeTomaso, MG Midget and Panther Lima. All this was only one side of the Meek story, however. As a businessman he was similarly driven, building up Leeds-based Titan Property Ltd into a highly successful business, which in turn supported Chris in Formula Ford in a Titan Mk 6 and sponsored Tom Pryce in the Token RJ02 for his Formula 1 debut races.

Later, in the eighties, Chris, through Titan, purchased the freehold of the Mallory Park Racing circuit – the scene of some of his greatest drives. He supported the Ginetta Owners' Club, arranging for them to use the facilities at Mallory for both the fortieth and fiftieth anniversary celebrations of the Ginetta marque. Chris also owned many exciting road cars, including Ferraris, a Porsche and a Bentley to name but a few. He died in 2016.

Chris Meek, a larger-than-life character, seen here after one of his many race wins. GINETTA OWNERS' CLUB

The Works G4R, 111NMD, on the front row of the grid with Meek driving. This car had huge successes in his hands. CHRIS MEEK

Meek leads Johnny Blades at Silverstone, both in G4Rs – two of the quickest to race these cars. CHRIS MEEK

received was of particular interest to the brothers: well-known and successful club racing driver Chris Meek wanted a G4 with the lightest bodywork the factory could achieve. Meek's car, which was delivered in December, was a hardtop version less engine, as he planned to fit his own Ford unit bored out to 1650cc. He had already established a reputation for hard racing and winning, and with the G4 he didn't disappoint.

Meek achieved success straight away with his G4, winning races at circuits up and down the country, but on 19 July 1964, fate was to take a hand. Meek was at Cadwell Park in Lincolnshire when in practice his G4 spun and turned over, suffering a lot of damage. The brothers had gone to the event to support Meek and taken their prototype G4R in the hope of getting a little testing time on the circuit; it was important to test the new IRS set-up and the new Lotus Twin Cam engine they had acquired to fully exploit the extra grip they were hoping for.

Meek, shaken after his accident, asked if he could borrow this untested car for the race. The Walkletts were unsure if Meek was fit to race at all and took some persuading, but in the end he got the go-ahead and formed up on the grid. When the flag dropped, he took the lead and went on to win by a considerable margin. It was an amazing debut for the G4R and almost immediately Meek was asked to become the unofficial works driver. For the rest of the season he and the G4R were seldom beaten, racking up the impressive tally of eight wins and six second places from fourteen starts by the season end. In September 1964, it was announced that the G4R would now be available in limited numbers alongside the standard solid-axle model for competition use. Several orders were received immediately.

The G4 was now firmly on the map as one of the most competitive cars in GT club racing. The following season saw many established names driving a G4 alongside Meek, in particular Johnny Blades and Mike Reid, while John Burton, Paul Bryan and others new to competition immediately made a mark. Amid the excitement of just what the G4 was capable of on the track, there was a sharp reminder of the risks involved and the fine line drivers trod competing in these cars, when young Ginetta enthusiast Mike Whitehead turned his G4 over at Mallory Park and tragically succumbed to his injuries two weeks later.

Aside from the racing successes, publicity came from predictable sources. *Motor Sport* tested the G4 as early as 1962, soon after the price reduction, and concluded by saying, 'As a dual purpose car it is difficult to think of many cars at such a modest price which can compete with the Ginetta.' *Practical Motorists'* Chris Webb built a G4 kit, which was serialized over several issues, and he then had the completed car road tested by Graham Hill, the current world champion driver at the time; Hill was complimentary. Less predictable perhaps was a request from the BBC for the loan of a G4 to appear in an episode of the acclaimed series *Play for Today.* When aired, the programme featured the car being driven around Brighton by the main character.

The successes of the G4 were reaching far and wide. Orders were now coming in from Europe, but it was in the USA that the early faith shown in the G4 by Jack Walsh

The US Ginetta importer, Competition Car Engineering, with their transporter fully loaded and ready to leave for the Sebring 12 Hours in 1965. GINETTA OWNERS' CLUB

A pit visit for the G4R during practice for the Sebring 12 Hours. Jack Walsh drove, with Canadians Peter Keith and Gord Brown sharing the car. GINETTA OWNERS' CLUB

paid dividends. Walsh and his business partner, ex-patriate Englishman George Kipps, imported G4s, usually in pairs, from mid-1963 onwards. Cars often had a high specification, including some with Cosworth- or Holbay-tuned engines. They found customers across the east coast of the USA and Canada; many owners were competition-minded, and the Sports Car Club of America accepted the G4 as a production car for the 1965 season.

In March 1965 a very special G4R left the Witham factory for shipment to Walsh, who had asked Ginetta to enter the car for the Sebring 12 Hours race. It arrived just in time. Driven by Walsh and two Canadian drivers, Peter Keith and Gord Brown, the specification included a Vegantune Lotus Twin Cam engine, disc rear brakes, which were now standard on all G4Rs, and oil cooler to go with the standard dry sump G4R arrangement.

The G4 was also a popular race car in Canada. Here Allen Hickling sits on the grid at St Jovite in 1965; just visible alongside is the similar Citation Motors-sponsored car of Barry Rosenburg. ALLEN HICKLING

A group fitted this G4 with a Saab two-stroke engine and gearbox, emulating the G6 project in Europe. GINETTA OWNERS' CLUB

In practice it ran well until the engine blew, but with the loan of a Twin Cam from Jim Clark's Lotus Cortina, which competed in a supporting race, it was running strongly until this engine also broke at just past the six-hour point.

Championship wins in Canada by Allen Hickling and Peter Roberts further cemented the appeal of the G4 across the North American continent.

Around the same time, a G4 minus engine and gearbox was imported by Walsh for some rather special attention. A group on the east coast had set up a race series for cars powered by the Saab two-stroke engine; with this in mind, one of these units was installed in the G4 together with its gearbox, clearly mirroring the DKW-engined G6 in its concept. This interesting car is known to survive, but we don't have a record of how many times it raced or if it had any success.

THE GINETTA G10 AND G11

The G10

The strong relationship with US importers Jack Walsh and George Kipps led to discussions about the possibility of Ginetta building a model powered by an American V8 engine that could compete head to head with similar hybrid cars, such as the AC Cobra and TVR Griffith. The idea appealed to the four brothers and Ivor immediately set about drawing up a suitable chassis design to accommodate the popular Ford 4.7-litre V8 engine and gearbox. He realized that the power and torque generated by this unit would require a suspension design to cope with the forces being

The G10 chassis was light and strong. Here the fabricated front suspension can be clearly seen, complete with twin coil spring damper units. Note the thick radiator to cool the big V8 engine. ROTHGALLERIES.COM

At the rear, the G10 featured a rigidly mounted differential and inboard brakes, together with more purpose-made wishbones and specially cast hub-carriers. ROTHGALLERIES.COM

generated if maximum use was to be made of the performance available.

Following the success of the G4, Ivor again planned a multi-tube frame on which the body would be fully bonded to further increase rigidity. The chassis frame was welded up in square tubing, with twin-wishbone front suspension fabricated by Ginetta utilizing Triumph TR4 uprights and – unusually – a pair of coil spring damper units to each wheel.

At the rear, a Salisbury differential unit was rigidly mounted to the chassis, while specially cast hub-carriers were hung on wishbones and, again, a pair of spring damper units supported each corner.

When it came to the body design, Trevers and Ivor came up with an idea that would both speed up the development of the new body and also make the assembly of cars in production quicker. They had found that door assemblies were time-consuming, both in design and manufacture, and so they decided to use the complete door carcass, handles, latches, glass, winding mechanism and interior trim, from a production car. Using a proprietary door skin determines the body lines of the car and features of the chosen door, such as swage lines and curvature, need to be incorporated into overall body design. For this new car (to be known as the G10), they settled on doors from the MGB, which incorporated everything they needed – the bodyshell was developed from these and the aluminium-framed MGB roadster windscreen. The finished car had a muscular appearance unsurprisingly echoing the shape and some proportions of the MGB.

The completed G10 ready to go on display at the Racing Car Show, January 1965. GINETTA OWNERS' CLUB

The skills and experience the brothers had gained were now paying dividends, and Trevers was able to sculpt the new body from Ivor's drawings very quickly, enabling moulds to be taken ready for production. In the USA, Walsh and Kipps were delighted; they felt it would find customers for both road and competition use, and placed an initial order for six cars.

The brothers felt the market in the UK would be limited for such a car but to test the sales potential they once again took a stand at the Racing Car Show in London, where the G10 was launched in January 1965 priced at £2,250 (£2,729 with purchase tax added).

The car was a prototype and hastily finished for the show with open bodywork, although a coupé top was also planned as an alternative. During the show the car was highly praised and visitors to the stand included Lord Snowdon, husband to the Queen's sister, Princess Margaret. Bob Walklett proudly showed Lord Snowdon the Ginetta display and some time was spent discussing the G10.

Back from the show and with the US market in mind, the brothers decided to start building up a second G10 with the proposed coupé top, which was fully bonded to the main body and not detachable, incorporating purpose-made front and rear screens.

GINETTA G10 (1965–6)

Layout and chassis	Two-seater sports car with space-frame chassis
Engine	
Type	Ford
Block material	Cast iron
Head material	Cast iron
Cylinder	V8
Cooling	Water
Bore and stroke	101 × 473mm
Capacity	4727cc
Valves	Overhead valve operated by pushrods, 2 valves per cylinder, hydraulic tappets
Compression ratio	11:1
Carburettor	4-barrel
Max. power (DIN)	27bhp
Max. torque	314lb ft at 3,400rpm
Fuel capacity	16gal (73ltr)
Transmission	
Gearbox	Ford 4-speed and reverse
Clutch	263mm-diameter plate
Internal Gearbox Ratios	
First	2.36:1
Second	1.78:1
Third	1.41:1
Fourth	1:1
Reverse	2.36:1
Final drive	3.31:1 limited slip
Suspension and Steering	
Front	Twin wishbone, twin coil spring damper units, anti-roll bar
Rear	Rigid differential, wishbones, twin coil spring dampers
Steering	Rack and pinion
Tyres	5.90 × 15in
Wheels	Wire knock-on
Rim width	5.5 × 15in
Brakes	
Type	Disc front and rear
Brake size	11.5in (290mm) front, 10.5in (263mm) rear
Dimensions	
Track, front	51in (1,295mm)
Track, rear	51in (1,295mm)
Wheelbase	90in (2,286mm)
Overall length	160in (4,063mm)
Overall width	61in (1,549mm)
Overall height	47in (1,206mm)
Unladen weight	2,183lb (990kg)
Performance	
Top speed	155mph (249km/h)
0–60mph	5.7sec

Lord Snowdon discusses the G10 with Bob Walklett at the Racing Car Show. To the left in this photograph is Alec Issigonis (designer of the Morris Minor and Mini) and behind him John Cooper (famous head of Cooper Cars).
GINETTA: THE INSIDE STORY – BOOKMARQUE PUBLISHING

The Ford V8 engine is a snug fit in the G10 engine bay. GINETTA OWNERS' CLUB

Racing the G10

The show car was taken to one side and prepared for racing, including tuning the engine and fitting wider wheels, which involved wheel arch extensions. For their G4R they had made magnesium alloy wheels to their own design, even going as far as making the patterns for the castings; matching wheels were fitted to the racing G10 in place of the standard wire wheels for road cars. Once the car was completed, testing was a priority. The budget for circuit hire and the like was limited but a suitable 'test track' was available closer to home.

The new Witham bypass, which had recently been completed, navigated around the outskirts of town with three straights and two steady curves. By modern standards the road was deserted and, picking the quieter times of day, Ivor and Trevers would drive out to the road and hang back over the joining flyover to wait for a long, clear break in the traffic before unleashing the G10. In the days before speed limits on these roads the car could touch 150mph (240km/h).

A young Londoner, Dennis Featherstone, was on the bypass one morning as a passenger in his brother's Aston Martin and, as the pair settled into rapid 110mph (177km/h) cruising speed, the Aston was suddenly rocked violently as the G10 hurtled by 20 or 30mph (32–48km/h) faster. What was this car? They gave chase as it left the bypass and headed back into Witham only to discover the Ginetta car factory at the end of the High Street. Dennis was smitten and soon bought a G4: more than fifty years and a number of Ginettas later he still drives one.

Ivor Walklett also remembers those test runs on the bypass. On one occasion, after a 150mph (240km/h) dash to check suspension settings, the G10 was driven back to the factory and parked in the yard outside the main workshop. A group were stood together talking when they heard a loud bang outside; on investigation it was noted the G10 had a flat tyre and on closer examination it turned out that the magnesium rim had split wide open. Later it was found that this particular rim had been badly machined, leaving the material too thin, and the increased pressure due to heat build-up from its high-speed run had caused it to rupture. Had this occurred at 150mph the consequences would have been unthinkable.

It was time to test the G10 on the track and an entry was made at Brands Hatch for Chris Meek to drive the G10 in a GT car race on 28 November 1965. The G10 had been well tested but in its first competitive challenge Meek placed it

Chris Meek drives the works G10 to a famous first-time-out win at Brands Hatch in November 1965. CHRIS MEEK

firmly in pole position. In the race there was a fierce battle with a lightweight competition E-Type Jaguar which led the G10 for several laps before Meek slipped by to win first time out.

The American Deal Falls Through

It was a bittersweet victory, however. Weeks earlier Bob Walklett had received a phone call from George Kipps in Massachusetts to say he wanted to fly over and discuss their order for the six G10s. Bob sensed all was not well, and when Kipps arrived he was nervous and flushed. It transpired that all the orders he and Walsh had taken were cancelled due to the AC Cobra being homologated and re-categorized into

The interior of the left-hand drive G10 road car sold to American William Moyka. GINETTA OWNERS' CLUB

Exported to New York in 1967, the Moyka G10 was found in the mid-eighties, as seen here, in poor condition but still original. BRUCE LYON

the GT class by the Sports Car Club of America (SCCA), whereas the Ginetta had been placed into the Sports Racing class. The G10 would be like a fish out of water against this opposition and the buyers knew it. Kipps was afraid Ginetta would sue for their losses, but Bob knew it was pointless – only the legal profession would benefit from such an action. Kipps flew back to America, and no further Ginettas were sold through their dealership.

With engines and gearboxes specially imported through Ford sitting on the factory floor and a part-completed left-hand-drive car already in production, the situation was serious, but nothing could be done.

Eventually Bob managed to find a buyer for it at a discounted price. He was William Moyka, an American oil man working temporarily on Teesside. He took delivery in August 1966 of a car that was to road specification and registered on temporary import plates. One condition of the deal was that the car would be made available for two magazines to road test; this was eventually done in early 1967, before Moyka returned to the USA later that year taking the car with him.

Around the same time, the factory sold their race-winning G10, now fitted with a coupé top at the request of the new owner.

The ex-works G10 as presented in the late 1970s by Rod Leach, proprietor of Nostalgia, the well-known high-end classic car specialists. CLIVE BERRY

In recent years the ex-works G10 has been the subject of a painstaking rebuild. Here it can be seen looking superb at Oulton Park. JOE GOWAND

So ended the G10 story. It had promised so much but in the end delivered little apart from the impressive Meek race win. The cars are much admired today and, over the last twenty years, several continuation cars have been built using bodies from the original moulds.

The G11

As previously noted, the brothers were under no illusions that the G10 would sell in numbers in the UK. The number of potential buyers for raw V8 high-performance sport cars was small and already covered by the few specialist manufacturers making such cars. In addition Bristol and Jensen could make small numbers of high-end luxury V8 cars successfully. Notwithstanding this, the brothers were also very aware that the look and general package of the G10 were much admired and there had been comments that if it had a smaller engine it would sell well in the UK.

It was decided to rework the G10 chassis to enable the fitting of a 4-cylinder engine, while at the rear the expensive independent set-up of the G10 would give way to a live axle located with radius arms and an A-bracket all suspended on coil spring damper units. A change at the front involved

GINETTA G11 (1966–9)

Layout and chassis	Two-seater sports car with space-frame chassis
Engine	
Type	MG
Block material	Cast iron
Head material	Cast iron
Cylinders	4
Cooling	Water
Bore and stroke	80.3 × 89mm
Capacity	1798cc
Valves	Overhead valve operated by pushrods, 2 valves per cylinder
Compression ratio	8.9:1
Carburettor	Twin SU
Max. power (DIN)	95bhp
Max. torque	110lb ft at 3,000rpm
Fuel capacity	10gal (45ltr)
Transmission	
Gearbox	Ford 4-speed and reverse
Clutch	Single dry plate
Internal Gearbox Ratios	
First	3.64:1
Second	2.214:1
Third	1.374:1
Fourth	1:1
Reverse	4.76:1
Final drive	3.9:1
Suspension and Steering	
Front	Twin wishbone, coil spring damper units, anti-roll bar
Rear	Solid axle, radius arms, A-bracket, coil spring dampers
Steering	Rack and pinion
Tyres	5.90 × 14in
Wheels	Wire knock-on
Rim width	4.5 × 14in
Brakes	
Type	Disc front and drum rear
Brake size	9.5in (238mm) front, 10in (250mm) rear
Dimensions	
Track, front	50in (1,270 mm)
Track, rear	50in (1,270 mm)
Wheelbase	90in (2,286mm)
Overall length	160in (4,063 mm)
Overall width	60in (1,524mm)
Overall height	47in (1,206mm)
Unladen weight	1,623lb (736kg)
Performance	
Top speed	110mph (177km/h)
0–60mph	9.8sec

The prototype G11 was sold in September 1966 and is seen here soon after. The whereabouts of this car is currently unknown. GINETTA OWNERS' CLUB

The second GT11, originally coloured British Racing Green, now painted metallic blue. JOHN ROSE

fitting the complete suspension, including wishbones, from the Triumph Herald/Spitfire range in place of the fabricated G10 set-up. The whole exercise was quick and simple to do; the only dilemma was which engine, gearbox and rear axle to instal, and here the brothers made an error that they would later regret. Because of the MG input with the doors, obtaining these major components from the same source seemed to make perfect sense, particularly when the package would bring the added benefit of an optional overdrive. Bob got a positive response when negotiating with BMC, the MG parent company, and was able to purchase the parts required at good discount.

They decided to go ahead and, with only very minor changes to the bonnet and internal mouldings, the body was pure G10. A coupé body was built up on the revised chassis and this new derivative became the Ginetta G11. The first car was painted white and proudly displayed on the Ginetta Cars stand at the Racing Car Show in January 1966. Priced at £1,098 in component form and £1,325 fully built and tax paid, it was competitive and half the price of the G10: how could it fail?

Initial interest was encouraging, and back at the Witham factory a batch of chassis frames were made ready for production. When the Walkletts ordered the necessary MG parts to build up a second car, however, it wasn't long before they realized they might have made a wrong decision. The engines, gearboxes and axles, all parts that were used on a variety of cars in the BMC range, were delivered promptly from BMC at Cowley, Oxford, but after weeks there were still no doors. As Bob pressed for delivery, he discovered that these were coming from MG at Abingdon and they were dragging their heels in meeting the order. It soon dawned on the brothers that MG had no interest in encouraging a company like Ginetta to build cars so similar to their own MGB but with every chance of outperforming it. Eventually they received some door assemblies but they were all for one side only, which meant not even one car could be completed. It was abundantly clear that cars couldn't be manufactured in this haphazard way and the G11 was doomed right from the start.

Disillusioned, the brothers sold the prototype to a dental student from Sheffield, who had owned a G4 previously. It was road registered NWA56D in September 1966, while a second car, another coupé, was eventually finished off and painted in British Racing Green for a customer. Just before it was delivered to its new owner in January 1967, it was displayed on the Ginetta stand at the Racing Car Show. This car

Russell Madden built several G11s from body/chassis units supplied by Ginetta. Here the first car he built, VON620J, is seen close to completion with Madden's Series 3 G4 parked behind. RUSSELL MADDEN

was fitted with overdrive and Armstrong adjustable shock absorbers as a special order.

This wasn't quite the end of the G11 story. Several G4 owners were interested in moving up to a G11, and in 1968 three open cars were built, two of which were part complete for the owners to fit MG components they had sourced. One of these cars went to Birmingham-based Russell Madden, who finished his car off to a very high standard, including a tuned engine.

Another Madden-built G11 unusually fitted with a Riley 1500cc engine. TOM KENNY

Madden had the car featured in several motoring magazines during 1970 and 1971, with the result that VON620J became quite a celebrity. By now Madden had well and truly caught the G11 bug, and in 1969 he purchased another body/chassis unit which he built up with a Riley 1500 engine for his wife to drive. In 1971 he persuaded Bob Walklett to sell him the remaining chassis from that original batch, and supply him with bodywork as and when required.

This latter move was regretted by Bob in later years, in that it rather watered down the 'currency' of the G11 model when such a percentage of cars had not been factory finished. Just one further G11 body/chassis unit was built, as late as 1990, to special order for a Ginetta enthusiast. The total number of G11s built totalled just ten cars and all are known to survive today with the exception of the original prototype; some have now been adapted to G10 specification with Ford V8 engine and independent rear suspension in homage to the original concept.

This G11 has been rebuilt to G10 V8 specification and is seen here with proud owner, Dennis Featherstone, and his wife, Ellen. DENNIS FEATHERSTONE

THE SQUARE-TUBE G4

Back on the Racing Car Show stand in 1966, as well as the launch of the G11 there was another new development that was a lot more low-key and so mostly went unnoticed. Alongside the G11, there was a new G4R destined for delivery to racer Johnny Blades immediately after the show – his second G4R and another G4 road car. Externally the car was the same as the G4 the company had now been making for some years but under the skin there was a new square-tube chassis.

When the G4 was designed in the fifties, Ivor's designs all featured round-tube chassis, but for ease of fabrication, it soon became clear that square-tube chassis were much quicker and easier to produce. With that in mind, from the G3 onwards all the production car chassis were of square tubing. In order to keep the price of the G4 competitive and to improve the company's profit margins on G4 sales, Ivor redesigned the chassis in square tubing and incorporated the Triumph Herald/Spitfire wishbones and uprights in place of the original fabricated wishbones. The new chassis was still very rigid and the handling of the highest order, but for those wanting a G4 for serious racing, the G4R remained in production with a round-tube frame. The car on the show stand was fitted with wire wheels; this feature was a new optional extra offered with the G4 and the appearance was very pleasing, but at £35 extra these were expensive and only three cars were sold in this form.

THE G4 SERIES 3

Despite the G4 having been in production for five years, sales remained reasonably strong; however, as mass-produced sports cars evolved, they became increasingly refined and the G4 was raw by comparison. As 1966 progressed and the troubles with the G11 played out, it was clear that the G4 would need to remain the company's main product for rather longer than had been anticipated.

There was another problem looming, too. The construction and use regulations now stated a minimum height above ground level that headlamps should be mounted and the low G4 lamps were marginal on this. Ivor set his mind to the challenge of the headlamps, whilst Trevers looked at improving the model's creature comforts. The fruits of their efforts were unveiled at the 1967 Racing Car Show with the launch of the G4 Series 3. This version featured a new bonnet moulding incorporating headlamps that lay flush on the bonnet for daylight use, and which could then be manually raised upright when required at night – a similar idea in appearance to the Lamborghini Miura. The interior had been improved with a contoured dashboard with neatly arranged

The Ginetta stand at the 1966 Racing Car Show. In the foreground is the prototype square-tube G4 with the new wire wheels option fitted. Bob Walklett is seated right with Sherry and Ivor is reading a newspaper.
GINETTA OWNERS' CLUB

The new Series 3 G4 with lay-down headlamp bonnet. This open car was originally red and was the first Series 3 delivered to a customer. COLIN HARDS

matching instruments, a centre console and more comfortable moulded seats. The show car also featured exterior door handles and a new unique side window arrangement for hardtop cars, now called the Series 3 coupé, designed to make the windows more rigid and stop them sucking out at speed. It was a good idea, but the downside was a complete lack of ventilation, and the feature seems to have been dropped.

With a Ford 997cc engine, the car was priced at £668, while the new option of a 1300cc crossflow engine put it up to £691 10s and the 1500cc pre-crossflow unit cost £699; it is thought no cars were supplied with the 1300cc unit. The new bonnet featured a curved front edge that mimicked a bumper, but a chrome-plated bumper to fit over it was an extra £5 10s. This was a significant increase in price over the earlier series of G4 but now cars came fully painted, trimmed and carpeted and disc brakes were now standard. As before, a full range of tuning equipment was available at extra cost.

Although the prototype coupé was ready for display at the January show, G4 production had been temporarily halted due to a volume of orders for another new model, the G12. It was May 1967 before the first customer G4 Series 3 was delivered, an open-top car, but shortly afterwards orders were dispatched for a mix of coupé and open-top cars in roughly equal numbers. By the end of 1967, however, another new development occurred – Ford made their 1600 crossflow engine available to Ginetta.

With this, the 1500cc option was dropped and the 1600 became the flagship model, priced at £739 with the standard 74bhp engine and £785 with the 95bhp GT version fitted. Interestingly, the price for the coupé version was the same as the open car with hood and side screens. Wide steel wheels of 5½J section had always been an optional extra on the G4 at £3 10s extra each, but with the 1600cc model for the first time Cosmic alloy wheels were also offered, at £8 10s each.

In Series 3 guise the G4 was by far the most refined

A Series 3 coupé G4 with 1600cc Ford crossflow engine, a striking car on the road. GINETTA OWNERS' CLUB

Chris Meek once famously told Ivor Walklett that 'the road is just a guide'; here he demonstrates what he meant as he puts all four wheels of his G4R off track on his way to another win. CHRIS MEEK

version yet, but it was starting to lag behind its natural competitors and, truth be told, it was not selling in the volume that had been achieved a few years earlier. Part of the sales decline may have been due to the frontal appearance – the lay-down headlamps were not universally liked by all – but there was no getting away from the fact that the G4 had run its course and a replacement was needed.

The last production G4 left the factory in June 1968, but in racing the model was still a winning car. Meek had raced his last season with the G4R in 1966, but there were many owners active in club racing throughout the sixties and early seventies.

In the north of England John Absalom was extremely quick through nearly a decade of G4 racing, while in the south the Gould brothers, John and George, enjoyed much success, including a national Modsports (modified sports car) championship win for John in 1970. Overseas, Monty Wells won the New England Region SCCA championship in 1966, and in 1968 Gerry Hunt, based in Malaysia, won the unofficial Far Eastern championship.

John Absalom was one of the fastest and most successful G4 racers well into the 1970s. JIM EVANS

PETER 'LEIGH' DAVIS

Warwickshire-born Davis enjoyed large motorcycles as a teenager. The chance sighting of a Ginetta G4 while waiting at a zebra crossing on the outskirts of Birmingham changed all that. He followed the car home, where he met the owner Ian Jennens, who had driven his G4 since 1963 and was happy to explain its virtues. Jennens himself still owns a Ginetta and may well lay claim to the record for longest continual ownership of a Ginetta, currently fifty-four years.

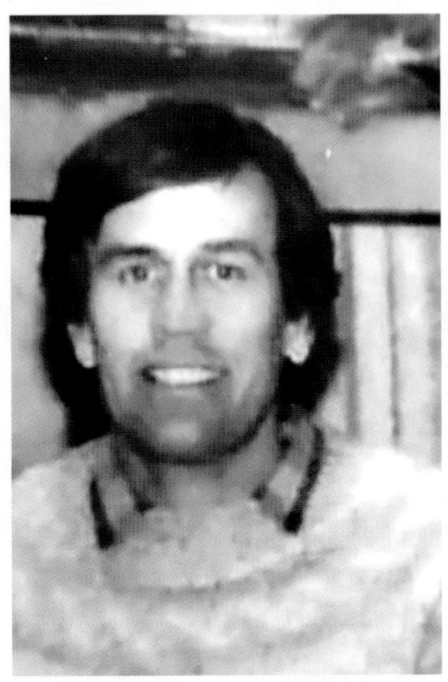

Leigh Davis has raced his G4 for over fifty years in many forms of the sport, a Ginetta legend. AUTHOR

Davis wasted no time in placing an order at Witham for a G4, which was delivered in component form in October 1966 and subsequently registered LAC64E in January 1967. Later that year he entered it for his first race at Castle Coombe and was totally bitten by the racing bug.

Davis has competed in a range of racing categories in his G4 with a variety of engines fitted. Starting in Special GT racing, he progressed to Modsports before turning to international sports car racing, entering the Barcelona 1000km sports car race in 1971 and the Targo Florio in 1972. In the eighties he rebuilt the car as a rally machine and twice entered the Himalayan Rally in India, a hugely gruelling event, before trying his hand at the Pirelli Marathon in 1988.

Enjoying the challenge of rallying, Davis and co-driver Duncan McNiven entered the ADAC Rallye Tour d'Europe later the same year. The event, covering 4,500 miles (7,200km) and taking in ten countries, was a huge challenge in the eight-day time frame, but they won their class against very tough opposition. Despite his many adventures in the G4, Davis looks upon this class win as his greatest achievement. Two more attempts at this event failed to achieve equal results – retirement sidelined them on both occasions.

In between he found the time to become a car manufacturer himself, designing and manufacturing the Liege sports car, which has proved very successful: over sixty were built between 1997 and 2005. He has enjoyed several competition successes driving his own Liege cars.

However, the draw of a competition challenge in his Ginetta can't be easily resisted by Leigh Davis, and in 2003 he entered his G4 in La Carrera PanAmericana, taking twenty-eighth place against mostly large American V8s. Most recently he also ran in the 2014 Daytona 24 Hours Classic.

Despite over fifty years of racing the same Ginetta, he continues to look for challenges in which to test himself and the car in an unparalleled story of Ginetta ownership.

Prepared for the Himalayan Rally, this G4 competed in two of these gruelling events in the hands of Leigh Davis. GINETTA OWNERS' CLUB

Gerry Hunt was Far Eastern GT champion in Malaysia, here driving his second G4, a Series 3 1500. GINETTA OWNERS' CLUB

Leigh Davis at speed in his Modsports G4. GINETTA OWNERS' CLUB

One driver, Leigh Davis, deserves a special mention: he purchased his G4 in 1966 and is still competing with it fifty years later.

Despite production coming to an end, the G4 was still popular with many fans, and the model was later revived in a variety of forms, as we will see later in the book. Production figures from factory sources state around 500 cars were built, but for various reasons it is impossible to verify this figure. Around 150 cars are known to have survived; many of the remainder were destroyed in racing accidents, while others were broken up to supply spares in the seventies before the cars started to rise in value.

Tony Lambert, driving the ex-John Burton G4R, took the 1970 Shell/RAC Leaders Hillclimb Championship outright. GINETTA OWNERS' CLUB

CHAPTER FOUR

SERIOUS RACING

Having finally got the G4 selling in the numbers that they had hoped to achieve, the minds of Ivor and Trevers inevitably turned to their great love of racing. They were already starting to get noticed with the G4 and during 1963, as we have seen, the DKW-powered G6 saw their marque find international credibility. The G4R was their first exercise in making a car that was biased more to race than road use and the early lessons learned here made them consider building their first single-seater racing car. Their 'can do' approach gave them enormous confidence and in their world it was straightforward: if Lotus could build single-seater cars successfully, then so could Ginetta.

By the autumn of 1963, Ivor had drawings for a Formula 3 car ready and it was ground-breaking. Glassfibre had shown its strength over a decade by now and both the Lotus Elite and Rochdale Olympic had proved the material could successfully be used to produce ultra-lightweight monocoque bodies to which the mechanical parts could be fixed with minimal steel mountings for key components. In racing, Lotus had once again shown the way by introducing monocoque construction into their cars, and the Lotus 27 Formula Junior car featured a partly fibreglass and aluminium construction. In fact, the Lotus wasn't a success initially, proving too flexible, and was reworked with an all-aluminium structure, but Ivor sensed that a fibreglass monocoque would be the way to go with his new car.

The G8 fibreglass tub was moulded in two pieces – an inner and outer shell with a minimum of steel reinforcement.
DEAN PETLEY

THE GINETTA G8

He came up with a radical concept where the main structure of the car was moulded in two halves. The outer tub was conventional in appearance, but laminated up to a significant thickness in key areas for strength; into this, a very light and simple steel frame was bonded, to which major components could be bolted. The other half was the internal skin of the tub, which comprised side panels, seat fuel tank and bulkheads. This dropped inside the external tub and was bonded with it to make an exceptionally rigid structure.

In practice, this design produced its challenges. Once the brothers had moulds and the first body was made, they really did struggle to bond together the outer and inner tubs, as well as the steel inner frame, and keep everything in perfect alignment. To this structure they added a one-piece front panel and an engine cover. The whole car certainly looked the part, although despite its glass-fibre underpinnings it was still heavier than they had expected. The torsional stiffness of the unit was exceptional, though, and they fabricated twin-wishbone front suspension utilizing the Triumph uprights as with the G4, but with strong cantilever top wishbones acting on inclined inboard spring damper units. This piece of design was favoured by Ivor to minimize obstructions and improve aerodynamics by removing the spring dampers from the air stream; there was also a small reduction in unsprung weight.

The rear suspension was developed more or less alongside the G4R. The models were being built up in tandem, and a special casting was made for the rear hub-carriers used on both. The G8 single-seater featured a different wishbone arrangement to the G4R, utilizing a reversed lower wishbone with a single joint to the chassis, while at the top a single transverse arm supported the top of the hub-carrier. Fore and aft movement was taken care of by a pair of long radius arms fitted each side, everything being fully adjustable. Inclined coil spring damper units were used together with outboard disc brakes front and rear. The G8 was finished with a set of Ginetta's own cast magnesium alloy wheels.

The brothers considered their options for the engine and gearbox and settled on a Holbay-tuned engine; they had supplied several of these to G4 customers and they

A bolt-on steel front sub-frame was another feature of the G8. Note the original cantilever wishbones were much lighter fabrications than the units showing in this recent photograph.

DEAN PETLEY

The G8 chassis fully assembled. Note the specially cast rear hub-carriers.
DEAN PETLEY

enjoyed a good reputation. For the gearbox a Hewland unit was specified. At the time these were derived from a Volkswagen transaxle and had become commonplace in single-seater racing cars, where the engine sat forward of the gearbox and axle line.

Publicly announced at the end of June 1964 at a price of £775 less engine and gearbox, the car needed to prove its potential to prospective buyers, and the brothers immediately booked a testing session at the Snetterton circuit in Norfolk. They invited assistant editor Mike Twite of *Motor Sport* magazine to join them at Snetterton, as he had become an acquaintance of the brothers and they often socialized, usually over a drink or two in the public house next to the Witham factory.

For this first test the car performed very well, meeting all hopes and expectations. The Snetterton circuit was fairly deserted except for Graham Hill, who was testing his Formula 1 BRM. One problem that had shown itself was a tendency for steering judder under heavy braking, which was disconcerting and prevented the driver from achieving the best lap times. The brothers had already attempted to cure this by firming up the front wishbone bushes but with no real improvement. The BRM mechanics servicing Hill's car

Completed and ready for testing, the G8 stands in the yard at Witham. Note the two Simca cars in the background, a business sideline at the time.
GINETTA CARS

Trevers Walklett sits in the G8 during the first test session at Snetterton. GINETTA OWNERS' CLUB

The G8 in the paddock at Snetterton awaiting its first race. CHRIS MEEK

Ivor Walklett, kneeling, talks tactics to Chris Meek on the front row of the grid at Snetterton. Car 31 near the pit wall is a Brabham driven by Frank Williams, later to find fame as a Grand Prix team owner. CHRIS MEEK

showed an interest in the G8 and suggested that the problem might be the lower forward wishbone arms flexing under braking and that some stiffening might be the answer; apparently a similar problem had been experienced with their car. Despite this minor problem and a tendency to oversteer, one of the brothers managed to post a time of 1 minute 55 seconds, less than 10 seconds off the Formula 3 pace at that time. Twite was a little less comfortable in the car and came through a little under the 2-minute mark; he found the lack of any seat padding and the feeling that he was sliding on the seat a little disconcerting.

Clearly this was all very positive, and so the next step was to race the car with an experienced driver. Chris Meek was the obvious choice, as he had already started to establish himself in the G4, and an entry was made for Chris to race in a Formula 3 event at Snetterton on 30 August 1964.

A rear anti-roll bar was in place to counteract the oversteer and Chris, in typical form, set a blistering pace in practice, putting the car on the front row of the grid. In the race he drove very hard but couldn't make headway against strong opposition from Lotus 31s and a Brabham BT9 driven by none other than a young Frank Williams, later to become Formula 1 team owner Sir Frank. Meek finished fourth to Williams' third but he felt the engine wasn't delivering all it should. After post-race discussions with the drivers of the winning cars it soon became clear that the engine they had fitted was not up to the current specification available. Despite a solid showing the brothers were very disappointed, as they couldn't afford to spend more money on the engine; so they turned all their attention to the new G10 V8 they were developing.

The fate of the G8 was sealed; it was wheeled back into the factory destined never to turn a wheel again in their hands. Orders from customers did not materialize. Eventually it was offered for sale in October 1966 less engine and gearbox. It passed through various hands but never realized the potential the brothers had hoped for; it survives as a one-off today, although not race-worthy at the time of writing.

THE GINETTA G9

Despite this hard lesson, the company still had an appetite to make competition cars. By now the G4R was performing extremely well and the brothers were still confident they could make other race-winning competition cars. Soon after building the G8, Ivor had also produced a similar design for a Formula 2 car, to be known as the G9, but this time it was more conventional, with a separate space-frame chassis with aluminium panels to stiffen it. The complexity of the G8 fibreglass monocoque had its drawbacks; as we have seen, it was incredibly difficult to make and, if damaged in an accident, almost impossible to repair. As Ivor commented to the author only recently, sometimes simplicity in design is best – complex designs can sometimes prove effective but invariably throw up problems that render the effort futile. Aside from its space-frame chassis, the G9 was very similar to the G8, including the inboard front spring damper units operated by rocker-type top wishbones. The disappointment of the G8 engine choice and the fact that the company had also started other projects, such as the G10, meant that G9 development was very slow.

A young racing driver called Willie Green got to hear of the idea and placed an order for the first car. He sourced a Cosworth SCA engine ready to be fitted, but as the car neared completion he visited the factory and decided to switch his order to a different Ginetta model. Effectively this was the finish of the G9; by now Ginetta were so stretched developing other ideas that no progress was made and eventually the car was sidelined and never fully completed.

THE GINETTA G12

Much of 1965 had been spent on the G10 and G11 projects, but with the G11 launched, the restless minds of the brothers had moved on to yet another idea for a competitive competition car. In Europe the Porsche 904 had demonstrated that a mid-engine layout could be extremely successful in a GT car and not just in single-seater and sports racing cars. Ivor had considered this layout as early as 1963, when designs for the stillborn G7 were being evaluated. The use of the DKW engine and transaxle behind the driver and in front of the rear axle were a favourite option; only the time needed to produce an entirely new chassis and body design led to the G7 being based on the G6 concept.

Inspired by these thoughts and hearing through a trade contact that Lotus were already working on a mid-engined GT car of their own – later to be revealed as the Lotus 47 and its road-going twin, the Europa – a new design was prepared. At the time Ivor and Trevers were working on the new square-tube G4 chassis frame, and elements of this frame were used to speed up the development of the new mid-engine chassis to be known as the Ginetta G12. The chassis featured front suspension of twin wishbones with Triumph uprights and rear suspension similar to that of the G8. This comprised reversed lower wishbones, single-link upper arms and a pair of trailing arms each side, all anchoring specially cast alloy hub-carriers. The suspension was fully adjustable, with oil spring damper units, anti-roll bars and disc brakes fitted all round.

The bodywork was inspired by that of the G4, with a bonded central section forming the cabin, a one-piece tilt-forward bonnet and a one-piece tilt-back engine compartment cover. This was topped off with a hardtop incorporating the windscreen and rear window, with a flying

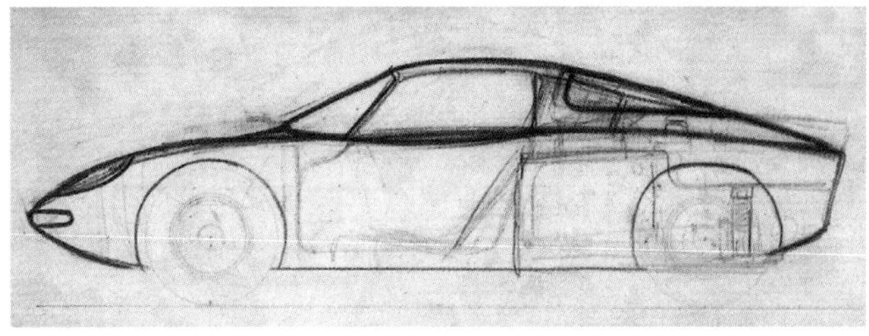

Notated in Ivor Walklett's sketch book as G12/ G16, this drawing in fact dates back to the G7 DKW project; his idea for a mid-engined coupé was revived to emerge three years later as the G12. IVOR WALKLETT

buttress streamlined rear section to the hardtop, which was split behind the rear screen and lifted with the engine cover.

The hardtop was derived from the G4 top, but the windscreen featured sharply angled top corners rather than the rounded corners on the G4. In 1966 this was quite an unusual design feature and was later adopted for the G4 with the introduction of the Series 3 in 1967, the two models sharing the same screen. This became a feature of Ginetta models over the next decade and gradually became increasingly mainstream, with the major car design studios adopting similar lines as time passed. Headroom in the G12 was limited as with the G4, but to accommodate taller drivers, a streamlined head fairing, roof mounted above the driver's seat, was made available, and at least three cars were fitted with this from new.

Under the lift-up front of the G12 were the radiator, fluid reservoirs and space for a tiny spare tyre – a compulsory requirement for Group 6 competition regulations. At the rear the large engine cover exposed the engine, Hewland transaxle, twin panier-style fuel tanks and compulsory luggage box, again a Group 6 requirement. The whole car was designed to meet the minimum size as laid down to be eligible in the Group 4 and 6 categories, with the chassis designed to accommodate units from 1000cc right up to 2 litres, depending on customer requirements and which Group they wished to race.

Work on the G12 had been progressing steadily, but as it gradually dawned on the Walklett brothers that the G11 was going to be difficult, if not impossible, to make successfully, there was a great deal of dismay. Trevers and Ivor, in particular, were even more convinced that their efforts should go into building racing cars. Bob and Doug understood their point of view but felt that concentrating on racing was too high-risk. The business needed sales volume for its income; sales of competition cars could be patchy and competitive drivers were always looking for the latest car that gave them the best chance of winning at any point in time, meaning sales could go from satisfactory to nothing almost overnight. Nonetheless the G12 looked to be very good, and they all

Willie Green enjoyed huge success in his Cosworth SCA-powered G12. He's seen here with his car. GINETTA OWNERS' CLUB

THE GINETTA G12 (SERIES 1 1966–9)

Layout and chassis	Two-seater mid-engined GT with space-frame chassis
Engine (customer choice; below is typical example)	
Type	Lotus Ford
Block material	Cast iron
Head material	Cast iron
Cylinders	4
Cooling	Water
Bore and stroke	82.5 × 72.7mm
Capacity	1558cc
Valves	Twin overhead cams, 2 valves per cylinder
Compression ratio	9.5:1
Carburettor	2 × 40DCOE Webers
Max. power (DIN)	105bhp
Max. torque	108lb ft at 4,000rpm
Fuel capacity	6gal (27ltr); double tanks available
Transmission	
Gearbox	Hewland 5-speed and reverse
Clutch	Single dry plate
Internal Gearbox Ratios	
Ratios	Ratios interchangeable
Final drive	Limited slip
Suspension and Steering	
Front	Twin wishbone, coil spring damper units, anti-roll bar
Rear	Lower reversed wishbones, upper transverse link, radius rods, coil spring dampers, anti-roll bar
Steering	Rack and pinion
Tyres	5.50 × 13in
Wheels	Magnesium alloy
Rim width	7 × 13in
Brakes	
Type	Disc front and rear
Brake size	9.5in (237mm) front, 9.5in (237mm) rear
Dimensions	
Track, front	51in (1,295mm)
Track, rear	51in (1,295mm)
Wheelbase	90in (2,286mm)
Overall length	140in (3,556mm)
Overall width	61in (1,549mm)
Overall height	42in (1,067mm)
Unladen weight	950lb (431kg)
Performance	
Top speed	130mph (209km/h)
0–60mph	7sec
Both these values dependent on gearing	

agreed that as the G4 was still selling well, they should throw all their efforts into the G12 and build the prototype as quickly as possible.

The car was completed by the summer of 1966 and was probably the first British-made mid-engine GT car to be marketed. The prototype was fitted with a Lotus twin-cam engine for testing. In the meantime, despite the car being secretly planned and built, G4R owner John Burton was already aware of its development and had ordered the first customer car, while Willie Green, waiting patiently for the completion of his G9, visited the Witham factory to see progress and stumbled upon the part-complete G12 after entering an area of the factory he shouldn't have been in. Willie was completely captivated by the car and there and then switched his order to the G12 with Bob's agreement.

Burton and Green planned completely different strategies with their cars. Green would fit his 1000cc Cosworth SCA Formula 2 engine, which had been destined for his G9; while Burton, having successfully run a Martin-tuned 3-valve Ford engine in his G4R, planned to fit the new Martin-built 2-litre V8 in the G12.

The driver's workroom of a G12; note the right-hand gear shift. GINETTA OWNERS' CLUB

Racing Success

Initial testing was extremely positive and so it was decided to give the car its debut race at Mallory Park in a Special GT event taking place on 10 July 1966. Chris Meek was to drive and, following practice, he was ecstatic at how well the car performed, placing it on pole position with a time quicker than all other cars, including single-seaters, in the Formula Libre race. Meek was keen to enter the Libre race as well but the Walkletts were not so enthusiastic. They wanted to clean up in the Special GT race to show what the car was capable of, but the Libre event was first in the programme, so if any disasters befell the G12 in that race, it would not be able to start in the GT event. Meek was persuasive, though, and worked on the brothers one by one, gradually convincing them he should give both races a run.

The clerk of the course allowed the G12 to start from the rear of the grid in the Libre event even though it had not practised. Meek scythed through the field, getting up to third place in no time. Now he was running with the quickest cars, big, open-wheeled single-seaters. He got a bit close to the rear wheel of one of these cars and in an instant the G12 was flicked up by the wheel and flew through the air before crashing down, luckily on all four wheels.

Back in the pits, it was clear the car was a mess, although the chassis appeared undamaged. The front bodywork was in pieces and the radiator smashed – there seemed no chance of it racing in the Special GT event. However, John Burton, less than a month away from taking delivery of his own G12, was entered in the same race with his G4R and keen to see how the G12 was going to perform. In a generous gesture he offered to scratch his car from the race so the G12 could use his radiator; this meant that if the bodywork could be repaired, they might just still race. The bonnet was literally taped together with the hope it would hold up.

With the car ready just in time, Meek started as planned from pole and never looked like being beaten: it was a triumph for a new car at its first meeting, even though bits of bodywork were flapping off by the end and some competitors launched a protest that it should have been black flagged. This luckily came to nothing, partly because Peter Creasey, who came second in a Lotus Elan, refused to join the protest. He was highly impressed by the G12 and placed an order; his was the third production car built.

Already Bob sensed the G12 could be a sales success. Although Burton was out on track in his car early in August, it was Willie Green taking delivery of his car at the beginning of September who really made the racing world take the G12 seriously. Green had already entered his first race before the car arrived but with the screaming SCA engine fitted, he savaged the opposition in his class. He raced every weekend, usually taking the class win, and despite the small 1000cc engine took some overall wins as well: by the end of the season he had eleven class wins from twelve starts and had broken the lap record at every circuit he had raced.

Mike Twite, now editor of *Motoring News*, the sister publication of *Motor Sport*, arranged a track test of the Green G12 back to back with the works Twin Cam car. He was more than impressed. *Motoring News* had arranged to sponsor a championship of its own in 1967 to be called the Motoring News Special GT Championship, and he convinced the magazine owner, W. J. Tee, to purchase a G12 to race in their series. The car would be driven by both Twite and one of

The Cosworth SCA engine suited the G12 well – many successes were achieved with these engines installed. ANDREW WARREN

G12 sales were strong. A number raced in 1967: the cars of Alan Harvey (foreground) and Keith Jupp are seen here being prepared for a race at Crystal Palace. STEVE WYATT/ QUILTER HOUSE

Tee's sons, Ian. Orders for the G12 started coming in thick and fast, and the small Witham factory was struggling to cope with demand. With the Racing Car Show coming up in January, further orders were likely and everyone wanted their car for the start of the 1967 season; the only solution was to stop G4 production to fill G12 orders and then resume the G4 with the start of the Series 3 model as soon as possible. In fact, it was May 1967 before the first customer G4 Series 3 left the works, by which time over twenty G12s had been delivered.

The G12 was massive for the tiny company, not just because it was so good on track but also because the profit margins were large. The G12 sold for £1,225 less engine and gearbox so, while it cost about the same to make as the G4, it sold for twice the price. Of course this brought a smile to Bob's face but he knew it would be short-lived. The G12 dominated the end of 1966 but for 1967 there were new adversaries to battle. The Lotus 47 had appeared and the G12 was a match for it, but Chevron produced their B8, which was a class act and pushed the G12 hard.

The 1967 Racing Car Show stand featured three cars: the G11, the new G4 Series 3 and a G12 in silver. An American from California, called Art Allen, had contacted Ginetta about the possibility of representing them on the west coast of the USA, an agreement had been reached and a G4 ordered. Allen flew over to the Racing Car Show to view the cars and was totally amazed by the G12, ordering one immediately. His was the first car to race in the USA, the start of fifty years of G12 competition in America.

The silver car on display was ready to be delivered to John Bamford, a friend of John Burton, and the pair, together with Paul Ridgeway, formed the Worcestershire Racing Association. This group would race G12s, pooling knowledge, administration, such as race entries, and overnight accommodation as well as some use of mechanics. Burton's V8 Martin car was joined by the Bamford Lotus Twin Cam-powered car and Ridgeway's Cosworth SCA car.

The three could compare cars, and it quickly became clear that the Martin V8 was not as reliable and or as competitive in class as the other two. It was Ridgeway's little SCA-powered car that seemed to be the best. Burton eventually ordered a new car and fitted an SCA but it was too late for

The works Lotus Twin Cam G12 being prepared for Willie Green to drive at Castle Coombe in May 1967. TED WALKER

America's West Coast importer, Art Allen, in pole position at Riverside in his second race in the G12 ahead of a Lotus 23. ART ALLEN

Motoring News Championship honours, where Ridgeway won the up-to-1150cc class from another G12, belonging to Andy Mylius; while Peter Creasey, in a Coventry Climax-powered G12, won the 1600–2000cc class. Frustratingly for Ginetta, despite such domination it was John Lepp who won the 1150–1600cc class in a Twin Cam-powered Chevron, and with it the overall championship.

The G12 never ruffled feathers on the international race scene as much as Ginetta had hoped. Peter Creasey took his car to the Nürburgring 1000km race but it crashed; and Mike Twite and Ian Tee took their car to Mugello, as did Paul Bryan and co-driver Taggart for the international event, but both retired. Later in the model's life, Swiss driver Walter Fluckiger did well in the Swiss hill-climb championship in his ex-John Burton car, actually winning the championship in 1969.

There was, however, one car that did enjoy a long spell in international racing, owned by entrant Richard Groves. His car was prepared with a 1300cc version of the Lotus Twin Cam engine and contested events in the up-to-1300cc class. At various stages Groves offered drives to John Moore, Rhoddy Harvey-Bailey and Martin Davidson, and was a regular at the Oulton Park Gold Cup, Nürburgring and Spa, often taking class wins. This car was taken over by Jack Wheeler and Martin Davidson when Groves sold it on and continued to be used in similar events.

In 1970, with an eye to a Le Mans entry, the car was modified with new front and rear bodywork in aluminium, panelled by renowned body specialists Williams & Pritchard. The design was by Dr Tom Boyce at Imperial College in London and developed in their wind tunnel. Wheeler and

Walter Fluckiger won the Swiss hill-climb championship in 1969 in his ex-John Burton G12 SCA. GINETTA OWNERS' CLUB

G12s had a lot of success in hill-climbs too. Shown here is Maggie Blankstone in her Twin Cam-powered car. Note the head fairing – several cars were so fitted for increased headroom. MARGARET BLANKSTONE

Davidson were focusing on the Le Mans Index of Performance Trophy but their entry was not accepted due to a high level of works entries for the event. With a drag coefficient of just 0.28 the car should have been very competitive, and in this form, nicknamed the 'Jerboa', it did notch up class wins and high placings in European Championship events at Mugello in Italy, Spa, the Nürburgring and the Targa Florio during 1970 and 1971.

This wasn't the only time G12s got close to racing at Le Mans. In 1967 a journalist friend of the brothers called Ted Wilkinson also had a foot in the PR business, and among his contacts were executives at John Player, part of the giant Imperial Tobacco Company. With sponsorship restrictions for motor racing being relaxed for the 1968 season, Wilkinson suggested to Players that they should consider advertising through the medium of motor sport. He suggested to them that a team of three Ginetta G12s should be entered for the 1968 Le Mans 24 hours race with their sponsorship, which would give the Players brands a very high profile. His suggestion was provisionally agreed by the relevant board subject to approval of the main John Player board. This was exciting news for the small Witham-based company and three chassis were laid down in anticipation.

However, when the proposal was put to the main board, they queried why the company should sponsor a relatively unknown company like Ginetta, when higher-profile racing makes were also in the market for such a deal. What followed was the historic decision to sponsor Lotus in Formula 1 and 2, when the company saw their Gold Leaf brand name on the world championship-winning Lotus 49 at the end of the 1968 season: doubtless the right decision for John Player but a near miss for the Ginetta company. It was forty-two years before the Ginetta name would finally appear on a Le Mans entry list, when an LMP1 Ginetta-Zytek, driven by former world champion Nigel Mansell and his sons Greg and Leo, competed in the 2010 event, sadly as non-finishers.

This G12, fitted with special bodywork designed by Tom Boyce at Imperial College London and known as the 'Jerboa', was very successful racing internationally. GINETTA OWNERS' CLUB

The G12 on the Road

In the earliest days of the G12's public debut, Ginetta received enquiries from several potential customers wishing to buy the car for use on the road. Enquires included one from the well-known popular singer turned actor, Adam Faith. They were all advised that the car was not suitable as a road machine and their orders declined. At this point in time, sports cars and ex-racing cars of many kinds were being put on the road by owners keen to make a statement and, with the advantage of hindsight, dissuading these customers was not the best business decision. The positive effect of having Adam Faith, who in the 1960s enjoyed a very high profile, driving your product, would massively have outweighed any negative publicity such a car might attract, however difficult the rear vision, right-hand gearchange and Hewland gearbox might make the car to drive.

The irony was, however, that as these cars became uncompetitive on the track they were often purchased by enthusiasts who registered them for the road and enjoyed the exhilaration of driving them for what they were, despite the many shortcomings, particularly in traffic. Records show that more than 75 per cent of the G12s built during this period found their way onto the road at some point by the mid-seventies. One G12 that definitely didn't get used on the road was purchased second-hand by David Render, who fitted a Buick 3.5-litre engine and competed in sprints and hill-climbs for several years, including outings at the, then new, UK drag strip Santa Pod.

The migration of G12s during this period from race to road car might in part have been due to a venture by two friends who had the idea to sell new bespoke G12s tailored to customer requirements for road use. Essex-born Bruce Giddy had met lifelong friend Richard Robarts at school and, while Giddy became a successful London estate agent, Robarts was keen to become a racing driver. Giddy drove a G3 and later a G4 on the road and in 1968 Robarts took a job at Ginetta, by which time the G12 was old history at the

David Render sprinted his G12 fitted with a Buick V8 engine.
GINETTA OWNERS' CLUB

ROAD GOING
G 12 GINETTAS
AVAILABLE FROM
GIRO RACING DEVELOPMENTS

ENGINE
GEARBOX
MAGNESIUM/STEEL WHEELS
RACING/ROAD TYRES
COLOUR
INTERIOR
EXTRAS
Your choice

PRICES FROM £1600
6 WEEKS' DELIVERY
Telephone 01-435 0066 (24 hour service)
TEST DRIVE BY APPOINTMENT

Bruce Giddy and Richard Robarts offered road-going G12s in 1969 through a company they named Giro Racing Developments.
GINETTA OWNERS' CLUB

factory. Robarts noticed a partly finished G12 there, which his friend Giddy purchased. They fitted a Ford 1600cc cross-flow engine to the chassis and a properly silenced exhaust and trimmed the interior; the car was ready for the road and registered WYN2G in January 1969. When Giddy got out on the road in his new car they hit on the idea of selling similar versions to customers using Giddy's car to demonstrate their offering.

The G12 was offered to *Car* magazine for road test and featured in the August 1969 edition in an article entitled 'A Racing Car on the Road'; while the tester enjoyed the car, they were clear that there were many shortcomings, making it far from the ideal road offering. Together Giddy and Robarts formed a company, Giro Racing (taken from the Gi and Ro at the start of their names) to market the cars. It is noted in the *Car* magazine article that the Walklett brothers were not particularly enthusiastic about the venture, but they must have agreed to manufacture the cars to meet any orders received. In the event, priced from £1,600 depending on engine and trim packages specified, this was not a cheap car and given its failings, it is not surprising that no sales were made. WYN2G was sold early in 1970 and could be seen being driven by the new owner around the roads of central Essex well into the seventies.

RICHARD PETIT

Richard Petit, right, discusses the design of the G12P with Dave Ash, a design director at Ford HQ Dearborn. RICHARD PETIT

Richard Arthur Petit was born in the mid-thirties in Erie, Pennsylvania on the southern shores of the Great Lakes. He enjoyed close links to the UK as his grandparents were Cornish. Educated at East High School, Erie, he then spent three years in the US Army Security Agency serving on Okinawa. With his service completed, he attended Cleveland Institute of Art and was hired on graduation by the Ford Motor Company, an achievement of which to this day he remains immensely proud. Before taking up a year assignment to work at Ford Advanced Vehicles at South Ockendon, England in 1966, he had reached agreement with Wilfred Becker, director of Wayne State University, that he could design and build a sports car to attain a master's degree in Industrial Arts. For this project he picked a Ginetta G12 chassis.

Returning to Ford at Dearborn as manager of Ford's Fairlane and Torino design studio, Petit was awarded his master's degree in 1969 before secondment to Ghia in Italy, working with DeTomaso for a year. Back at Dearborn he worked under Lee Iacocca, who is famed for designing the Mustang and Pinto at Ford before he departed to head Chrysler. Petit also spent time working in Japan at Mazda developing Japanese products with Matasaburo Maeda, the leader of Mazda Design. He retired from Ford in 1996 after a distinguished career.

One other road G12 should be mentioned here. This was something very different and was destined to hit the highways of the USA in the same year. Richard Petit was a stylist for the Ford Motor Company looking to attain a master's degree; to achieve this, he decided to design and build his own sports car. Having researched a number of possible chassis suppliers for a mid-engined layout, he decided on the Ginetta G12. By good fortune he was due to come to Ford of Britain for a year during the period 1966–7 and would be based in Essex, less than 20 miles (32km) from the Ginetta factory. After discussions, Bob Walklett signalled he was ready to supply Petit with a rolling G12 chassis fitted with a Lotus Twin Cam engine and Hewland gearbox and would be happy to keep in contact with Petit over any technical issues he might encounter. The rolling chassis was collected in May 1967 and shortly after Petit returned to Ford at Dearborn in the USA, taking it with him.

Having previously made a scale model to evaluate the shape of his car from all angles, he now started the hard work of making the new glass-fibre body. Working in his double garage at home with his cousin and Ford clay modeller David Conley, the pair needed thirty hours a week for twenty-two months to produce the finished car while still doing their day jobs. The process included making a timber and clay buck from which the moulds were taken before the body could be laminated. The interior received similar treatment, and in total fifty individual moulds were produced to make the car, which on completion was a triumph of superb quality and style. Petit was awarded his master's degree in May 1969.

Afterwards, Petit offered the moulds to Ginetta and, despite the fact that until then all their models had been designed and developed in house, the brothers did give this offer serious consideration. They decided that the Ford V6 engine would best suit it as a road car but an expensive ZF transaxle would be needed, and when Bob Walklett

The finished Petit G12, known as the G12P. Ginetta themselves considered building this car as the Ginetta G20, with a Ford V6 engine. RICHARD PETIT

The engine bay of the G12P complete with lotus Twin Cam engine and Hewland gearbox. RICHARD PETIT

costed an individual car they felt it would not be competitively priced in its natural market. Doubtless the fifty individual mouldings would also have made it difficult and time-consuming to make in production, another factor they would have considered. Had the car been built by Ginetta it would have been coded the G20, and this number was set aside for this aborted project. The Petit-built car was eventually sold and in the eighties was briefly in the UK before being exported to Japan. The moulds also ended up in Britain and have been used to produce several replica bodies.

The G12 had a meteoric rise to prominence on the race track but, once the competition caught up, sales nose-dived, and by 1969 the model had been sidelined with twenty-nine cars made – although it would be revived many years later, as we shall see in chapters to follow.

Jersey-based enthusiast Brian Moody campaigned his G12 for forty years in sprints and hill-climbs. GINETTA OWNERS' CLUB

This beautifully restored G12 is displayed by its Swiss owner Marcel Spiess at the Altbaron hill-climb in 2013. BRUNO MEIER

THE GINETTA G16

As the G12 got rapidly outpaced by newer mid-engined machinery during 1967, Ivor and Trevers were keen to replace it with a new car to carry on where the G12 had left off. They realized that the G12 had been very successful in the smaller-engine classes but less so in the classes with a larger engine. It was these larger engines that often produced the race winners and in consequence got the greatest exposure. With these thoughts firmly in mind, Ivor enlarged the G12 design and generally beefed it up to handle engines of greater power. The bodywork was taken from the G12, widened slightly with a similar bonnet incorporating a radiator air extraction panel, and at the rear a long lift-up tail section was produced. These changes enabled 8in-wide wheels to be used at the front and 10in at the rear; this had been one of the restricting factors of the G12 design. This time the car was open-cockpit, but a stout roll-over bar was incorporated and a windscreen with a T-bar that braced back to the roll bar. To slightly reduce frontal area, the top corners of a standard G12 windscreen were cropped off, giving quite a distinctive look.

The chassis and suspension were strengthened from that of the G12 and at the rear the driveshafts and hub-carriers were taken from the contemporary front-wheel-drive Triumph 1300 saloon. The whole package was designed to meet the Group 6 regulations and certainly looked the part. The price of a rolling body/chassis unit was around £1,800 depending on exact specification, but the cost of a Hewland FT200 transaxle and a racing engine needed to be added, meaning there would be little change out of £3,500 to be race ready.

There was a sense of urgency about the development of the G16, partly to capitalize on the momentum they had garnered with the G12 but also to get the car out ready for the 1968 season. It is probably not unfair to say it was rushed out

John Burton was the first to race a G16, but here he carries a passenger following a Swiss hill-climb ascent. GINETTA OWNERS' CLUB

The Burton G16 FVA was sold to Gerry Tyack in late 1968 and has remained in the Tyack family ever since. It is currently campaigned by son Edward. AUTHOR

with very limited testing, but orders were already on Bob's desk and the first cars were promised for delivery in February 1968; although in fact the first production car was not delivered to John Burton until May. Fellow Worcestershire Racing Association (WRA) member John Bamford received his car a few weeks later. The development was effectively left to the WRA to sort out and they struggled with the cars. The prototype car had been purchased by Art Allen in California but he requested that the car was not to be dispatched to him until testing development modifications had been made to it.

Burton's car was fitted with a Cosworth FVA engine while Bamford opted for a 2-litre BMW engine following its successful use in several leading Chevrons. The G16 showed flashes of promise in Burton's hands but never came close to achieving the successes of the G12. To the Walklett brothers the problem was clear: the car needed further development but WRA were unable to make headway and the schedule at Ginetta's works in Witham was at that time too demanding to assist.

Burton was keen to up his racing programme to international events but, in the club races he entered, the G16 was struggling to be completely competitive, or indeed reliable. Burton and Bamford entered the Martini International at Silverstone but both failed to finish and, after a few more club events together, they went all the way to the Nürburgring to share the driving of Burton's car in the 500km race only for the engine not to start in the pits before the race. Back home, a seventh place in a club event at Crystal Palace was the final straw for Burton – two weeks later the car was sold to Gerry Tyack, a Cotswold garage proprietor who promptly went out and won his class at the Weston Super Mare Speed Trials. Burton had owned the G16 for just four months, but the car remains in the Tyack family to this day. Bamford carried on with his car but Paul Ridgeway, the other WRA partner, cancelled an order he had placed for a similar car.

Living a mile down the road from the Ginetta factory was a young driver, Jeremy Richardson, who had motor sport in his blood. His parents were keen on the sport – indeed his father, Karl, drove a variety of wonderful cars, including a Ford GT 40 and a Ferrari 275 GTB, while his brother had purchased the ex-Andrew Mylius G12. During the autumn of 1968 Jeremy ordered a G16 to which he fitted a Climax 2-litre engine. He was keen to further his motor sport ambitions and planned an assault on the European GT Championship in 1969. When the car was ready it made its debut at a freezing Boxing Day meeting at Mallory Park in 1968. It was then run at various club meetings before Richardson and another Witham-based friend, Bernard Farthing, tackled the European events.

During the following summer they travelled backwards and forwards all over mainland Europe, from the Jyllandsring in Denmark to the fearsome road circuit at Vila Real in southern Portugal. At Mugello in Italy, a missed gear on the Giogo in practice saw the G16 fly over the top, and only being caught in the trees saved Richardson from a 100ft plunge down the mountain. Despite the effort, results were mixed: a few good placings were interspersed with mechanical failures.

Jeremy Richardson's second time out in his new G16 Climax, at Brands Hatch in December 1968. STEVE WYATT/QUILTER HOUSE

The G16A

Meanwhile, freeing up a little time, Ivor set about tackling the developments needed to make the car more competitive, and by March 1969 the G16A had been announced. The car was improved in numerous minor ways; particularly the brakes were enlarged and made better. The windscreen had been removed and replaced by a small Perspex wind deflector placed in front of the driver to take advantage of the new 1969 Group 6 regulations and the driveshafts were replaced with stronger items; otherwise, visually, the car was the same. Two G16As were built in parallel, one works car and one for *Motor Sport* and *Motoring News* proprietor, Wesley Tee, for his son Ian to drive. As it turned out the G16A would be launched on a world stage when the Ian Tee car was entered for the BOAC 500km at Brands Hatch in Kent, a round of the World Sports Car Championship. This time it was decided to fit both cars with a very special engine – the 2-litre unit built by BRM, which was basically a stretched version of the 1.5-litre world championship-winning Formula 1 engine. These engines were very expensive but promised to give the new G16A the kick in the tail it needed to compete at the highest level.

Jeremy Richardson at speed in his G16, now upgraded to G16A specification. STEVE WYATT/QUILTER HOUSE

Arrangements were made through Wilkie Wilkinson at BRM for the supply of these engines and, when the time came to collect them, Ivor went along personally to the iconic BRM works at Bourne in Lincolnshire. On arrival he was told that BRM chief and motor sport legend Raymond Mays would very much like to meet him before his departure; such recognition from one of his heroes was a great moment of pride for Ivor. Back at Witham the engines were installed and testing commenced. The car was now all they had hoped for and enormously quick, but they found it almost impossible to get the engine to run reliably for any length of time. The BRM engine ran on an early form of electronic transistorized ignition and this seemed to be

The G16A BRM of Ian Tee ready for its first time out at no lesser event that the 1969 BOAC 500km sports car race at Brands Hatch. TONY STYLES

the problem: after a short period of running, the car would misfire and then very quickly the plugs would oil up. Despite a lot of effort by the time the BOAC race date arrived, no permanent cure had been found. As it happened, in the race Tee and co-driver Willie Green were sidelined by an oil leak.

Undaunted, Ian Tee continued to enter club events. When the car did run reliably, it was very quick. Leading by some margin in a race a Snetterton in June 1969, Tee was forced off the track at Russell Corner and the car crashed very heavily. Tee was badly injured and the car virtually destroyed, but despite this it was rebuilt and he was able resume racing by August.

Meanwhile, the works car was ready to go, and one of its first outings was in the hands of Jeremy Richardson, who drove it at Snetterton to an outright win while his car was being overhauled. In August it was racing at Crystal Palace in the Daily Express Trophy with Bev Bond at the wheel. Bond had only raced single-seaters prior to this race but had proved himself a very fast driver; in the G16 he did not disappoint, but in this event accidentally flicked off the ignition switch with the back of his glove, delaying the car and spoiling what looked like a good result. Bond continued as works driver for the remainder of 1969 but he had attracted attention from elsewhere too. While Ginetta planned to enter their car in the 1970 BOAC 500km race, Lotus had offered Bond a works single-seater drive – an opportunity he couldn't refuse. Bob Walklett felt strongly that once again Ginetta had been outflanked by Colin Chapman: whether

The BRM V8 engine and Hewland FT200 gearbox in the works G16A. ANDREW WARREN

Snetterton August 1969 and Ian Tee borrows the works G16A BRM while his own car is being repaired following his serious crash at the same circuit. Doug Walklett checks the radiators as Ivor and Trevers talk to Tee. GINETTA CARS

Brian Alexander blasts his ex-Bamford G16 off the line at Prescott. The car is now fitted with an Oldsmobile V8 engine. TED WALKER

intentionally or not, Lotus had robbed Ginetta of a chance to show how good the G16A had become. Ian Tee continued to campaign his car through to the end of 1970 before giving up on racing, but not before he had got to know Trevers and Sherry Walklett's eldest daughter, Gayle, who he would later marry.

Two other chassis were built. One was sold to Norman Moffett, who had won the Irish GT Championship in both a G4 and a G12, while another car remained unsold and was finally completed forty-five years later when built up for Ginetta enthusiast Patrick Ward-Booth. By the end of 1970 the G16 had disappeared from the circuits, but was reborn on the hills and in sprints, where Gerry Tyack, together with son Edward and another driver, Brian Alexander, kept the flag flying, the latter driving the ex-John Bamford car, which was now fitted with an Oldsmobile V8 engine.

In more recent times the G16 has shown well in historic racing, where Trevor Needham, Simon Hadfield, James Dodd and George Douglas have developed the model to contend with the best.

Even a raw racer like the G16 attracted some to attempt road use. The Brian Alexander car was road registered in 1970, although maybe only for special events, but a Suffolk-based engineer, David Eustace, acquired the ex-Jeremy Richardson car in the early seventies and fitted an Audi engine and transaxle to power it. In respect of the bodywork he created an attractive hardtop, sweeping over the rear engine cover, and the doors were converted to gullwing type. Despite all the work, however, it is thought the car was never fully completed in this form and may never have actually been used on the road.

This G16 was modified with a coupé top and Audi engine and transaxle with the thought of turning it into a road car. GINETTA OWNERS' CLUB

THE GINETTA G17 AND G18

One of the reasons that the factory were unable to find the time to develop the G16 initially was that they were engaged

One afternoon in March 1969 at the Witham factory a selection of cars were lined up for an impromptu photo shoot. Of special note are: left front, the works G16A; centre, two G18s; middle right, the ex-works G12; and left rear a G11. GINETTA CARS

The prototype G17 on display in the Witham showroom. ALEX BROWN

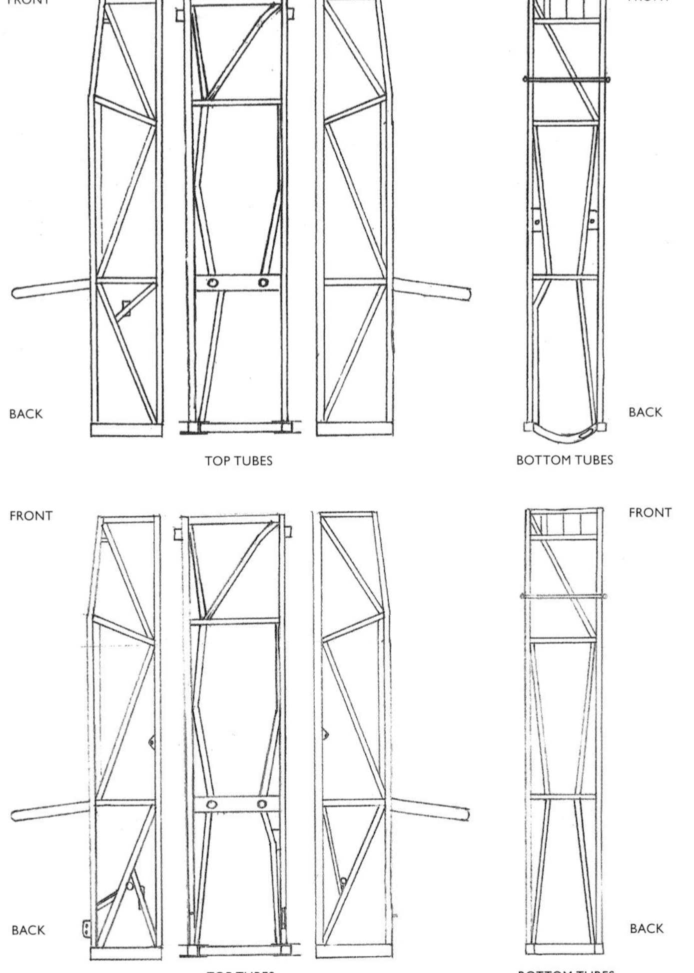

The G17 (above) and G18 (below) chassis frames are identical forward of the rear bulkhead. A study of the two drawings shows the differences between the two designed for the installation of the Imp and Ford engines of the G17 and G18 respectively. MARK SMITH

The Imp transaxle mounted in the G17, inverted to enable installation behind the engine. ALEX BROWN

Driver's-eye view of a G18 cockpit. GINETTA OWNERS' CLUB

in another racing project: they had decided to make a further attempt at building a single-seater Ginetta. This time they focused on two new Formulas that had been launched at the lower end of the racing ladder, Formula 4 and Formula Ford. In the case of Formula 4, it was the amendment of the rules to allow the Rootes Imp engine to compete that opened up the field, while Formula Ford had quickly established its position as a stepping stone into single-seater racing.

Ivor had designed a space-frame chassis that varied behind the cockpit so that an Imp engine with the transaxle fitted upside down or a Ford 1600cc engine with Hewland transaxle could be fitted. The Imp version, fitted with an 88bhp, highly tuned unit capable of revving to 9,000rpm, was named the G17, while the Ford version was known as the G18. Suspension was conventional and much the same at the rear as the G8, while the front suspension was more conventional, with twin wishbones and outboard coil spring damper units. The bodywork was developed from the G8, but at the rear a neat engine cover featured a small 'kick-up' to act as a spoiler. The long cigar-shaped nose now incorporated a radiator air extraction panel, mirroring the design seen on the G16. Wheels were in line with the regulations for the Formulas – wider alloy on the G17 and skinny steel wheels for the G18.

Once the chassis jigs were ready, Ginetta took on a young local motor sport enthusiast to build the first cars: his name, Richard Robarts. It was the end of 1968 before they had body moulds and initially one example of a G17 and one of a G18 were built before the cars were launched to the public. The factory G17 was displayed on the Paul Emery Racing stand at the Racing Car Show held at Olympia, London in January 1969, but no orders were placed.

Meanwhile, the G18 was tested at Snetterton following which some suspension modifications were made, before Chris Meek was once again drafted in for its race debut. This time the chosen venue was Rufforth in Yorkshire. Meek shot into the lead before the engine went 'sick' and his race was run.

With the Formula Ford market spoiled for choice of chassis to buy, the only G18 sold in 1969 was to Robarts' friend, Bruce Giddy, of road-going G12 fame.

RICHARD ROBARTS

Richard Robarts during his racing days, which took him from Ginetta to the Brabham Formula 1 team. RICHARD ROBARTS

Richard Robarts was born in Essex in 1944. At the age of eighteen, he purchased a pre-war M45 Lagonda, which from 1964 onwards he raced in sprints, hill-climbs and Vintage Sports Car Club events. Having been apprenticed in motor engineering and later learning panel-beating skills, in August 1968 he went to work for Ginetta Cars, making chassis and components for their new single-seater cars.

With racing experience coming only from competing in the Lagonda, he made the leap to single-seaters relatively late in life, with a debut in 1969 driving a Formula Ford Ginetta G18 belonging to an old school friend, Bruce Giddy. He took a break from racing in 1970 but returned to Formula Ford in 1971 in a Palliser and 1972 in an Eldon. In 1973 he upgraded to a Formula 3 GRD with success and by the season's end he had amassed enough points to win the Lombard North Central British Formula 3 Championship jointly with the highly rated Tony Brise, and take third place in the Forward Trust British Formula 3 Championship.

Eagar to maintain this momentum, he paid for a seat in Formula 1 for 1974 in the Brabham team, at the time run by Bernie Ecclestone. He contested the Argentinian, Brazilian and South African Grand Prix and two non-championship races before Rikky Von Opel offered more money for the seat. Shortly after, he was taken up by the Williams team and was entered for the 1974 Swedish Grand Prix but failed to start the race due to the seat being given to Tom Belso, who had crashed his car in practice.

In 1975 he contested four rounds of the World Sports Car Championship and in 1976 entered Formula 2 in a March 752 but crashed seriously at Vallelunga, destroying the car; he bought another and continued, but with no significant results. He also contested the Shellsport G8 International Series, coming second at Brands Hatch in the last but one round.

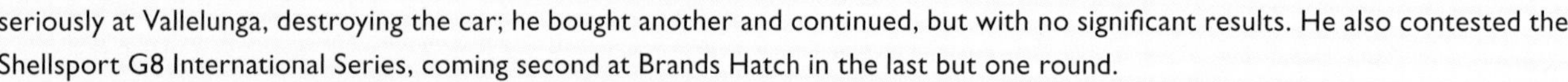

He retired from racing in 1978 and later went on to be a director of a large Essex-based coachbuilding company.

The first production G18 owned by Bruce Giddy and raced by both him and friend Richard Robarts. RICHARD ROBARTS

Ex-Formula 1 driver Richard Robarts started his single-seater career in a Ginetta G18, seen here in one of his first races in the car. RICHARD ROBARTS

Peter Voigt slides his G17 at the Harewood hill-climb in 1971. JOHN ROSE

Alex Brown prepares for the start at Bouley Bay, Jersey during his Leaders Hillclimb Championship-winning season. ALEX BROWN

The plan was for Robarts to maintain the car and for the pair to share it for racing. Robarts debuted the G18 at a Cadwell Park meeting in May 1969, and during the season posted a number of very credible results for a novice driver, while Giddy only did two events and, despite a fifth place at Lydden Hill, decided racing wasn't for him; the car was sold at the end of the season. By this time Robarts had left Ginetta's employ and sales seemed to have fizzled out. The G17 was, however, displayed on the Ginetta stand at the 1969 Motor Show and this may have kick-started sales, because for the 1970 season new orders were received, in particular for G17s.

Sussex-based violin maker, restorer and master craftsman Peter Voigt debuted his G17 at the Braunton hill-climb in Devon in April 1970, taking a class win. The car, fitted with the same tuned Imp engine previously installed in Voigt's DRW sports racer, was extremely successful, and in the first two seasons Voigt clocked up twenty-one wins and nine seconds in class in thirty-seven starts, a performance that got both driver and car noticed.

In Scotland, Alex Brown heard from Voigt that Ginetta had other chassis available and, after speaking with Bob Walklett, made the long journey down to Essex, returning home with the body chassis on the roof of his Mercedes. Brown used local engine builder Hugh Shannon to build an engine using a tuning kit from Paul Emery Racing, which resulted in a capacity of 1068cc; this engine proved extraordinarily strong and reliable. Brown used the G17 for all rounds of the National Leaders Hillclimb Championship for several seasons and shared the car with friend David Fyfe, some feat in itself from their Scottish base. At one point Brown held the up-to-1100cc record on eight different hills; his record at Prescott remained for fifteen years. The culmination of Brown's success came in 1973, when he and the G17 took the National Leaders Hillclimb Championship outright.

It is a strange irony that there is no record of a G17 competing in a Formula 4 race for which they were designed, but as a hill-climb and sprint machine it has seen considerable successes, which continues to this day.

In 1970, a young driver, Alex Durrant, campaigned a G18 in Formula Ford events, the car being prepared by a Canterbury-based company trading as Ennerdale Racing, run by former racing driver David Saville-Peck. Ennerdale acquired several G18 chassis from Ginetta and prepared them for customers, as well as selling them ready to race in Formula Ford. The cars that passed through the Ennerdale concern were modified by them to what they called 'B' specification, calling the cars G18B. These modifications included an externally mounted oil cooler and the raising of the flap on the front radiator air outlet.

Ken MacMaster drives the ex-Peter Voigt G17 at the Gt Auclum Hillclimb. TED WALKER

This G18 was modified into a specialist hill-climb car, complete with BRM V8 engine by Ginetta. Here it is photographed in the Witham showroom – the three young ladies are Bob and Anne Walklett's daughters. WALKLETT FAMILY

As a result of this, the number of G18s racing in Formula Ford in the early seventies was as many as four, and some continued to be raced right through the decade. In 1972, a young man with racing ambitions purchased a G18B and took part in several races that season. His name was Adrian Reynard, and he went on to design and build his own For-

G18s featured at many race meetings in the early 1970s; this is Phil Gazeley's. JOHN ROSE

mula Ford car, which became the forerunner of the highly successful Reynard Motorsport business that was at one time one of the largest makers of racing cars in the world.

In 1974, a G18B, owned and raced at the time by Doug Wood, featured in a long-running television drama called The Brothers. One storyline involved a leading character in the series taking up motor racing, and the G18B, along with several other Formula Ford cars, was filmed for 'racing' scenes. Wood asked Ginetta for some financial backing as the car would be featured on the TV programme, but Bob Walklett politely declined this opportunity; as it turned out this was a shrewd move, for when the car was in shot it flew by so fast it was quite hard even to identify it as a Ginetta.

Around 1971, Ivor and Trevers built an interesting G18 hybrid which they thought would make an effective hill-climbing car. They took a spare G18 chassis and modified the rear part of the frame to mount a 2-litre BRM V8 engine and Hewland FT200 gearbox. The chassis was strengthened where necessary and they even discussed the project with Peter Voigt, who at the time was performing extremely well on the hills with his G17. The bodywork of this car was new

G18s can still be seen racing in historic Formula Ford events. Here Paul Summerville races at the Historic Spa meeting in 2012. PAUL SUMMERVILLE

too, featuring a 'shovel' nose that was gaining popularity in single-seater circuit cars. In many ways it was a strange step away from their other work and designs and the sales potential would have been extremely limited. When asked, Ivor explained that it was a useful exercise in design and parts evaluation and also a diversion from other work they were undertaking at the time. The car never ran in anger and sat for many years in the Witham showroom before being tucked away; parts of it still survive.

The G17 and G18 models had been yet another chance for Ginetta to show that they were capable of building competitive racing machines for a variety of categories, but with the exception perhaps of the G12, the work in building, developing and testing these cars was not really a profit-making exercise, if not exactly loss-making.

Nonetheless, five years of making racing cars had helped raise the profile of the Ginetta company and provided a lot of fun and excitement along the way.

CHAPTER FIVE

VOLUME PRODUCTION

As we have seen, attempts to produce a road car to replace the G4 and take the company forward had not worked out.

As 1967 arrived, this need was becoming ever more urgent. The reaction to the G4 Series 3 had not lifted sales, but perhaps fortunately G12 sales were strong and made a worthwhile contribution to the company's financial stability. Ginetta needed a product that would sell in reasonable numbers and be the bedrock that they could rely on while developing further new products. As always, Ivor had a selection of design ideas, but what was the best solution? Still with thoughts of building a new model that would slot into the market they had hoped to meet with the G11, Ivor had produced drawings for a Ford-engined two-seater with a backbone-type chassis along the lines of the by now iconic Lotus Elan.

This Ginetta Owners' Club display clearly shows the main G15 body moulding and its relationship to the chassis frame beneath.
DAVID DOOLAN

THE GINETTA G14

A G4 owner, Vic Howard, from Lowestoft in Suffolk, owned and ran a very well-equipped engineering business and, hearing of the brothers' dilemma, invited them to visit for the weekend. Together, using machinery to hand, they built two chassis of predominantly steel sheet. Full use was made of the large folding machines available, and Ivor and Trevers were impressed by the ease with which these chassis were fabricated; but back at Witham, all the brothers lacked confidence that this was the right way forward. The design reached the stage that it was allocated the G14 model number (G13 not being used for reasons of superstition) but further development was halted due to various worries, not least that there was already a selection of models available from other specialist makers catering for this market.

THE GINETTA G15

There was, however, another idea that they liked the look of for a small sports car, using the Rootes Imp engine and transaxle. Ivor even drew out the profile of the car on the workshop wall so they could all get an idea of the scale of the car and its proportions. The more they thought about it the more it appealed. Ivor had always admired the small Coventry Climax engines and the Imp unit was developed from exactly this line of engines. The benefits were clear: very small and made from lightweight aluminium, it developed 55bhp in Sunbeam Sport form from just 875cc. Not only did this free-revving engine have a sporty feel but it was also capable of excellent fuel economy for the times; even better, it was canted over from the vertical, enabling the body line to be kept low – ideal for a sports car.

Bob made contact with the manufacturers in Coventry, where the Rootes Group (as it was known) had recently been taken over by the American Chrysler Corporation, to see if they would be prepared to supply components to Ginetta and if so at advantageous prices. Chrysler were very open to Bob's enquiries and offered a supply deal that made the project look even more attractive.

Ivor set to work on producing detailed designs for what was now designated the G15. For the chassis he chose a larger-section steel tubing than previously used for his designs and the construction was a much simpler platform layout and, as a result, much easier to fabricate. At the front he resisted the temptation to use the Imp swing-axle suspension, electing to stay with the Triumph-based twin wishbone and vertical link arrangement in the interests of better handling and importantly the ability to use disc brakes, rather than the drums that were part of the Imp package. For the rear suspension, the Imp trailing arms and driveshafts were used, complete with their drum brakes, hung from a steel Imp cross-member welded directly to the Ginetta chassis. Coil spring damper units were used at the front, along with an anti-roll bar, while at the rear, coil springs with separate telescopic dampers completed the package. The chassis frame swept up at the rear, with the engine and Imp aluminium transaxle effectively hung from the rear.

Design Innovations

Close examination of the G15 chassis frame will show that there is a small degree of torsion flex – one of the reasons why the space-frame chassis was at the time considered more desirable for serious sports cars. Ivor was fully aware of this and so he ensured the new body would compensate by affording additional rigidity when the two were bolted together. This was another departure from previous Ginetta designs, where bodies had been bonded to chassis frames.

The design of the body was special in a number of ways apart from this; for the first time Ivor and Trevers, working closely together, came up with a shell that could be moulded in one piece. This one-piece shell included the floor as well as internal bulkheads and was made possible by making the mould split along the waistline and side window apertures, enabling the body to be released from the mould once cured. Externally, doors, bonnet lid and opening rear engine cover needed to be added to complete the package. Internally, a dashboard and a handful of trim panels completed the entire body assembly. It was a triumph of design for speedy and low-cost fabrication.

Due to the low stance of the car the headlamps were set too low to meet construction and use regulations and these were mounted in separate binnacles that could be raised to the minimum regulation height if required. In practice, few owners ever raised them but they met the regulations should anyone ever be challenged.

The rear engine meant the car had a low frontal area but the classic good looks were not spoiled by the rear-mounted engine – many have been surprised, on seeing a G15, to learn that it is a rear-engine machine.

Speaking to Ivor Walklett fifty years after this design, the author was interested to hear that Ivor considered the G15 to be one of his greatest design achievements, in that it represented a major step forward by the Ginetta company in production engineering. Not only was the chassis relatively simple to fabricate, but the fibreglass element involved the minimum number of mouldings, making it quicker and more cost-effective to build; and, importantly, the car could be assembled by unskilled labour. As a result of using their now considerable experience and applying this to the design, Ginetta were able to manufacture the G15 at a lower unit cost than anything they had done up to that time, and these savings meant the car could be offered at a very competitive price while still making the company a handsome profit. In addition, for the first time with a Ginetta design, the car was engineered to be built in either right- or left-hand drive layout.

With the G15 almost ready, Bob Walklett sat down to cost the product. This was an element of the business that he took responsibility for and he always looked to achieve a selling price that would be both competitive and attractive to potential purchasers. With the G15 he arrived

GINETTA G15 (1967–74)

Layout and chassis	Two-seater sports car with platform chassis
Engine	
Type	Chrysler Imp
Block material	Aluminium
Head material	Aluminium
Cylinders	4
Cooling	Water
Bore and stroke	68 × 60.4mm (G15S 72.5 × 60.4mm)
Capacity	875cc (G15S 998cc)
Valves	Single overhead cam, 2 valves per cylinder
Compression ratio	10:1
Carburettor	2 Stromberg
Max. power (DIN)	55bhp (G15S 65bhp)
Max. torque	52lb ft at 4,300 rpm
Fuel capacity	Fibreglass tank 5.75gal (26ltr), steel tank 4gal (18ltr)
Transmission	
Gearbox	Chrysler Imp 4-speed and reverse
Clutch	Diaphragm
Internal Gearbox Ratios	
First	3.41:1
Second	1.83:1
Third	1.174:1
Fourth	0.852:1
Reverse	2.84:1
Final drive	4.857:1
Suspension and Steering	
Front	Twin wishbone, coil spring damper units, anti-roll bar
Rear	Trailing arms, coil springs, telescopic dampers
Steering	Rack and pinion
Tyres	5.20 × 13in
Wheels	Steel (alloy optional)
Rim width	4 × 13in (4.5 × 13in optional)
Brakes	
Type	Disc front and drum rear
Brake size	9in (225mm) front, 8in (200mm) rear
Dimensions	
Track, front	49in (1,244mm)
Track, rear	48.5in (1,238mm)
Wheelbase	82in (2,082mm)
Overall length	144.5in (3,670mm)
Overall width	57in (1,448mm)
Overall height	44.5in (1,130mm)
Unladen weight	1,232lb (559kg)
Performance	
Top speed	100mph (160km/h); G15S 115mph (185km/h)
0–60mph	12.5sec; G15S 9sec

at a component form price of just £799 (or £983 10s with purchase tax added for factory-built cars), which represented outstanding value for money for a specialist-built sports car with this level of equipment. Within this figure the buyer could look forward to a fully carpeted and trimmed interior, adjustable sports seats, leather-rimmed steering wheel, oil cooler, matching oil, water temperature and fuel gauges, plus a matching speedometer and rev-counter and a cellulose-painted finish in Moonstone White, Ginetta Red, Monaco Blue or British Racing Green. Extras that could be added were a heater (£16 10s), seat belts (£10 10s), special colours (£7 10s), Dunlop SP41 radial tyres (£10) and wheel trims (£3 15s) – these last items clipped between the hub caps and steel wheel rims and were a popular aftermarket fitment to cars in this period in general. These became an irrelevance very quickly as customers were offered the Cosmic Mk I cast alloy wheels at £35 extra for a set and these became a popular addition, if for no other reason than their appearance.

First Earl's Court Motor Show

Bob Walklett's thoughts turned to the launch and marketing of the car, and the perfect opportunity had presented itself, with Ginetta exhibiting at the International Motor Show at London's Earl's Court for the very first time. To exhibit at this show in the vehicle hall, not only did a company have to be a manufacturer or concessionaire of an overseas manufacturer, but also a full member of the Society of Motor Manufacturers and Traders (SMMT). Membership was not straightforward and, while long-established specialist car makers were part of this elite, the newer generation such as Gilbern, Marcos, TVR and of course Ginetta, found it hard to gain acceptance. While there was obviously competition between these makers, there was also some limited dialogue, due to the fact they were all in the same boat.

One competitor the brothers did get on well with was Jem Marsh of Marcos. Bob and Jem would regularly compare notes, and together they formed a group under the banner of the British Specialist Sports Car Manufacturers Association, which was joined by several of these small companies until slowly, one by one, they became SMMT members; Ginetta membership was granted in 1965. Even after membership, the company had to wait two years until they could exhibit and had been granted their first small stand for the October 1967 event. However, in August 1967 it was announced that Alvis cars would cease production and as a result they cancelled their stand at the show. The SMMT were in touch with Bob and asked if Ginetta would like to take over the larger Alvis stand, placed next to Jensen and Rolls-Royce,

The prototype G15 press release photograph, showing the original design without front radiator and the aluminium wheel trims. GINETTA CARS

Temporary Leaflet

Introducing the 1968 – GINETTA G15
Luxury Sports Coupé

SPECIAL FEATURES

- Tubular Steel Chassis.
- Non-Corrodible Bodywork.
- Rack and Pinion Steering.
- Powerful Front Disc Brakes.
- Independent Suspension to all four wheels.
- Wishbone Front Suspension.
- Collapsible Steering Column.
- Laminated Screen.
- Competition Leather Alloy Steering Wheel.
- Matching Speedometer and Tachometer.
- Aluminium Alloy Engine.
- Diaphragm Clutch.
- Twin Stromberg Carburettors.
- Overhead Camshaft.
- Competition Air Filters.
- Four Branch Exhaust Manifold.
- Oil Cooler.
- Carpets.

SPECIFICATION

Tubular steel chassis developed from the G.4 and G.12 with glass reinforced plastic bodywork.

Engine
875 c.c. Sunbeam Sport Engine.
O.H.C. developing 55 bhp at 6100 rpm.

Gearbox
All synchromesh, four forward speeds and reverse.

Suspension
Independent front and rear.

Steering
Rack and Pinion.

Brakes
Front Disc. Rear Drum.

Tyres
520 x 13.

Colours
Ginetta Red, Moonstone White, B.R.G. and Monaco Blue.

Dimensions
Wheelbase: 6ft. 10in. Track: front 4ft. 1in. Track: rear 4ft. ¾in. Overall Length: 12ft. ⅜in. Width: 4ft. 9in. Height: 3ft. 8⅛in. Ground clearance: 6in.

Performance
100 m.p.h. Consumption approx. 40 m.p.g.

Price
£983. 10. 0. Tax paid. (£799. 0. 0. in component form) plus heater and seat belts.

Hire Purchase
25% deposit, balance up to 36 months.

GINETTA CARS LIMITED, West End Works, Witham, Essex
Telephone: Witham 2143

mga

Such was the rush to finish the G15 prototype before the Motor Show that this temporary leaflet was hastily printed days before the launch. GINETTA CARS

The Ginetta stand at Earl's Court in 1967: a G12 features in the foreground with the brand new G15 in the background. GINETTA CARS

and Bob accepted without hesitation. For a small company like Ginetta the cost of exhibiting at the show was very large but the status it gave a maker in those days was significant, and effectively lifted the Ginetta name to a whole new level.

The prototype G15, painted Moonstone White, was ready for testing in mid-October. Despite being the only car and destined for the show stand, it was tested on the road just days before the show build-up. The author, on his way home from school that afternoon, was astonished to see this new car – launched in the Motor Show preview magazines days before – being driven down the busy High Street in Maldon a few miles from Witham. It had been photographed and pictures were sent to the press, and a temporary leaflet was hastily put together and printed.

In order to fill the stand they decided to place the G15 alongside a new G12, one of the last made. The G15 was well received and it was reported in the press after the show that 100 orders had been taken; this figure was a fantasy but it is possible that it might have referred to expressions of interest rather than firm orders.

The G15 wasn't the only Imp-powered sports car there, though. Rootes themselves had considered a sports version and a prototype had been built, while Paul Emery Racing had built a car called the Emery GT with an Imp engine mounted ahead of the transaxle, though only four were built. More relevant was the TVR Tina, which by chance was exhibited on an adjoining stand to the Ginetta at the Motor Show. This was still in prototype form, having been publicly revealed the year before, and was designed by Trevor Fiore, who was also responsible for the TVR Trident. The body was mounted directly to the Imp floor pan, and for the Motor Show it was shown in both coupé and spider form. It's not known if the Walklett brothers saw this as serious competition at the time but for sure they would have known that TVR were recovering from a sticky financial patch and would have wondered if TVR had the funds to get it to the production stage. One thing is for certain: they would have been confident that the chassis and suspension of the G15 would be far superior to the Imp floor pan of the Tina and hoped that potential buyers recognized this. As it turned out, this became irrelevant when TVR decided not to continue with the Tina project and the G15 had the Imp-powered sports car market virtually to itself for several more years.

Jem Marsh dropped in on the stand of course and, after close inspection of the new G15 and its price, the straight-talking Marsh commented. 'Well, Bob, you can keep that,' to which Bob replied, 'We intend to, Jem!' One wonders what Marsh thought years later when the G15 was still selling well.

A lot of interest was shown in the G15 but actual orders were quite slow in materializing: by May 1968, only five orders had been placed. This caused some worries, but in another sense this was a blessing because putting the G15 into production was an extremely slow process. It wasn't until August 1968 that the very first customer G15 left the factory, and by this time there had been further development incorporated into the prototype as well as all production cars. In testing it had been decided that more weight was needed at the front, and so the previously

Very early G15 dashboard layout. Note the left-hand column stalk for dipping and flashing headlamps, as found on early Imps. GINETTA OWNERS' CLUB

fitted standard rear-mounted Imp radiator and fan were discarded and replaced by a front radiator mounted in an extra moulding hung below the front bumper. This radiator was fed by pipes running through the chassis and, although no fan was fitted, cooling seemed adequate for most conditions. The prototype was converted to this layout and as a result all production cars were sold with the front radiator too. Despite such a radical change, the appearance of the G15 was not marred and many think it improved the looks of what was already an attractive shape.

Orders Take Off

On another positive note, the motoring magazines were keen to get their hands on a G15 to test. *Car* magazine were first to try it, taking the still unregistered prototype for testing near Witham. At the beginning of August 1968 the prototype was road registered BHK47G and immediately went on test with several magazines, all of whom were very complimentary about the car and felt the asking price to be very competitive for the package on offer. Perhaps potential customers had been waiting to read tests on the G15, for around the time these reports appeared the orders started to arrive thick and fast: suddenly the G15 was in demand and the brothers realized they had a hit on their hands.

The first few cars made often varied from car to car in small ways – for example the first three cars used early MGB pull-out external door handles, but from car four these were substituted for push-button handles. Cars seven and eight were supplied without engine and gearbox; these went respectively to an associate of Paul Emery Racing and Brian Tavender, an engineer in Chrysler's own competition department. These two orders were particularly encouraging, as they showed the G15 was attractive to competition-minded buyers, and indeed Brian Tavender fitted a specially tuned Imp engine and competed in sprints and hill-climbs for a number of seasons with much success.

With a dozen cars supplied, it was time to prepare for the G15's second Motor Show appearance. This time three cars were displayed in standard red, white and blue colours. The price had been raised by £50 to £849 in component form (£1,087 fully built and tax paid), but this did not deter buyers and demand was now strong. The price rise

The G15 Imp Sport engine has unparalleled access due to the entire rear body section lifting.
NEIL SAYER

This 1968 Motor Show car, the first Series 2 G15, became a factory demonstration vehicle and was tested by *Motor Sport* magazine. AUTHOR

This early G15 was purchased new by motoring journalist Peter Dron. Note the 41/2 J Cosmic alloy wheels, which were a very popular optional extra. JOHN ROSE

probably reflected the fact that the original launch price of £799 was trimmed a little too much to make the car an attractive proposition, but the new price was explained away by small but significant upgrades. The show cars were the first to receive some alterations made by Chrysler on the launch of their Mark 2 Imp, the most obvious being an all-in-one steering-column-mounted indicator, headlamp flasher, horn push and dip switch lever. As Ginetta used the Imp steering column, they inherited this feature, which superseded the two dashboard-mounted levers with an electric column-mounted pawl unit for cancelling the indicators found on the early G15s. There were also alterations to brake and clutch pedal positions to try to improve their ease of use, a very real issue on those first dozen cars.

Several purchasers had requested a tuned and bored-out 998cc version of the Imp engine be fitted to their car. Ginetta could purchase these from the Chrysler competition department as Rallye Imp engines and they were supplied for an additional £100. This was an expensive option but somewhere between 5 and 10 per cent of G15s sold were fitted with these units, and this version later became known as the G15S.

After the show, the white G15 was appropriated and retained by the factory as a demonstration car and road registered in November 1968 as CTW14G; following this, the car was immediately taken by *Motor Sport* magazine for an extensive test, which was published in the January 1969 edition. This test of what had been dubbed the Series 2 G15 was another strong influence in drawing the attention of potential buyers, although comments about what the tester thought would be a typical G15 owner – 'quite possibly you will have a beard and a big woolly jumper and almost certainly you will not have a wife. No woman in her right mind would put up with such a car' – alienated a lot of readers, as the letters column in the next issue clearly attested.

One early purchaser of a new G15 kit was Mrs Beatrice Naylor, perhaps better known by her maiden name, Beatrice Shilling. Working at the Royal Aircraft Establishment before the war she invented Miss Shilling's Orifice, which enabled Hurricane and Spitfire fighter planes with Merlin engines to fly without losing power or completely cutting out while making high-speed and sudden manoeuvres. It was a huge breakthrough and she went on to work as a highly skilled engineer at the RAE until her retirement in March 1969. In her spare time she raced motorcycles. Riding a Norton, she became the first woman to lap Brooklands at over 100mph. She later took up motor racing, and the G15 was a retirement present to herself. Bob Walklett made sure he delivered her kit personally so he could meet her. Miss Shilling may not have been a typical female car buyer, but the G15 model appealed equally to both genders, with female teachers, aircrew and housewives, among others, purchasing them.

The G15 in Racing

It was, however, a young wife from Berkshire, Alison Davis, who would go on to leave an indelible mark in Ginetta history.

Alison's brother-in-law Chris Davis had been an early G15 owner and her husband Roger had seen the potential of the G15 for racing. Together, Roger and Chris worked on a plan to build a G15 that would be suitable and highly competitive in Modsports racing. Alison borrowed Chris's road G15 and competed in a sprint at RAF Odiham in Hampshire and agreed it would be ideal for her to race. At Witham, Bob Walklett was happy to supply an ultra-lightweight body chassis unit with key components and Roger and Chris built up a beautifully prepared car fitted with a Carter engine.

The main G15 body mould. The split joints enabled the bodies to be moulded in one piece. DUNCAN CAMPBELL

ALISON DAVIS

From a young age, farmer's daughter Alison enjoyed motor racing and had a very competitive spirit, competing in sprints and some rounds of the RAC Hillclimb Championship.

Following marriage to husband Roger Davis, they decided to try their hand at circuit racing and purchased a Diva GT, which was used for several seasons and which, while not being particularly competitive, taught Alison a great deal about race craft. Working as a graphics co-ordinator for a firm of structural engineers by day, her leisure time was largely taken up by racing.

In 1971 she graduated to a Ginetta G15 in Modsports events and drove well, taking third place in the British Women Racing Drivers' Club Championship that season; this was followed by another strong season in 1972. Leaving the Ginetta behind, she raced a Fiat 124 and BMW 3.0 in Touring Car events and then a Triumph TR7 in Prodsports (production sports car racing).

It was the Prodsports experience that led her back to Ginetta, and in 1979 she won the Prodsports Championship outright in another G15, becoming the first woman to win a national racing championship in doing so. Alison went on to jointly win the Donnington Championship for Production GT Cars in 1981.

Turning to a one-make series for BL Metro cars, she raced for three seasons very competitively in a Melitta Coffee-sponsored Metro, which was later immortalized by Scalextric, who made a model of her actual car. An outing in the TT at Silverstone driving an Alfa Romeo GTV was among her last races before she turned away from motor sport to horse riding – she competed for many years thereafter in equestrian events.

Alison Davis was highly successful racing G15s. ALISON DAVIS

Alison Davis in her Modsports G15 leads the pack. The car was supplied by Ginetta to lightweight racing specifications and further modified by her husband and brother-in-law.
ALISON DAVIS

With sponsorship from Crookes Anestan promoting their Femfresh brand Alison was extremely competitive in 1971, and in 1972 she again showed great form, taking fourth place in class for the Chevron Oils Modsports Championship. In 1972 the sponsors ran a competition in *19* magazine, a publication aimed at teenage girls and young women, the first prize being a new G15 road car. This was only part of Alison Davis's triumphs behind the wheel of a G15, as we shall see.

Looking back to 1969, the company were preparing for the third G15 Motor Show appearance. During the summer, for the first time, a Weathershields fabric sunroof had been added as an optional extra; this special short-length version had been developed for the small roof area of the Marcos car and it suited the G15 equally well, proving a popular fitment at an additional £35.

Motor shows were now Ginetta's main marketing forum. They took the occasional advertisement in magazines and there were now regular road test features, but the shows were the real expenditure to drive sales. The problem Bob faced as he pondered what to do for the 1969 event was how, with nothing new to show, would Ginetta grab the attention of the public and press alike? One answer was to place an example of the single-seater G17 on the stand but the real show-stopper would be a specially painted G15. Three G15s were on display but one car was fitted with Minilite alloys and the car and wheels were painted with gold metal flake, a finish up to that point only used by customizers and hot-rodders. It really stood out and so it should have – the whole paint job took days and involved twenty-two coats of lacquer to produce a mirror finish.

The plan worked and the press lapped up the display; the gold car was sold off the stand to a teacher, but those ordering cars normally faced a twelve-week wait for delivery. At least they could now enjoy a fresh air heater, a new development to replace the previous recirculatory type, which by now was rather outmoded.

With well over 100 cars sold, it was necessary to consider making new moulds. Releasing the bodies from the moulds was quite brutal, often involving wedges and sometimes even club hammers on the front wing areas to break the seal. Naturally this took its toll and once the quality of the finished mouldings started to suffer, replacements were required, so an opportunity was taken for a facelift of the G15 ready for the 1970 Motor Show.

This involved enlarging the small side window behind the doors, perhaps one of the least pleasing features of the original design; the new larger window suited the shape perfectly. Other changes included a reshaped radiator air intake, a small divider between the two halves of the front bumper and a revised dashboard with space for an additional gauge and a deeper central section that could house a radio if required. At the show Ginetta had also announced a new model, the G21, but more orders for G15 were taken than ever before and they were struggling to cope with the demand. A further price rise to £899 in component form did little to slow the sales and delivery was now eighteen weeks and rising.

In 1970, the G15's side window was enlarged, improving its appearance still further. AUTHOR

A revised dashboard was also introduced in 1970. There was now space for a radio. AUTHOR

This drawing shows the anatomy of the G15 – a very compact package but offering plenty of interior space. GINETTA CARS

G15 production at Witham. The capacity was at its limit at this time. GINETTA CARS

BARRY WOOD

Barry Wood started racing in 1960 and soon graduated to racing Austin Healey Sprites, while working for well-known tuning expert Paddy Gaston. In 1963 he set up Surbiton Motors in the Surrey town of the same name and raced the new Lotus Elan under their banner.

Together with a local company, Shapecraft, Barry designed a coupé top which was bonded to the Elan shell. These Elans, with bodies modified by Shapecraft and marketed by Surbiton Motors, went into limited production and one of the first was famously bought by Peter Sellers for his new wife, Britt Ekland.

With the Shapecraft Elan project coming to an abrupt end late in 1964, Wood returned to racing Sprites, a Lotus 27 Formula 3 car and a Ford GT 40 at a few events. He also moved to Essex, where he was sales manager for a small garage business. Through this he got to know the Walklett brothers, who invited him to drive the works G15 in Modsports racing.

After a serious crash in the G15 he later raced another and has continued to race in a variety of cars, more recently in historic events while making a living in the motor trade.

The experienced Barry Wood was extremely quick in the works G15. GINETTA OWNERS' CLUB

The Witham factory was too small, though everything possible was done to create space, even to the extent of stacking partially completed bodies on end. The fabrication of some chassis frames was subcontracted out to Vic Howards' business in Lowestoft as another means of freeing up factory space and manpower. Despite all this, the Walkletts still found time to indulge in some motor sport, and prepared a G15 for Modsports racing. Maybe the idea came from the Davis team or perhaps Ginetta were planning this anyway; either way, a lightweight G15 shell was prepared with large wheel arch extensions and a car built up with wide wheels, minor chassis modifications and a highly tuned engine. It was still relatively close to the cars that customers were driving on the road but when it raced for the first time in the summer of 1971, shortly after Alison Davis's G15 debut, it made an immediate impact, driven by an experienced club racer, Barry Wood.

Despite starting mid-season, the works car was quick from the outset in the up-to-1150cc class, which ironically had been dominated up to that point by Ginetta G4s, and by the end of the season Wood had come close to winning the category. The less experienced Alison Davis had also given Wood a hard time on occasion, and now, for the first time since its introduction, the G15 was making a significant mark in circuit racing.

Barry Wood again, now sporting a Bevan Imp engine. GINETTA OWNERS' CLUB

A special G15, this is one of only three 'Racing' specification cars built, the other two being those of Alison Davis and Barry Wood. GINETTA OWNERS' CLUB

In 1972, Barry Wood was leading his class in both the STP and Chevron Oils Modsports Championships at mid-season and went on to dominate for the rest of the year. He continued to race the G15 until 1975, although less intensely, but at Castle Coombe that season a huge crash destroyed the car and hospitalized Wood. As we have seen, the cars raced by Wood and Davis were very lightweight and built specifically for racing; these cars were designed as 'Racing' G15s and noted as such within their chassis number. In total just three such cars were built.

For some time the Walklett brothers had been searching for larger premises and in early 1972 they took a lease on a factory in Edgeworth Road at Sudbury on the Essex-Suffolk border, around 25 miles (40km) north of Witham. Previously occupied by Sudbury Factors, vehicle component suppliers, it had the space both inside and out, and was quickly readied for production to transfer from Witham.

There was debate among the brothers as to whether the Witham site should be sold, but it was still home to Trevers and his family, as well as Doug and Ivor and their sister Dorothy. In the end it lay dormant as a factory although still storing some old moulds, jigs and spares, while at Sudbury

The new factory at Sudbury in Suffolk that Ginetta took over in early 1972. AUTHOR

G15 production at the Sudbury factory; compare this to the earlier photograph of G15 production at Witham. GINETTA CARS

production was ramped up to a highly creditable five cars a week. For the first time in the company history, Ginetta had the space to run production lines, and prospective purchasers visiting the offices would see the company was a well-organized and thriving business.

Challenges

From the outset the G15 had few challengers in the Imp-powered small sports car market, although Davrian, a small south London company, had come on the scene around the same time with their Davrian Imp, but this was a body chassis unit for using recycled Imp parts. The Davrian, while a very capable car that improved by development over time, held a slightly different place in the market.

However, in 1971 a real challenge to G15 supremacy did materialize when ex-Lotus engineers Paul Haussauer and stylist John Frayling introduced their Clan Crusader to the public. The Crusader was a quirky-looking car and not to all tastes, but it was well made, nicely finished and with government funding to set up in Washington, Co. Durham it quickly established a place in the market once production got under way between July and September 1971. The Clan, although trimmed to a slightly higher quality and more softly sprung, was aimed straight at G15 buyers and was fitted with the Sunbeam Imp engine and suspension; it was, however, significantly more expensive at £1,118 in component form. The four brothers were particularly incensed when they discovered that an employee at Chrysler had handed Clan a copy of the list of parts they supplied to Ginetta, information which was commercially sensitive and no doubt saved Clan a lot of time and effort while working on the design.

The market for specialist component cars had never been stronger than in 1972 and, while sales of the G15 were at record levels, it could not be denied that the Clan was selling well too and Bob Walklett could not escape the feeling that every Clan sold might have previously been a G15 order. He lost count of the number of customers visiting Ginetta's new factory for a test drive who were weighing up whether to buy a G15 or a Clan. They knew the Clan was more expensive but many couldn't see that with its twin-wishbone disc-braked front end, compared with the Imp swing arm drum-braked Clan, the G15 was giving a lot more for less as well. But in the end the brothers had never been afraid of competition and so long as it was fair competition they were confident they could meet any challenge.

The G15 was engineered to be available in right- and left-hand drive. Here a left-hand drive car sits in the Sudbury factory awaiting dispatch to Canada. GINETTA OWNERS' CLUB

Major revisions were made to the G15 in the summer of 1972. External clues to the changes can be seen here in the flush external door handles and stand-forward indicator lamps. This car, owned by the author for forty years, is one of only five cars fitted with 5J Cosmic Mark 2 alloy wheels. AUTHOR

There were certainly more challenges to come. Firstly, the tax concession on cars supplied in component form would be removed on 1 April 1973 with the introduction of Value Added Tax (VAT) and a special car tax that would increase the 10 per cent VAT up to a similar level that the old purchase tax delivered to the exchequer. Secondly, there was a new raft of legislation, mainly safety-related, that car makers needed to adhere to. There were many minor changes made to the G15 throughout its production run, but in the summer of 1972 the last major change came when legislation decreed the fibreglass fuel tank was no longer acceptable and it was replaced with a steel item. At the same time, new flush burst-proof door handles and locks had to be fitted; these were sourced from suppliers Wilmot Breeden and were the ones used on the new Morris Marina saloon. Another change at this time was that the front flashing indicator lights were now required to face forward, and these were mounted in small pods on the front body edge.

However, the real obstacle was new crash safety testing, which all new vehicles were required to undertake. This was very expensive and the G15 was never designed with this test in mind, although with its separate chassis construction Ivor felt it would meet the requirements.

The various tests were carried out at MIRA, the Motor Institute Research Association centre, and perhaps the crash dummy test on the steering column and the final destruction test, when the car was launched into a concrete block at 30mph (50km/h), were the most challenging. The G15 passed both but the 30mph impact test did do a lot of damage, including fracturing the offside screen pillar; the cabin remained intact, however, and the steering column didn't intrude, so a major hurdle had been overcome.

The G15 saw a further price increase to £949 (£1,175 including tax) just before the 1972 Motor Show and by now production had become manic, with customers rushing to order their new G15 to enjoy the tax-free component form price before the April cut-off point. In the year since

The moment of impact. This is a video screenshot of the G15 crash test at MIRA. The bonnet is flung forward and the windscreen pops out as the body compresses on the 30mph (50km/h) impact. WALKLETT FAMILY

FPU37H was a 1969 Motor Show car and long-term demonstration car. It was crash tested at MIRA only to be rebuilt into a new body chassis unit. MARK SMITH

The final series of factory-built G15s were the most refined versions; this car is factory fresh. GINETTA OWNERS' CLUB

production had got under way at Sudbury up to the VAT cut-off, some 250 G15s had been built and Ginetta was now a serious player. With VAT and special car tax added to the price, customers could now drive their cars away from the factory rather than having to finish building them at home, but the new price of £1,395, which included alloy wheels, was less attractive.

The End of the Line

There was still a demand for the car but it was far lower, and now Chrysler were making noises about dropping the Imp, which could mean the loss of major components they needed to make the cars. It was difficult to know what to do for the best, but before the 1973 Motor Show, the brothers sat down and made the tough decision to stop making the G15. A final large batch was made before the show and the cessation of production was not formally announced until April 1974, with the very last new G15 sold leaving the factory in May 1974.

One of the last cars made was purchased by a British couple living and working in Abu Dhabi in the Gulf; they decided to pick up their car in Sudbury and drive it the 5,500 miles (8,851km) home. Loading their G15 up to the roof, they crossed into France before going down through the former Yugoslavia into Greece and Turkey. They crossed over the Bosphorus into Asia at Istanbul and traversed mountain passes in eastern Turkey and parts of Iran at 4,000–5,000ft (1,200–1,500m) in ice and snow on road surfaces only suitable for a four-wheel drive vehicle before running down through the Gulf states to their destination. The G15 ran almost faultlessly with only minor tinkering required to offset problems caused by the at times harsh conditions.

Final production is stated by the factory at 804 units but records suggest the actual figure was nearer the 600 mark. A high percentage of cars made still survive.

In racing, the success of the G15 had barely begun, though, and two south London-based owners were determined to

GINETTA G15 EXPORTS

Angola	1
Canada	2
Hong Kong	1
New Zealand	1
Northern Ireland	5
Portugal	1
United Arab Emirates	1
USA	2

G15s have found their way all around the world. This Japanese owner is passing Mount Fuji, just visible in the background.
GINETTA OWNERS' CLUB

make their mark with the G15, initially in production car trials. Gary Taylor and David Beams both bought new G15s in 1971 and by 1974 had become enthusiastic competitors, but for Beams even this was not enough and he tried his hand at sprints and other forms of competition. He decided to rebuild his car for Prodsports racing, a category for which the G15 was eligible, and in 1976 made an impressive debut season.

Returning for 1977 he was regularly winning his class and even vied for the overall lead on occasion, before winning the Championship outright. This inspired others to try their hand, and Alison Davis in particular watched with interest. It was time to return to unfinished business. She purchased a well-used road G15 in south London, which husband Roger and his brother Chris meticulously rebuilt to the highest standards. In 1979 Alison took Prodsports by storm, winning the class and overall Championship to become the first woman in history to win a national racing championship – an enormous achievement.

She raced the same series again in 1980 but the classes had changed and her G15 was now in the same class as a V6-engined Panther Lima, and if that wasn't enough to take, it was driven by none other than Chris Meek.

The G15 had been a really significant success for Ginetta, but all good things come to an end. The brothers had bright hopes for the future; with hindsight it might have been worth continuing with the G15 for a few more years, but at the time they couldn't predict what a turbulent period in history the seventies would become for car makers.

The immaculately prepared Prodsports G15S of David Beams. AUTHOR

THE G15 SUPER S

The G15 story wasn't quite over yet. Due to United States emissions regulations, the car wasn't suitable for export with the Imp engine. However, the West Coast importer Art Allen was keen to test the market with a VW engine and transaxle in place of the Imp unit. The brothers weren't that enthusiastic, but when Allen put the money on Bob's desk to build two complete cars minus engine and gearbox they couldn't ignore it.

They modified the rear suspension to accept the VW driveshafts and the chassis to mount the engine and

David Beams sideways In the G15S pushing the Modsports G15 of Ron Woods. GINETTA OWNERS' CLUB

Alison Davis was queen of Prodsports in 1979 in a G15. ALISON DAVIS

transmission. The bodywork came in for a small amount of upgrading with an engine cover that was split horizontally to provide a lift-up top panel, while the wheel arches were widened like the factory Modsports G15 to allow wider wheels to be fitted. The final touch in place of the chromium bumpers was a combined air dam and bumper moulding at the front, while at the rear the bumper was substituted for a deeper glass-fibre item. It was a smart update of the G15 form, and the bumpers in particular caught the imagination of those driving G15s in the UK: an unintended spin-off of the Super S model were useful aftermarket sales of these bumpers to G15 owners.

The cars were delivered to California in 1977 and Allen fitted VW 1600cc engines on arrival, but the hoped-for further sales did not materialize and no further cars were ordered.

The Volkswagen-powered G15 Super S – no radiator cutout at the front for this air-cooled machine.
GINETTA OWNERS' CLUB

Rear of the G15 Super S. Note the shut lines at the top of the engine cover – on these cars the top section of the engine cover lifts, unlike on the traditional G15.
GINETTA OWNERS' CLUB

CHAPTER SIX

TAKING ON THE ESTABLISHMENT

Ginetta may have been a relatively small company but the four Walklett brothers delighted in punching above their weight, whether on the race track or in the road sports car market. With the effort of getting the G15 into production, finishing off the G16 and building the G17 and 18, 1968 had been a frantic year. It's worth at this point reviewing just what had been achieved over the period from 1964 to the end of 1968. Ivor had designed and, with Trevers, built three different single-seater models, two sports GT models, three road cars and put them all into production except the G8 single-seater. Some would argue that this was too much and that more time should have been spent perfecting particular models rather than moving onto the next, but the sheer achievement of their labours cannot be overlooked.

During this period Trevers had become the bodywork specialist, developing and creating the shapes and turning them into actual car bodies, while Ivor developed the chassis and suspension; they worked closely together and overlapped with each other as they arrived at the end product. Bob and Doug also played a major part, perhaps not so much in new model development, but they oiled the wheels by ensuring the company was well organized and funded and that production could continue unhindered; and in so doing created the environment in which this development work could flourish.

THE GINETTA G19

Perhaps in 1969 they should have relaxed a little, but they were always looking towards the next model and in racing it was always a struggle to stay on top. Ivor had planned one more single-seater car to project Ginetta into the highest levels of motor sport.

The G19 was designed as a new Formula 1 car and this was a serious project that Ivor and Trevers were keen to progress. There is no question that they had the capability and the skills to build this car – the chassis, suspension and bodywork would have presented no major challenge to them. The design was relatively simple, with a space-frame chassis and fully adjustable wishbone suspension all clothed in a conventional cigar-shaped body; in many ways it was an enlarged and beefed-up version of the G18.

It could have become a reality in 1969. The plan was for Ginetta to further their association with BRM and instal the 3-litre V12 engine and gearbox. Bob Walklett had been in touch once again with BRM and agreed a price of £3,000 for the engine, but in reality 1969 was a bad season in Formula 1 for BRM and Bob was far from sure they should commit. The engine to have seemed instead to be the Cosworth DFV. Although BRM did turn things around in 1970, even achieving a race win in the Belgium Grand Prix with Pedro Rodriguez driving, by then the brothers had abandoned the project and the G19 never got beyond the advanced drawings stage.

The reality was that while the construction of the car and engine purchase was something they could have afforded, the cost of racing the car and the team that would be required to run it was beyond their means without major sponsorship. Bob was generally unhappy that the racing was drawing the company's attention away from what he considered the relative stability of road car manufacture and the steady profits this side of the business had produced. It seems doubtful that there was total agreement between the brothers over scaling down the racing, and in particular the development of racing cars, but Bob's view finally prevailed.

That is not to say that Trevers and Ivor abandoned their love of racing – far from it, as we shall see – but such activities were for a long time consigned to the sidelines. The truth was that they could not stop themselves from coming up with ideas and developing them; often, after a long day's work, the evenings would be spent on the latest project. These developments were diverse and not always associated with racing: one idea that came about was a uniquely

Ford Zodiac with camper van conversion top, one of many ideas from the fertile minds of the brothers. AUTHOR

clever take on the camper van. At the time Trevers had been running a Mark 4 Ford Zephyr family car. He planned a glass-fibre bolt-on top where the bootlid was removed and became the entrance to the camping compartment, containing a sink and cooker with access to the sleeping area above the Zephyr's normal roof. While the camper part was hardly commodious, the Zephyr remained a normal full five-seater car. Not only was this one-off built, but it was later sold and amazingly it still survives, albeit now sitting on a Mark 4 Ford Zodiac after the original Zephyr rusted away.

Another project during the seventies was a design for a 1.5-litre two-stroke Formula 1 engine, a revolutionary idea with twelve tiny cylinders, horizontally opposed and turbocharged. Trevers made a lot of progress with the prototype, having specialist castings made, before other work caused it to be set aside and never completed.

The brothers even came up with an electric car design where the batteries could be charged, if required, by a small petrol motor while the vehicle was being driven along. It very much foreshadowed the hybrid cars that have gained popularity in recent years, and was yet another example of their inventive minds running ahead of the pack. Only the lack of investment capital held them back.

In business, the strength and determination of the brothers should never be underestimated either. With G15 production in full swing and at record levels, the brothers were astonished to hear that the new rival Clan Motor Company had homologated their Crusader with the RAC and thereby gained a passport to international racing. The

This two-stroke Formula 1 engine design reached an advanced stage of completion.
GINETTA: THE INSIDE STORY – BOOKMARQUE PUBLISHING

Clan had been in production for little over year, against the G15's four years, so to think they could have built the units necessary for homologation was frankly ridiculous, when Ginetta themselves had barely passed that figure.

A challenge was made to the RAC Motor Sport Division but dismissed out of hand, so the brothers had to either back down or risk everything they had worked for by taking on the RAC. When Bob spoke to a contact at Chrysler, he was tipped off that at no time had Clan purchased more engine and gearbox assemblies than Ginetta, so they took on the establishment with an appeal to the FIA in Paris. This resulted in the RAC being instructed to rescind the homologation and Clan being publicly embarrassed. They were unhappy but when, in October 1973, Clan went into liquidation, it was revealed that they had built just 315 cars.

THE GINETTA G21

With the Formula 1 car set aside and with thoughts of producing the Richard Petit take on the G12, designated the G20, now dismissed, Ivor turned his mind to designing another road car, the G21. He and Trevers were keen to make a larger-engined sports car but with more appeal in the UK than their V8 G10 could ever have achieved. They set their sights on the Ford 3-litre V6 engine that had been available since the mid-sixties, having been introduced for the Mark 4 Zephyr/Zodiac range of cars. Specialist makers had been quick to pick up on this engine, with Reliant fitting it to their Scimitar GT and Gilbern to their new Genie model as early as 1966. A small Suffolk-based specialist, Trident, were also using the engine in their Venturer from 1967. For 1969, both TVR and Marcos adopted the V6 by fitting it to their Ford 1600cc chassis, thereby giving their customers the option of much more powerful versions.

The V6 was a smooth, torquey unit and came with a four-speed gearbox that had the added advantage of an overdrive option. It was a good package for a sports car, perhaps the only disadvantages being that the engine was quite tall, due to its centrally mounted carburettor, and the fact that there was quite a large gap between the second and third gear ratios; the later not really an issue for the large Ford saloon but was more noticeable in a sports car.

Work on the prototype development started in autumn 1969, with the chassis developed from the principles used on the G15. It was constructed of 2in (5cm) square-section tubing swept up at the rear to accommodate axle mountings and with a platform centre section. The front of the chassis was similar to the G15 but lengthened and braced to cradle the front-mounted engine. Returning to the design they had envisaged for the aborted G14 project, the brothers provided extra stiffness with a sheet steel backbone doubling as a transmission tunnel fitted between the upswept rear section and the framework cradling the engine. The result was a very rigid structure with a high degree of torsional stiffness, which, by virtue of its full-width platform central section, gave good perimeter protection.

The G21 chassis. Note the strong sheet steel backbone. STEVE FIDLER

Front suspension was by the Triumph wishbones and uprights as on previous models, with coil spring damper units and rack and pinion steering, but for the rear Ivor wanted to ensure the full power of the V6 engine could be exploited and opted for an independent layout, the cost of which they felt was fully justified. The rear axle comprised a Salisbury differential rigidly mounted and driving through fixed-length shafts to specially cast alloy hub-carriers, retained by twin trailing arms and a single transverse link each side. Rear springing was by a pair of coil spring damper units to each wheel, while disc brakes were fitted all round, mounted inboard at the rear.

The design of the fibreglass bodywork again owed much to the style of the G15, although the roof line was extended back into a fastback style, not seen on a Ginetta before, but liked by Ivor for the increased interior space that could be achieved without compromising the overall sports package. Forward of the windscreen, a front-hinging, tilt-forward bonnet produced a long flowing line, finishing with a discreet radiator air intake tucked under the curved chrome-plated front bumper, as found on the G15.

By taking panels and shapes from the G15 bodywork and adjusting the dimensions, the main body buck was quickly sculpted by Trevers, working largely alone in a separate building to the rear of the Witham site. Now that Ginetta had achieved a higher profile, it was important that new developments were kept under wraps and away from prying eyes. Details such as door hinges and fittings, bumpers and many other items were shared with the G15, giving the dual advantage of parity in component supply and, critically, no time-consuming and costly development work in these areas.

As work progressed, Bob Walklett wanted the G21 to be made available with the 1600cc Ford engine as well as the 3-litre. He thought this would broaden the market appeal of the model, although Ivor and Trevers felt it would water

GINETTA G21 (1970–8)

Layout and chassis	Two-seater sports car with platform chassis	Reverse	3.323:1
		Final drive	3.7:1 (3.9:1 optional)
Engine		*Suspension and Steering*	
Type	Chrysler Sunbeam Rapier	Front	Twin wishbone, coil spring damper units, anti-roll bar
Block material	Cast Iron		
Head material	Aluminium	Rear	Rigid axle with trailing arms and Panhard rod, coil spring damper units
Cylinders	4		
Cooling	Water	Steering	Rack and pinion
Bore and stroke	81.5 × 82.5mm	Tyres	165 × 13in
Capacity	1725cc	Wheels	Cast alloy
Valves	2 valves per cylinder, pushrod operated	Rim width	5.5J × 13in
Compression ratio	9.6:1		
Carburettor	2 × Stromberg (G21S 2 × 40DCOE Weber)	*Brakes*	
		Type	Disc front and drum rear
Max. power (DIN)	79bhp (G21S 98bhp)	Brake size	9in (225mm) front, 9in (225mm) rear
Max. torque	95lb ft at 3,800rpm (G21S 106lb ft at 4,000rpm)		
		Dimensions	
Fuel capacity	10gal (45ltr)	Track, front	50.5in (1,283mm)
		Track, rear	51in (1,295mm)
Transmission		Wheelbase	91in (2,311mm)
Gearbox	Chrysler 4-speed and reverse (overdrive optional)	Overall length	156.5in (3,975mm)
		Overall width	63in (1,600mm)
Clutch	Diaphragm	Overall height	46in (1,168 mm)
		Unladen weight	1,792lb (813kg)
Internal Gearbox Ratios			
First	3.122:1	*Performance*	
Second	1.993:1	Top speed	112mph (180km/h); G21S 117mph (188km/h)
Third	1.296:1		
Fourth	1:1	0–60mph	10.0sec (G21S 9.2sec)

down the macho image carried by the 3-litre. As was often the case, Bob's view prevailed, but to make the 1600cc version price competitive in what was a fairly crowded area of the specialist sports car market, a live axle was developed for it with a drum-braked Ford axle located on a pair of trailing arms, coil spring dampers units and a Panhard rod to take care of lateral location. Dunlop light alloy road wheels were specified for both versions.

Development of the G21 took longer than previous new models, which was probably in part due to the volume of work G15 production was creating but also because the brothers put everything they knew into the G21. They wanted the product to have a level of finish and equipment in line with anything similarly priced available in the mass-produced and specialist car market: the G21 was built to take on all comers, including cars such as the MGB and Triumph GT6. The interior trim was neatly finished in leather cloth and carpet complete with full instrumentation under a deeply hooded dash top. The horizontally sliding windows above the doors on the G15 had become electrically operated wind-down windows on the G21, while the boot was large enough for two small cases although the spare wheel and 10gal (45ltr) fuel tank restricted the total amount of space available. Large loads could be carried inside the car as well on the carpeted area behind the seats; in the design stage making the model a two-plus-two had been considered but in the end this idea was not pursued.

The Walkletts built two cars initially: a 1600cc version in orange and a white 3-litre, and both were ready in time for the 1970 Motor Show.

Motor Show Debut

Two weeks before the show, Bob invited the press to view the cars, and on the eve of the show *Motor* magazine ran a detailed article entitled 'Fast New Ginettas' – welcome publicity indeed as Ginetta prepared their stand at Earl's Court with the two G21s and two G15s. At the show there was a great deal of interest shown. Bob had once again priced the car competitively at £1,395 in component form (£1,869 4s 9d with tax paid) for the 1600 and £1,795 in component form (£2,411 tax paid) for the 3-litre. The TVR Vixen S3 1600 and Tuscan V6 were significantly cheaper but less well specified, while Marcos, who had dropped their 1600 in favour of a 2-litre, had their 3-litre V6 priced at £1,790. Some extras were also made available, including overdrive for the 3-litre at £95, and generally for both models, sunshine roof at £39 10s, electric cooling fan £18 10s, heated rear screen £25, radio £25, fog and spot lamps £6 6s. For the 3-litre, a purchaser could opt for an automatic gearbox in place of the manual for £120.

The problem was that, as previously mentioned, so many G15 orders were taken it was going to be impossible to fit in any G21 production at Witham and so the model was effec-

The G21 3-litre at its launch. Members of the Walklett family active in the business can be seen in the front row: from the left, Douglas, Trevers, Ivor, Bob and Dorothy, together with the factory staff. GINETTA CARS

The G21 3-litre as first displayed at the 1970 London Motor Show. JOHN ROSE

This is the prototype Ford 1600cc G21, difficult to distinguish from the 3-litre version. DENNIS FEATHERSTONE

tively on ice. In February 1971, the 1600cc car was registered for the road as MPU20J, and further testing and development was carried out on it. Even if production capacity had been available, a major long-running strike at the Ford Motor Company during 1971 froze the supply of V6 engines for a time and would have been a major disruption to the build programme.

The relationship between Ginetta and the Chrysler company had grown from strength to strength. The component prices they offered to Ginetta were very attractive, and this started a train of thought that resulted in consideration being given to installing a 1725cc Chrysler Arrow range engine into the G21 chassis. The engine chosen initially was the twin carburettor version, as fitted to the Sunbeam Rapier and Humber Sceptre models in the Chrysler range. Rated at 80bhp, it was a heavy unit but was smooth, well engineered and, importantly, came with a four-speed gearbox to which an optional overdrive could be added. It was soon apparent that this package fitted the chassis with only the most minor of modifications – it was a little tight around the alternator but otherwise a neat installation. By switching the rear axle for an Arrow range unit for which there were several suitable ratios available, the Chrysler content of the G21 was virtually at the same level as that of the G15.

The 1725cc engine from Chrysler became the standard offering; here in Sunbeam Rapier form, the H120 Holbay version was fitted to the G21S. AUTHOR

The one area where further development was required to the G21 to enable this engine installation was the bonnet moulding. The 3-litre and 1600cc versions featured a broad bulge down the centre line of the bonnet, which on the 3-litre actually ducted air from an area just behind the radiator directly to the top of the carburettor. With the Chrysler engine installed, this bulge was removed from the bonnet and replaced with a smaller offset 'blister' to one side, the purpose of which was to give clearance for the air filter box.

A year after the launch of the G21 range, Ginetta's 1971 Motor Show stand once again featured two each of both the G15 and G21 models, but this time the Ford 1600cc version had been replaced by the Chrysler-engined version billed as the G21 1800. Perhaps due to the sporty image always associated with the Sunbeam brand, the G21 was always referred to as being powered by a Sunbeam Rapier engine, but in fact the first batch of G21s were fitted with engines carrying Humber supply tags. As the Rapier and Sceptre engines were identical this is academic, but it is nonetheless interesting that Ginetta preferred to refer to the Sunbeam marque.

Type Approval

Finally, with the move to the 40,000sq ft Sudbury factory as previously described, there was capacity to build the G21. The brothers made many inspired decisions, but occasionally they did make a wrong move, and one was surely deciding not to push forward with G21 production in component form during the summer of 1972. There is little doubt that during the pre-VAT buying frenzy the G21 would have sold well and achieved a high level of market awareness. As it was, the Walkletts were so pleased with the mainstream standard achieved in the execution of the design, they decided to hold over production until after the imposition of VAT and special car tax, when the cars would leave the factory fully built.

In order to sell fully factory-built cars, the G21 – like the G15 – would need to pass the type approval tests and the G21 was presented at the same time as the G15. Like the G15, it was upgraded to include the new flush external door locks and forward-facing front indicator lights and it passed; in fact, the results were among the best ever seen at the time on the 30mph impact test. The crumple zone created in the nose of the car ahead of the chassis absorbed the shock, leaving the chassis virtually undamaged, the cabin and doors unaffected.

It wasn't all plain sailing, though: on the crash dummy tests, steering column movement was outside required limits, leaving Ivor and Trevers to come up with a simple on-the-spot solution to arrest the movement. Working inside the MIRA premises, they decided to weld a small steel hoop to the steering column under the dashboard and fix it back to the internal structure. This proved enough to bring the test within limits and so gain a pass. The cost of these tests was so high for a company of Ginetta's size that failure would have been a huge blow. Once again the brothers' ingenuity had carried them through.

Launched at the 1971 Motor Show, the G21 1800 took over from both the V6 and 1600 Ford versions. GINETTA CARS

Prototypes outside the Sudbury factory in early 1973: the 3-litre is flanked by the 1600 (left) and G15 demonstration car (right). TIM WALLACE

As the model tested had to be the heaviest version, it was the original 3-litre prototype, veteran of two Motor Shows and much testing that was used for the crash test, and so for the G21's third Motor Show appearance in October 1972, a new 3-litre car was built. In an effort to make an impact, the car was painted yellow and up-specified with, wide for the times, 7in Revolution alloy wheels, giving the car a macho appearance befitting its 3-litre power. Also – and importantly – it was fitted with an automatic gearbox, a first for Ginetta, who were demonstrating to the public that as well as building cars with a racing bias, they could now make high-end road cars for doctors, accountants and other professionals who wanted to cruise in comfort in a stylish sports car that was that little bit different.

This, the first production G21 with 1725cc engine, left the factory in July 1973. It has been owned by the author for nearly forty years. AUTHOR

Also on the show stand was a red 1800cc car. For the first time, orders were being taken with a delivery early in 1973 quoted. Back at Sudbury, both show cars were road registered as demonstration cars in January 1973, BCF767L for the 3-litre, BCF768L for the 1800. After more than two years, the brothers were still refining the product and in an effort to make the interior look more production quality, a new vacuum-formed plastic material was used for the dashboard and door panels in place of the leather cloth-covered panels; the G15 had similar treatment in some areas. Also, the Dunlop alloy road wheels were substituted for similar-looking wheels made by the Exaction Company and used on the range-topping Hillman Avenger Tiger, thereby adding more Chrysler content to the package. Finally, the seats, which were made by Restall in Birmingham and originally designed for the G10 and 11 models and into the G21 from the outset, were substituted for a cloth-upholstered seat made by Huntmaster following supply issues with the former.

At the rear, the G21 fastback style offered useful boot space for the spare wheel and luggage. GINETTA OWNERS' CLUB

Despite everything, it was not until 11 July 1973 that the production prototype car, featuring all the upgrades except the seats, was finally delivered to a customer. Three weeks later, the 3-litre automatic demonstration car was sold too. By coincidence both lucky owners lived within a few miles of one another in rural Essex and the author, spotting both cars out on the road, gained the false impression that the model must be selling in significant numbers. How wrong could I have been – these were in fact the only two outside factory hands. Several years later I had the opportunity to purchase the first car to leave the factory, which I still enjoy nearly forty years later.

Production Under Way

Full deliveries finally got under way in September 1973, almost three years after the G21's public debut. By now the idea of the 3-litre had been put on hold, but in its place Ginetta announced the G21S, fitted with a Holbay version of the Rapier engine, as fitted to the Sunbeam Rapier H120 model. This engine, tuned by Holbay, featured twin Webber carburettors in place of twin Strombergs, and a different camshaft and exhaust among other upgrades. The Holbay produced around 95bhp and, while not giving the outright performance of the Ford V6, was a quick car and included overdrive as standard. Priced at £1,975 plus £115 for overdrive, the standard version was significantly less expensive than the S version, at £2,355. Approximately one in three cars ordered were the S version, but the marketing of the G21 was another area where changes were taking place.

Ginetta had always sold cars in the UK market direct to the public from their factory premises. In the early days of the G15 they briefly flirted with selling cars through Paul Emery Racing and a Lotus dealership with branches in Northamptonshire and Leicestershire but it didn't work out. However, Bob had noted that potential customers were often keen to visit the factory to test-drive cars, meet the managing director personally and generally buy into the very exclusive experience of buying and owning a Ginetta. Saturday mornings were usually set aside for test drives, and in the heady days of G15 production, often five or more potential customers would present themselves to be driven around the block and often handing over a deposit cheque before leaving. On the Monday morning Bob would ask secretary Dorothy to confirm by letter receipt of the deposit, the extras ordered and colour and the cars would be placed on the production schedule. It was an efficient and very cost-effective method of selling.

With the dawn of VAT and fully factory-built drive-away cars, the dynamics had changed, however, so perhaps now was the right time to appoint a dealership network. It would mean offering a substantial discount to the dealer, which would either need to be added to the price or taken from profits, but on the plus side it would put the cars in showrooms local to customers and hopefully generate more sales as a result. Bob had even discussed with Chrysler the possibility of them putting a G21 in every one of their showrooms as they no longer had a sports car in their range; in practice Ginetta were not in a position to build sufficient cars for this to be feasible, but it remained on the table for future review.

During the summer of 1973, a network of dealers was established; some were well-known sports car dealerships, others were car sales businesses run by enthusiasts and keen to offer a specialist product. Initially, dealers took G15s into stock while waiting for G21 production to get under way, but as its production ramped up during the last few months of 1973, outstanding

The interior of the G21 was comfortable and well finished, with vacuum-formed panels to dash, transmission tunnel and doors.
AUTHOR

orders direct from the factory were soon filled. Dealership deliveries quickly followed, with most dealers taking two cars – one for the showroom and one for demonstration purposes.

As 1973 drew to a close, storm clouds grew rapidly over the economy of the United Kingdom. An energy crisis emerged as an Arab–Israeli war disrupted fuel supplies and pushed up the price of petrol at the pump by 50 percent, and this was quickly followed by a stand-off between striking coal miners and the Conservative government led by Ted Heath. By January 1974 businesses were ordered to work a three-day week in an effort to conserve energy. For Ginetta this was the worst possible environment in which to drive forward a new model. Despite the short working week, completed cars started to stack up at the factory as dealers failed to take cars previously reserved. With the last of the G15s also parked up awaiting sale, cars in stock quickly tied up a huge amount of the company's capital. Bob tried all he knew to move the stock, including offering discounts to customers considering buying cars directly from the factory, and even placing a full-page advertisement in a Sunday newspaper offering big discounts and immediate delivery.

As Bob would later comment, the problem with sales to dealers was that they were not real sales, in that you never knew when or if they would come back and take the next cars they had requested to be built, whereas a deposit from a customer directly to the factory was almost always a car sold.

The Sudbury factory with G21 and G15 cars stockpiled. Cash flow was a problem with so much money tied up in unsold stock. GINETTA CARS

Bob Walklett drove this G21 daily for several years. AUTHOR

Commercial Failure

With money haemorrhaging from the business they were forced to act. The four brothers sat down and reluctantly agreed to close down the Sudbury factory and return to Witham, which, two years on from the original expansion, they still owned. Ginetta weren't the only specialist car maker in trouble at this time. Many were going broke and indeed at one point there was a rumour that Ginetta had gone too, but Bob moved quickly to quash this while planning the survival of the business. The move back to Witham was completed by August 1974 and the Sudbury factory handed back to the landlord. A great deal of money had been lost but the money was their money – all suppliers were paid, as was the rent. Now, however, they faced a very different future to the one they had planned.

Before the closure of the Sudbury factory most of the workforce had been laid off but a large supply of components had been stockpiled. As G21 orders trickled through over the next year, cars were assembled on a built-to-order basis by the brothers and a very small workforce, while Bob was looking for ways to bring in more income for the business. As well as buying, selling and refurbishing used G15s and G21s, he also filled the showroom with used cars of all makes and types. Cars as diverse as a Hillman Avenger would sit alongside an E Type Jaguar or a Triumph TR6 in the Witham showroom. It was all a far cry from the mass production at Sudbury two or three years before, but it paid the bills and kept the business alive. The mood was very downbeat and the brothers had lost their drive and

Autocar **road tested this G21S, LNO54P. Here Doug Walklett stands with the car at the local Essex beauty spot of Heybridge Basin. Ivor later drove this car daily for nearly ten years.** GINETTA CARS

Never designed as a competition car, G21s have nonetheless been used effectively, none more so than by Steve Fidler, pictured here. STEVE FIDLER

enthusiasm. Furthermore Bob had married Anne and they now had three children while Ivor had met Vivien, so their whole focus was no longer on Ginetta.

Bob was particularly unhappy about what he perceived as bad treatment by the motoring press: he felt the G21 was never given the status it deserved or put head to head with cars like the MGB. Magazines had published articles on the G21, but it was not until 1976 that *Autocar* published a full road test of a G21S, by which time the model had almost run its course and a prolonged period of inflation had pushed the price up to £3,496 for that version.

Ironically, twenty years later a classic car magazine, *Practical Classics*, did finally put the G21 up against a mainstream competitor – the Triumph GT6; the article concluded the G21 was an easy winner, thereby making the point Bob tried so hard to get across all those years before. Back in 1976 the road test by *Autocar* had given a small boost to sales but it was all far too late and, with supplies of vital purpose-made parts like the vacuum-formed dash panels running out, Ginetta had no choice but to call a halt to G21 production. The last car was built late in 1977. In total just sixty-seven had been built, more than half of them during the first year at Sudbury.

In sales terms, the G21 was a failure and the brothers were always left wondering if continuing with the Ford engine might have given a different outcome, or indeed if selling the car in component form rather than holding it back to sell as a fully built car would have made a difference – they would never know. Among Ginetta enthusiasts today, the G21 model is held in high esteem and most of the cars built are thought to have survived.

GINETTA G21 EXPORTS

Eire	1
France	1
Hong Kong	1
Northern Ireland	3

THE GINETTA G22

While Trevers and Ivor continued to ponder the motor racing scene, they spotted a new series called Sports 2000 for cars fitted with a mid-mounted 2000cc ohc engine and thought it might take off in a similar way to Formula Ford ten years previously. Despite the G21 failure, Bob still felt the future lay in road cars, but agreed to the proposal put forward by his two brothers to build a Sports 2000 car to be known as the G22. Ivor designed a chassis frame of square tubing incorporating a stiff boxed area to support the twin-wishbone front suspension, while at the rear, sturdy outriggers supported the engine, gearbox and rear suspension. Rear suspension was by trailing arms, transverse links and specially made hub-carriers.

A full-width roll-over bar was incorporated into the chassis frame and the package included four wheel disc brakes. The bodywork was designed to meet the regulations for the Formula and was simple and lightweight, involving a number of flat panels which made the construction of the first body a fairly straightforward exercise.

THE GINETTA OWNERS' CLUB

In 1973 two G15 owners, Gary Taylor and David Beams, got together and formed an owners' club. This quickly grew and the following year boasted over 100 members, but it did not continue for long and was disbanded.

In 1978 another G15 owner, Jules Birch, proposed through magazine adverts a Ginetta Owners' Register with an occasional newsletter posted to participants as a means of bringing owners together in common interest.

The following year, and now with nearly 200 owners registered, a committee was formed and the Register formally became the Ginetta Owners' Club. Gradually expanding and representing owners of all types of Ginetta, the club soon had members throughout the world.

The club always pledged full support to Ginetta Cars, and in turn always received their approval and support. The club quickly became a useful sounding board for the company, representing as it did a pool of like-minded enthusiasts – and as such, potential purchasers of new models.

The club remains active today, boasting around 350 members.

Enthusiastic members meet with a variety of models in the early days of the club. GINETTA OWNERS' CLUB

The strong G22 chassis frame. GINETTA CARS

Dawn Walklett models the new G22 at its launch in Witham, January 1978. GINETTA CARS

The G22 proved a popular car for sprints and hill-climbs, as seen here. GINETTA OWNERS' CLUB

From the rear, the simple flat-panelled bodywork can be best appreciated. AUTHOR

A side view of the G23 prototype, with plain body sides as on the G21. GINETTA CARS

The car was finished and ready for testing by the end of 1977, and the services of two racing drivers were engaged – Sid Fox, who had experience in the Sports 2000 race series; and Phil Dowsett, a local driver who was starting to make a name for himself. The car was on pace but Fox felt it lacked the speed to be a race winner, and so Ivor and Trevers reviewed the body design and added more downforce in an effort to improve lap times. At a further test session, both drivers were impressed with the improvements made but were still unsure if it was a race winner.

From a commercial point of view, Bob had been taking soundings and wasn't convinced there was a real market for it. The races hadn't really captured the imagination of promoters and there was only one series, meaning potential sales were limited to little more than a grid full of cars from all the manufacturers building these cars. The money being spent on development and testing could simply not be justified and Bob reluctantly persuaded his brothers they should turn their thought to other products.

This spelled the end for the G22. Apart from the original prototype, only one other complete car was built and eventually used for sprints and hill-climbing, while some years later a bodyshell was sold and mounted to an OMS chassis and used for similar purposes.

THE GINETTA G23 AND G24

With the G21 out of production, a new road car was urgently needed. Refurbishment, car sales and spares sales were now the only real income for the business, but the brothers were seriously lacking in confidence as to what direction to take. They still felt there was mileage in the G21 concept and so went back to the G21 3-litre as a starting point for a major update on the design. Ivor created a smooth, flowing bonnet incorporating flip-up headlamps, which were very much in vogue at the time, while the fastback top was removed and the rear deck levelled to make the car an open-top, while the rear panel came in for a restyle as well. The appearance with the roof off was extremely pleasing, but the prototype with a standard G21 3-litre chassis, including independent rear suspension, was never fitted with a soft top. Instead a hardtop was made, rather oddly to many eyes, featuring a porthole-type window behind the doors, reminiscent of the fifties Ford Thunderbird and covered in vinyl.

Having completed this, Trevers thought some of the work could be applied to the standard G21. Taking a spare G21 bodyshell, he fitted the new G23-style bonnet to it, which involved little modification other than the removal of the heater air intake in front of the windscreen, the heater now being ducted from the extreme front of the car. At the rear, because the chrome-plated rear bumpers, derived from a contemporary Riley Elf, were no longer available, Trevers created a full-width bumper capping along the lines of the aftermarket moulding created for the G15 a few years earlier.

So pleasing was the G21 update that it was given a new model name, G24. The brothers decided as part of this update to improve the rear axle location, which had been sometimes criticized on the G21, where there was a certain amount of noise transmission to the cabin. At the time, one of their employees was driving a Vauxhall estate car and the eagle-eyed brothers noticed the Vauxhall lower trailing arms also formed the spring mounting partway along their length.

After much measuring, the G21 chassis jig was modified and the new G24 incorporated these lower suspension arms with the spring acting on the arm rather than directly on the axle. With the completed G24 out on the road, the result of these alterations to the axle mounting was very pleasing – axle noise transmission was eliminated and the ride and suspension compliance were much improved.

The two new models were announced to the public during March 1980 through a low-key article in *Motoring News*. Perhaps the half-hearted launch was symptomatic of the brothers' mood at the time or just the result of lack of confidence that these cars would sell any better than the G21 had done.

What is certain is that after a time, insufficient interest in the cars led to a decision not to proceed to production. This was a great shame as these were extremely well-engineered and thoroughly developed products. Before this decision was taken, however, there were a couple of interesting developments.

Firstly, work was started on a second G23 prototype, again fitted with a hardtop; but in order to reduce the cost of the finished product the brothers this time fitted a live Ford rear axle mounted in the same way as the successful G24 application using the Vauxhall trailing arms.

The use of this axle necessitated the widening of the body to accommodate it and this was accomplished with neat wheel-arch extensions. To balance the look, the front wishbones were lengthened to give an equal front and rear track and similar arch extensions were added.

The Vauxhall-derived rear suspension arms of the solid-axle G23 and G24 can be clearly seen here. DON ARMSTRONG

The G24 was a stylish update of the G21 with an improved chassis. GINETTA OWNERS' CLUB

From the rear, the G24 again displays updated styling over that of the G21. GINETTA OWNERS' CLUB

The second G23 prototype, as abandoned at the factory in the early 1980s. DON ARMSTRONG

To bring the car right up to date, the now obsolete Ford 3-litre V6 engine was replaced by the latest Cologne Ford 2.8-litre V6 engine. This car reached an advanced state of completion before being abandoned at the rear of the factory. It was here, three years later, that Ginetta owners Don and Sue Armstrong spotted it and managing to persuade Bob Walklett to sell them the project; they had the car on the road the following year.

The second development was even more offbeat and involved a G21 owner in Northern Ireland, who, in 1980, wished to purchase a new G21 without certain body panels, as he planned to design and make his own bespoke panels

The G23 with hard top fitted can be contrasted with the photograph of the car in open form. Note also the extended wheels arches to accommodate the wider solid axle on this second prototype. DON ARMSTRONG

With the hardtop removed, the G23 is transformed into a summer cruiser. DON ARMSTRONG

instead. A car was duly built up and dispatched as requested. However, this car was built on a G24 chassis and with body changes only found on the G24, even though it was sold as a G21 and carried a G21 chassis number. Well after the launch of the G24, as late as 1981, one further G21 body/chassis unit was also sold to the original G21 specification.

The fate of the prototype G24 was sealed in 1981 when it was sold into private hands. This car still survives, while the original 3-litre G23 IRS was sold the following year. Both G23s still survive. The G23/G24 episode only proved just how difficult it was for the brothers to find a new way forward to regrow their business.

The G23 interior, almost pure G21 but upgraded still further in the interests of added comfort. DON ARMSTRONG

CHAPTER SEVEN

SURVIVAL AND FIGHT BACK

Towards the end of the seventies, there was a growing interest in the G4 model, examples of which were racing and still very successful. Added to this the style and shape of the G4 had lost nothing despite being nearly twenty years old; it was still much admired and was clearly a timeless design. Several customers were pushing Bob to sell them a new G4, but knowing how basic the model was compared with the standards now considered acceptable he was reluctant to agree. The advent of the Owners' Club and the fondness many members felt for the G4 only added to the pressure.

As it became clear that putting the G23 and G24 into production was too much of a risk for the business, the brothers' thoughts turned to what else they might try to get back into serious production. It was becoming ever more urgent, as the supply of suitable used G15 and G21 cars for refurbishment was beginning to dry up and Bob knew this source of income would not last for ever. One idea was to cheapen the whole G21 concept and sell the model at a much lower and hence more attractive price; in practice this was easier said than done, and there was little enthusiasm for it. They also considered a very basic sports car with no doors and simple features, much along the lines of a Lotus 7, but again it never really got beyond the sketch stages.

Finally, after much consideration, they decided to take another look at the G4 model. Ivor felt that a major update would be required to make the car suitable, but came up with a plan for an updated version that took its styling cues from the old model but was in fact a completely new car. It was essentially a modern take on the old design in much the same way that in the twenty-first century major manufacturers bring out new cars with the look of past models, obvious examples being the BMW Mini and Fiat 500. Of the four brothers, it was Trevers who felt this wasn't the right way to go, still preferring the option to cheapen the G21, but he did throw his weight behind the new project and they quickly made progress.

The very first G4 Series 4 at its launch early in 1981. Note the lay-down headlamps – an idea carried over from the G4 Series 3. GINETTA OWNERS' CLUB

THE GINETTA G4 SERIES 4 AND SERIES 5

The chassis was completely new and had no similarity with the original G4 space-frame design. It had much more in common with the G21, being square tube, but instead of a sheet steel backbone, the new car featured sheet steel stiffening through the sill sections on either side. The front suspension was the time-honoured Triumph-derived twin wishbone and vertical link set-up, with anti-roll bar and coil spring damper units, steering by rack and pinion and disc brakes. At the rear, a Ford axle was fitted on twin radius arms each side, a Panhard rod and coil spring damper units; drum brakes came as part of the axle package. In order to evoke some of the passion created by the G4, the new car was not given a new G number but instead named the G4 Series 4. This was the first time such a radical design change had not been allocated a new number and showed just how much weight the company were giving to the G4 heritage.

The new bodywork was wider and longer than the old model and was based on the last of the old G4 line, the Series 3 with its lay-down headlamps. This may have been a mistake, as it was the look of the Series 1 and 2 G4 model that most regarded as the ultimate 'looker'. The new bodywork was far better than the original's, featuring returns on panel edges and wheel arches, external door handles and a glass-fibre windscreen surround braced back in a T-bar style to the roll-over hoop, much as they had designed way back for the G16. For the power unit they made room in the engine bay to accept a variety of engines from the Ford range, including the 1300cc and 1600cc crossflow units as well as the 1600cc and 2000cc Pinto ohc engines, all with their respective gearboxes.

The first prototype was complete and ready to test by February 1981 and was initially well enough received to encourage the brothers to prepare it for production. From the outset the design had made allowance for the car to be sold as a kit, both complete with all new parts or as a body/chassis unit for the purchaser to add their own second-hand engine and axles. The reasons for this were twofold: firstly, to make the car inexpensive enough to attract those unable to afford a brand-new car; and secondly, to avoid the costs of type approval that would have come with offering turn-key cars, something they simply didn't have the money for. In creating this new G4 it was inevitable that the design would not be able to be engineered into a few simple mouldings in the way the G15 and G21 had been constructed so cost-effectively. The G4 Series 4 was made from far fewer panels than its sixties predecessor but still comprised a lot of separate panels that needed to be brought together, and as such was more costly to build.

Anxious to ensure that kits were put together to a high standard, Ginetta encouraged purchasers to buy as a minimum the completed and painted body/chassis unit, fully trimmed and wired, with all new ancillaries such as a

THE KIT CAR REVIVAL

The origins of the kit car can be found in the fifties special building era described in Chapter 2, but following the demise of the Ford and Austin special the idea of building a car did not die for many enthusiasts.

There gradually evolved new products for recycling old, rusted-out cars that still had sound mechanical parts. At the forefront of this was the humble Mini, and products such as the Mini Marcos and Mini Jem catered for people who wanted to convert their old Mini into a sports car. Later Davrian made a similar product, initially for Imp components.

This small industry gradually gained momentum but a new company, Dutton, gave it a huge boost in the seventies, initially with a Lotus 7-style sports car for recycling Triumph and Ford models, and later with an estate utility-type car for Ford Escort components. Dutton became the largest kit car makers in the world at one point, making over 1,000 kits a year.

Magazines such as *Alternative Cars* and *Kit Car* gave the whole industry a shop window and legitimacy, which attracted people to the scene and in turn gave birth to kit car shows and other events.

Although kit cars were subject to VAT like any other product, when using second-hand components, cars were not liable for special car tax or other costs, thereby making them affordable albeit with plenty of work required to get them up and running – but then for many this was part of the fun!

For production, the bonnet was modified with small raised headlamps and a large bonnet bulge. AUTHOR

Comparison between the original G4 (right) and the new Series 4 was like comparing an early Mini and the current model: apart from the name, they were different vehicles in every way. DICK ELLINGHAM

From the rear the Series 4 was a pretty car, exemplifying open-top sports motoring at its best. GINETTA OWNERS' CLUB

windscreen and wiper motor, instrumentation, light units, door locks and latches ready fitted. The price of the car in this form was just £2,064 including VAT, and all the customer needed to finish it was an engine and gearbox, front suspension and brakes, wheels and a rear axle. It did represent something of a bargain, and even the complete kit, with all new parts, was only £5,175, including VAT and special car tax.

The lay-down headlamps, unlike the ones on the Series 3 G4, which required manual raising, were lifted electrically by a Triumph TR7-derived motor. This was an expensive item and, in an effort to reduce costs, the prototype was soon modified to delete these headlamps, which were replaced by small-diameter units mounted in a bug-eye style on the bonnet top.

Towards the end of production, this style of bonnet with pop-up headlamps was produced, without doubt the best-looking bonnet of the variants. This car was built and is still owned by Duncan Campbell, a former Ginetta employee.
AUTHOR

Indistinguishable from the Series 4, this car is in fact a Series 5 and features independent rear suspension.
GINETTA OWNERS' CLUB

GINETTA G4 SERIES 4 (1981–7)

Layout and chassis	Two-seater sports car with platform chassis
Engine (customer choice – typical example)	
Type	Ford
Block material	Cast iron
Head material	Cast iron
Cylinders	4
Cooling	Water
Bore and stroke	90.6 × 76.9mm
Capacity	1993cc
Valves	Single overhead cam, 2 valves per cylinder
Compression ratio	9.2:1
Carburettor	Weber twin choke
Max. power (DIN)	98bhp
Max. torque	111lb ft at 3,500rpm
Fuel capacity	8.9gal (39ltr)
Transmission	
Gearbox	Ford 4-speed and reverse
Clutch	Diaphragm SLP
Internal Gearbox Ratios	
First	3.65:1
Second	1.97:1
Third	1.37:1
Fourth	1:1
Reverse	3.66:1
Final drive	3.09:1
Suspension and Steering	
Front	Twin wishbone, coil spring damper units, anti-roll bar
Rear	Rigid axle with trailing arms and Panhard rod, coil spring damper units
Steering	Rack and pinion
Tyres	185/70 × 13in
Wheels	Cast alloy
Rim width	6J × 13in
Brakes	
Type	Disc front and drum rear
Brake size	9.6in (240mm) front, 9in (225mm) rear
Dimensions	
Track, front	50.5in (1,283mm)
Track, rear	51in (1,295mm)
Wheelbase	90in (2,286mm)
Overall length	142.5in (3,623mm)
Overall width	56in (1,420mm)
Overall height	37in (937mm) to top of windscreen
Unladen weight	1,512lb (686kg)
Performance	
Top speed	112mph (180km/h)
0–60mph	7.5sec

It was a styling compromise that never quite worked, and in fact four orders were received from customers who specified that the lay-down headlamp bonnet should be fitted. The new bonnet also featured a large, slightly offset bulge which allowed the engines to be fitted with the standard air cleaner. Getting everything ready for production took a long time, and the first car finally left the factory in March 1982.

The car had received some good publicity. In August 1981 *Motor* magazine published a feature test of the prototype, now road registered WHJ232W, in which ex-Formula 1 driver turned road tester and journalist John Miles gave it a good review. Miles, who had raced his Diva wheel to wheel against Chris Meek's G4 in the sixties, recognized the G4 offered good value for money, but equally noted that in order to achieve that, there were compromises such as high noise levels and poor ride comfort.

Initially quite a few orders were received, mainly for the fully specified body/chassis units less engine, gearbox and suspension, but by the end of 1982 sales had run out of steam although cars continued to be sold on an ad hoc basis, the last being built in 1989. The last car made was actually dubbed the G4 Series 5 and featured Ford Sierra independent rear suspension complete with differential in place of the live axle; this car remained a one-off and, apart from the axle, was indistinguishable from the G4 Series 4.

The headlamp arrangement had come in for a further revision in 1983 when the brothers again redesigned the bonnet, this time to incorporate manually raised pop-up headlamps sculpted into the curves of the front, a style that finally looked right and gained universal approval.

In total, thirty-three cars were built, but the Series 4 never looked like putting Ginetta back into full-scale manufacturing. It is likely that deep down the brothers knew this would be the case, and even while the finishing touches were being made to the first G4 Series 4 prototype, their minds were in another place planning something completely different as the next Ginetta model.

THE GINETTA G25

The mid-engined sports car had long been heralded as the best handling and balanced driving machine. These cars had

Building a small sports car out of Ford Fiesta parts proved a real challenge. The first incarnation of the G25 shown here featured headlamps mounted in fixed 'pods' above the bonnet line. GINETTA CARS

Improving the shape led to pop-up headlamps in this version of the G25 during its development phase. GINETTA OWNERS' CLUB

In its final form the G25 front was further revised with a small chin spoiler. AUTHOR

Access to the mid-engine involved lifting the whole rear window and surround on the G25. With so many major Fiesta parts, such as the doors, glass and tail lights, it looked too much like a Ford for most tastes. AUTHOR

proved themselves time and time again on the race track but there had been few successful road cars with that layout, at least in part due to the difficulty of providing adequate storage for luggage, a spare wheel and all the things a practical road car needed. Rearward visibility for the driver was another difficult area to get right in the mid-engine package. Lotus had some success with their Europa in the sixties, and various other specialist cars, such as the Unipower GT and Cox GTM, had proved it could be done in small numbers, but generally the mainstream manufacturers had shied away from the layout, except for Fiat with their popular X1/9. It was the X1/9 that attracted the brothers' attention: it had been around for a long time and surely by now there must be a market for a modern take on this little car.

Any new car would need to be type approved if it was to be sold as a complete drive-away model and so it was decided they must design for it to be sold as a kit, into which previously used components from a donor car could be installed by the owner in exactly the same way that the G4 Series 4 would be marketed. Wanting their new car to be Ford-powered, they decided to base the design around the Ford Fiesta, a popular model that had been on the market since 1977 and featured a transverse-mounted engine and gearbox – an ideal layout to mount across the car behind the driver and passenger but in front of the rear axle. They had in mind to use as many parts off the Fiesta as possible, and this would include, in addition to the engine and gearbox, the front and rear screens, dashboard, lights, steering gear, suspension struts and hubs and – harking back to an old idea of theirs – the doors and all associated components. It was a bold plan, and to incorporate all these diverse parts from a family car into a small two-seater sports car was placing tremendous constraints on the design. Compromises were inevitable.

The process of making the prototype of what they now affectionately referred to as the 'Omelette', due to its mixture of recycled parts, was very slow, and while they had the basics of it complete by late 1982, they weren't totally happy and many design details were revisited and improved.

At one point the design had the headlamps in little pods mounted on the bonnet and a Fiesta radiator grille at the front; later this was changed for pop-up headlamps activated by a sturdy cable from the driver's seat – a simple, cost-effective solution – and the grille was dropped completely.

Known as the G25, this car was finally ready by May 1983. The chassis was a square-tube structure incorporating wishbone front suspension with Fiesta hubs and uprights with rack and pinion steering and anti-roll bar, while at the rear the entire Fiesta front suspension of MacPherson struts was fitted, the hubs fixed from 'steering' by short tie bars each side. Brakes were Fiesta-derived discs on all four wheels.

More than anything, the use of Fiesta doors had affected the design in a negative way despite Ginetta's best efforts. The doors were too tall for a low sports car like the G25, and as a result the cabin height was a little too high and out of proportion to the rest of the car. The brothers had done their best to lower the doors as much as possible but in doing so they were low to the ground and vulnerable to opening against kerbs.

By now things had changed dramatically at Ginetta, as we shall see, but despite this they decided to make the new car public, alerting the motoring press in June and then displaying the new car at Motor Fair, which was effectively the Motor Show that year, in October 1983. The response was muted. The design limitations of the doors were not lost on the public and the brothers were left thinking they should review the whole package.

Showing their hand was a mistake in other ways too, and Bob became acutely aware that the car was of great interest to other car designers, particularly from Japan. At the Motor Fair they were photographing the car from every angle and many of its specific details. A year later, Toyota announced their own MR2 model, which bore a stunning similarity to the G25. It seems inconceivable that the MR2 was developed in little more than a year, so almost certainly Toyota were working on their product in parallel to Ginetta, but the G25 may have influenced some of the MR2 design. Whatever the truth, Bob and his brothers remained convinced they had gone public with the G25 too early, when it was not fully developed and they were not even in a position to build it. Despite another public showing at the 1984 Stoneleigh Kit Car Show, the G25 remained a one-off, but it would live again later in another form.

GRS – GINETTA'S UTILITY BRAND

The Tora

As 1982 dawned and deliveries of the G4 Series 4 were about to begin, Bob found himself in regular conversation with kit car magazine editors. They often made the point about the popularity of estate car designs in the kit car world (as did several other confidants), and in particular the Dutton Sierra, which had come to the market in 1980 and been a huge success, selling in large numbers. They told Bob there was definitely a gap in the market for a quality-made competitor to the Sierra and encouraged the brothers to give it serious thought. When Bob raised this with his brothers it was no surprise to him that there was little enthusiasm: after all, they were sports car makers, and were in any case reluctant to become even further involved in the kit car industry. However, they could all see the business sense in it, as they certainly needed a product that would sell well.

Ivor went to his drawing board and prepared plans for an estate car along the lines of a smaller version of the Range Rover and very similar to the Matra Rancho, which today would probably be best described as a sports utility vehicle (SUV). The donor vehicle for this new car would be the Chrysler Arrow range, which was dominated by the Hillman Hunter but also covered a wide range of badge-engineered models, including the Hillman Minx, Singer Vogue and Humber Sceptre. This choice was probably driven by the fact that they had large stocks of these parts still on the shelf, left over from G21 production, including a quantity of engines and gearboxes. The design would accept mechanical parts from any of these cars post-1966, and comprised a simple square-section steel platform chassis that rose up at the front to surround the engine and provide mountings for the MacPherson strut front suspension. The chassis was motorized with the donor car engine, gearbox, front suspension, rear axle and leaf springs.

Also straight from the donor car were the fuel tank, radiator and heater. For the body, Trevers and Ivor worked closely together to produce an angular, slab-sided cabin with a lifting tailgate and incorporating the standard steel doors and windscreen from the donor vehicle. The cabin was moulded in one complete piece, including the bulkhead with a separate tailgate moulding, while at the front separate mouldings bolted together to form the two wings, front panel and bonnet. The design perfectly met the criteria of manufacturing the body from a limited number of mouldings, making it quick and profitable to produce. The prototype body/chassis unit was constructed very quickly and proved once again just how skilled Trevers and Ivor had become in this field.

One of the most important factors in the design was to ensure that the parts transferred from the donor car could be bolted straight onto the new car without modification, thereby making the construction simple and trouble-free. They had heard that builders of some other kits on the market had experienced trouble during the build, with parts

The GRS chassis frame was sturdy and can be seen here with suspension and steering already attached. NICK LUARD

With the main body mounted to the frame, the fitment of bonnet, wings and front panel is a simple exercise. NICK LUARD

requiring modification, bolt holes not lining up and problems with panel alignment; the brothers' product would be a straightforward build, eliminating all such difficulties. For the interior of the car, unmodified donor car parts were again used, including the dashboard, wiring loom, steering column, front and rear seats and other minor fittings.

Back in 1968, Ginetta had purchased a Hillman Hunter through Chrysler as a company car. Bob drove it mostly and it was road registered at the same time as the prototype G15 and as a consequence had the consecutive registration number BHK48G. Eventually this car rusted through and was left at the rear of the factory, along with many other

This was the first GRS made and soon became the factory demonstration car. It was built up from a Hillman Hunter that Bob Walklett drove years earlier, and its registration number is consecutive with the prototype G15. AUTHOR

A GRS badge was designed exclusively for the brand although many owners fitted Ginetta badges instead.

GINETTA OWNERS' CLUB

GRS TORA (1982–7)

Layout and chassis	Five-seater estate utility vehicle with steel platform chassis
Engine (customer choice – typical example)	
Type	Chrysler Hillman Hunter
Block material	Cast iron
Head material	Aluminium
Cylinders	4
Cooling	Water
Bore and stroke	81.5 × 82.5mm
Capacity	1725cc
Valves	2 valves per cylinder, pushrod operated
Compression ratio	9.2:1
Carburettor	Single Stromberg
Max. power (DIN)	79bhp
Max. torque	103lb ft at 3,000rpm
Fuel capacity	10gal (45ltr)
Transmission	
Gearbox	Chrysler 4-speed and reverse (overdrive optional)
Clutch	Diaphragm SDP
Internal Gearbox Ratios	
First	3.353:1
Second	2.140:1
Third	1.392:1
Fourth	1:1
Reverse	3.569:1
Final drive	3.7:1
Suspension and Steering	
Front	MacPherson strut with integral damper, tie rods, anti-roll bar
Rear	Rigid axle, half-elliptical leaf springs, telescopic dampers
Steering	Burman recirculating ball steering box
Tyres	185/70 × 14in
Wheels	Steel
Rim width	7J × 14in
Brakes	
Type	Disc front and drum rear
Brake size	9.5in (237mm) front, 9in (225mm) rear
Dimensions	
Track, front	53in (1,345mm)
Track, rear	53in (1,345mm)
Wheelbase	99in (2,511mm)
Overall length	160in (4,063mm)
Overall width	64in (1,624mm)
Overall height	67in (1,700mm)
Unladen weight	2,183lb (990kg)
Performance	
Top speed	90mph (145km/h)
0–60mph	12.9sec

The interior was neat and well trimmed. This dashboard is one of several types found in the Hillman Hunter range and its variants, any of which could fit. AUTHOR

The high sill with the tailgate open was criticized by some, but was necessary to enable the use of the standard Hunter fuel tank. GINETTA OWNERS' CLUB

discarded items. This Hunter was now dragged into the workshop and dismantled. All usable parts were transferred into the prototype, and the finished car assumed the identity of its donor car.

Just as in the days of the Fairlite, the brothers didn't want to call this car a Ginetta as it was so far removed from what they thought of as a true Ginetta, and so they came up with the name GRS, with a model name of Tora. The origin of the name GRS is not actually known but the Walketts had circular badges produced with the letters GRS written over a Union Jack background to emphasize the British manufacture of the product. Despite all this, many purchasers would stick a Ginetta badge on the vehicle in place of the GRS one, wishing to be associated with what had now become the iconic sports car brand.

It had been some years since Ginetta had exhibited at the Motor Show but with the completed GRS ready for launch, it was agreed to display the product on the *Alternative Cars* magazine stand at the 1982 event, now held at the Birmingham National Exhibition Centre, and so reach the widest audience possible.

The press release prior to the show caught the attention of the *Daily Express* motoring correspondent David Benson, who gave the new GRS a good review in his column and included a photograph; a few days later, a similar write-up appeared in the *News of the World* by Barry Powell, their motoring scribe. Such announcements gave the new model a massive boost, reaching out to a huge newspaper-reading public, and this, combined with the show appearance, caused the floodgates to open: there was instant serious interest in the GRS. Dorothy Walklett, 'manning the fort' back in the office at Witham while Bob was on stand duty at the show, was inundated with enquiries and requests for information. There could be no doubt that at last they had another hit on their hands.

A simple order form was produced that doubled as a brochure, detailing the price of the unpainted body chassis unit, which included gas struts for the tailgate as well as glazed side and rear windows, at £1,249 plus VAT. There were a handful of extras available: headlamps and front side lamp/indicator units for £36.25, tow bracket £12.50 and external spare wheel carrier £11.25, all subject to VAT. Customers were encouraged to tick the extras required and return the form to the factory with a £250 deposit cheque, thereby placing a firm order to await delivery.

This is the only known photograph of production at a satellite factory set-up at Maldon, Essex. GINETTA OWNERS' CLUB

Factory Expansion

The race was now on to get a production line going and to start filling the orders that were rapidly mounting up. While the Walkletts started building the first cars at Witham, it was very obvious that, with the volume being ordered, additional manufacturing space would be needed. In the nearby town of Maldon, 5 miles (8km) to the southeast of Witham, an old ironworks dating from 1872 had been vacated by then owners, Boulton & Paul Ltd, and purchased by a local company and split up into units. These were on offer at relatively low rent with short leases to get the venture under way. Ginetta wasted no time in taking a lease and, once suitable power had been laid on, quickly started building GRS body/chassis units at this site.

Completed units were transported to Witham, where they were checked over, final adjustments made and they were readied for dispatch to the customer. By the end of the first year of production, 200 cars had been built, an astonishing turnaround in the company's fortune. There was now also a new Walklett family member involved with the business: Trevers' son Mark had now left school and was learning the skills of his father. Both Mark's elder sisters, Gayle and Dawn, had also worked in this close-knit family business for a time in the seventies. In the office there was a change too. The brothers' sister Dorothy, who had assisted Bob for so long, had married and moved away, and her place was taken by Bob's wife, Anne. Running the production on two sites 5 miles apart was far from ideal. Ivor visited the Maldon site almost daily and Mark spent time there as well as transporting raw materials and completed body/chassis units backwards and forwards between the two sites.

Once space had been freed up at Witham, thoughts turned to offering the GRS in a more complete form, and a range of interior trim panels, carpet kits, roof bars and a front 'cow' catcher were added to the extras available. In addition Ginetta also started offering the model as a 'super kit', initially at an additional £400, though by 1985 the price had risen to £1,999 plus VAT. This took a lot of the hard work out of the kit build, as this version was painted and trimmed before leaving the factory.

The GRS really worked as a design and concept; the only let-down were the length of the driver and passenger doors, which are relatively short, being derived from a four-door saloon. This made access to the rear seats a little tight, but many enterprising builders fitted front seats from other makes of car that folded in a way that gave better clearance and as a result eased this minor difficulty.

Near Witham was the Crittall window company, world renowned for the manufacture of durable galvanized window frames; as an offshoot they had established a galvanizing plant in the town. This was one of, if not the best, hot dip galvanizing plants in the country, and Ginetta decided to make use of it and offer the GRS with a galvanized chassis, thereby making it almost indestructible by the elements. A

Amateur constructors could still create a stunning looking car, as this example shows. GINETTA OWNERS' CLUB

A rare shot of a GRS supplied jigged up for the fitment of a Ford ohc engine in place of the standard Hillman unit. DEAN PETLEY

galvanized chassis was priced at £98 plus VAT, which seemed quite expensive until the purchaser realized the process involved far more than simply dipping it into a tank. Each chassis tube was twice drilled in specific positions to allow the galvanizing liquid to flow through the tube and for the air to be expelled, thus ensuring the chassis was protected on both the inside and outside of the tubing. This extra was popular with customers and cars protected in that way have chassis as good today as when they were made.

Although the GRS could run happily on standard 13in wheels from the donor vehicle, in practice the appearance was much improved by fitting wider wheels and tyres. The factory offered a choice, but a 14in-diameter Weller-made wheel proved a popular fitting and gave the car a stance and purpose that suited its go-anywhere appearance.

Another option offered was a pickup version of the GRS. This example was used by a professional fisherman working off the Essex coast. AUTHOR

The GRS Pick Up

Orders for the car continued to flow in, and it wasn't long before thoughts turned to improvements and variations on the theme, and top of the list was a pickup version. From the start there had been a strong emphasis on the GRS being a work horse, with adverts suggesting that it was ideally suited to people who wished to tow a caravan, trailer or even a horse box, so a pickup version seemed a natural progression. To achieve this, the brothers cut a standard body through behind the doors and fitted a flat rear panel, thereby making a two-seater cab; the rear bed was then made from a simple moulded tray with a drop-down flap at the rear. The prototype GRS Pick Up was displayed at the 1983 Motor Fair event alongside the new G25, with two new prototypes parked side by side. It was an indication of just how far Ginetta had come in the past year since the launch of the first GRS. Priced at £1,149 plus VAT, it was £100 less than the estate, but as it turned out the Pick Up wasn't a sales success and only three were ever completed.

One was sold to a local fisherman operating on the Essex coast. He had found that throwing all his fishing paraphernalia and catch onto the back of vans and pickups destroyed them in no time – as he said, if the crabs and lobsters didn't cut their way through them, the salt water certainly soon rusted them through. The GRS Pick Up with galvanized chassis was the ideal solution. As well as the factory produced Pick Ups, at least one homemade version was later built from a standard GRS estate car by an enterprising owner.

At least one standard GRS estate car was converted to a Pick Up by its enterprising owner. GINETTA OWNERS' CLUB

The GRS Mark 2

Some time after the Pick Up was developed an order was received from a customer who was known to the Walkletts as he was already a G15 owner and active in the Owners' Club. His order was for a GRS Tora with a difference: he wanted his car to have a full-length lift-up tailgate. For some this was another flaw in the GRS design – that it had a substantial ledge beneath the tailgate over which objects had to be lifted to get them into the rear estate section of the car.

This was identified by the brothers at the time of the original design, but it was necessary as the fuel-tank filler pipe exited through this panel and was a fixed part of the tank; eliminating this sill would have meant the standard Chrysler fuel tank could not have been used from the donor vehicle. A full-length tailgate was something they had considered for some time and so the order was accepted and the body modified accordingly. It proved a success, so they offered this version as the GRS Mark 2 at an additional price of £150 plus VAT; around a third of the cars built after its introduction were the Mark 2 version.

The GRS had almost been the saviour of the Ginetta business. Without it they would doubtless have soldiered on, but with it they were suddenly back on the crest of a wave, and their now vast experience in the business enabled them to make the most of this turnaround. By 1985, production had slowed significantly on the GRS, partly due to a drop in the supply of suitable donors, but also due to another new product taking over. Nonetheless, the last GRS was built as late as 1988, by which time some 317 of all types had been built.

The Mark 2 GRS featured a one-piece deeper tailgate, much more practical for loading. AUTHOR

With the tailgate open, the flat loading area of the Mark 2 GRS can be clearly seen; a side-mounted fuel filler was required, however. DEAN PETLEY

CHAPTER EIGHT

FRESH THINKING

The early reveal of the G25 was something the brothers lived to regret, but it did have one positive outcome. When the G25 was displayed at the 1983 Motor Fair, Bob lost count of the number of people who expressed the view that the GRS concept was appealing, but they preferred something a little more sporty. Gesturing to the G25, several commented that something like that, but with the space for a family, that could be built from a donor car, like the GRS, would be perfect.

This feedback was food for thought indeed; the brothers knew only too well from their regular contacts in the Owners' Club that there were many who had grown up with G15 and G21 models and who now had families to transport, but still wanted to drive a Ginetta. Some had built GRS kits but others preferred the traditional Ginetta line and the realization dawned there was a large gap in the kit car market ready for them to exploit. Up to this point in time the kits available were in general either two-seater sports cars, estate utility-type vehicles or buggies of various kinds. If Ginetta could build a five-seater, two-door sports saloon with a sporting character to the same high quality as the GRS, they would have a ready market.

A FAMILY SPORTS CAR

Immediately on their return from the Motor Show, work began on the new model. Ivor sketched the basic shape and the chassis drawings were prepared. For the donor car they chose the Ford Cortina in its Mark 3 form. This was an easy decision. The kit car market was only just beginning to wake up to the Cortina as a potential donor vehicle but it ticked every box – rugged, relatively simple in construction but comfortable and with a wide variety of engines to choose

THE FORD CORTINA

First introduced in 1962, Ford's Cortina range was an instant success. Aimed at the family motorist, it was relatively inexpensive to buy and run, but was modern and practical with a choice of either 1200 or 1500cc engines.

Ford's clever marketing also emphasized the sporting character of the model, referencing the iconic Lotus Cortina that proved so successful in saloon car racing.

In 1970 it had a complete redesign for the Mark 3 version with its stylish 'coke bottle' shape and revised range of engines, starting with the 1300 and 1600cc crossflow units. By far the most popular options, however, were either the 1600 or 2000cc ohc engines, which gave these cars a very good turn of speed for the period. As well as the engine options the range was offered with various trim packages to suit all pockets from a basic L version right up to the range-topping Ghia, which featured luxury seats, carpets and a wood veneer-look dashboard.

The Cortina had rivals – perhaps most notably the Vauxhall Victor FD, which beat it to the market by several years; yet stylish though it was, the Vauxhall never captured the public's imagination like the Cortina. Other makers tried to emulate the recipe of the Cortina, for example British Leyland with their Marina, which sold quite well but was inferior to the Ford and never looked like toppling the Cortina from its perch as the best-selling family car.

The Cortina was facelifted for the Mark 4 version and again for a Mark 5 before being discontinued and replaced by the Sierra in 1982.

from offering good performance with a slick gearbox. Furthermore it was a Ford, just what many kit builders were looking for. The supply of suitable donor cars was enormous. As Doug Walklett remarked to the author at the time of the model development, you could stand in the window at the factory when the morning commute was under way and virtually every other car passing was a Cortina – they were that popular.

THE GINETTA G26

The new model, named G26, had a strong family resemblance to the G25; the front of the car was pure G25 in fact, albeit widened and lengthened to give the shape balance and to clothe the front engine, while the side panels incorporated, once again, the Fiesta doors and also took the lines of the G25. At the rear, the bodywork was styled as a fastback with a flat tail panel. There is no doubt that having already produced the G25 aided the speedy development of the G26, but, as Trevers found when he cut and widened a G25 front panel for the new car, it wasn't always straightforward. The cable-operated pop-up headlamp pods made for the G25 should have been used as they were for the G26, thereby saving time and work. In practice the increased width and curvature of the G26 front meant the top surface of the lamp pods were not quite the correct shape, which necessitated adding a camber to the pod tops on each side and then producing a new mould for each.

Development of new models was certainly time-consuming, but the G26 wasn't just a new shape – it incorporated a whole collection of items from others cars into this one design. For example, as well as the Fiesta doors, Fiesta rear side window glass was used and a heated rear screen from the same source. The front screen, however, was from a Ford Cortina, which also provided the fuel filler flap, the dashboard and front and rear seats; in fact the whole floor pan of the G26 was moulded straight from the underside of a Cortina to make the fitting of donor car components easier. To include so many diverse features into one bodyshell with all the constraints that created and still manage to produce a cohesive and pleasing look was a masterclass in design.

The body included a lightweight steel frame bonded into the roof and screen pillars that offered some roll-over protection, as well as providing an anchorage for the front seat belts; the doors' latch plates were also bolted to it, offering a degree of side impact protection. In line with their desire to keep fabrication costs to a minimum, the brothers had the

The sturdy G26 chassis is clearly visible in this exploded diagram. The front sub-frame and suspension and rear axle and suspension are all Cortina items.
GINETTA CARS

main body, up to and including the front bulkhead, moulded in one piece in a split mould, leaving only the one-piece wings and front panel, headlamp pods, bonnet, bootlid and lower rear valance to complete the entire bodywork.

The chassis was a simple platform of rectangular-section steel, swept up at the front and rear and designed to accept every piece of the Cortina running gear unmodified. Care was taken to ensure that the builder of a kit would be able to bolt in every part; even special, time-consuming-to-fabricate brackets were provided on the chassis to take the handbrake cable rather than leave the builder to their own devices. A feature of the Cortina was a front sub-frame onto which was bolted the twin-wishbone coil sprung suspension, steering rack, anti-roll bar and engine mounts. This whole unit was bolted straight to the G26 chassis albeit without the rubber insulation blocks, which were discarded in the interests of stiffening up the structure and improving road-holding. Due to the underside being exactly the same shape as the Cortina, the standard exhaust system, fuel tank and propshaft could be fitted unmodified to the new Ginetta.

Promising Sales

The brothers made no secret of the fact that they were developing this car and there was a lot of interest expressed by potential customers – so much interest in fact that the brothers took the unprecedented step of taking a body/chassis unit to a show before it was fully completed. This was the 1984 Newark Kit Car Show, where they presented the new G26 body and chassis unit fully painted and trimmed but without any running gear. The idea was to show those contemplating building a kit that something new was soon coming to the market. The response was overwhelming and, despite the fact that no prototype had been fully completed or even driven, the first orders were taken. The race was now on to finish the car off, test it and ready the factory for production.

Two months later, at the end of August, the prototype had been completed, tested on the road and was shown in this form at a show for kit cars at Olympia in London. Again the response was extremely encouraging. Priced at £2,785 plus VAT for a fully trimmed, painted and glazed super kit complete with new Fiesta doors it offered an attractive package. For those requiring a basic unpainted body and chassis without doors, this was available at £1,495 plus VAT but generally Bob encouraged customers where possible to purchase a super kit, as this ensured the completed car was finished to the highest standards, thereby producing satisfied owners and upholding Ginetta's reputation for quality. A range of extras was also on offer, including stylish wide-rim wheels either in steel or alloy, retrimming the Cortina seats in materials to match the interior trim, a glass sunroof and a galvanized chassis.

The G26 model was launched at Olympia in London in August 1984.
STEPHEN GREENSWORD

The interior of the G26. The dashboard was Cortina in origin. GINETTA OWNERS' CLUB

The G26 engine bay with, in this case, a powerful twin cam version of the Ford Pinto engine installed. GINETTA OWNERS' CLUB

The order books were filling fast and the factory at Maldon was readied to commence production with all the necessary jigs and moulds prepared. The first kits were delivered to customers by Christmas 1984. At this point GRS production was scaled back considerably to allow the new model to be made.

Although the model had been designed around a Mark 3 Cortina, most parts from the Mark 4 and 5 were interchangeable and a number of builders used these as their donor cars with few challenges. It wasn't lost on some builders that the Ford Sierra five-speed gearbox was a direct replacement for the four-speed Cortina box, with only the gearbox mounting bracket in a different position; indeed, two of the first orders received were from people planning to fit this gearbox and so a gearbox mounting adaptor plate was developed and offered as an inexpensive extra to facilitate this. For those that wanted these cars, but didn't have the confidence to build one themselves, there were a few businesses springing up around the country offering a build service. Some of these companies had also offered

The first customer-built G26 to return to the Witham works is inspected by Ivor (left) and Bob Walklett in February 1985. The author built this car in five weeks from a super kit. AUTHOR

GINETTA G26 AND G30 (1984–91)

Layout and chassis	Five-seater sports saloon with platform chassis	*Suspension and Steering*	
		Front	Twin wishbone, coil spring, telescopic dampers, anti-roll bar
Engine (customer choice – typical example)		Rear	Rigid axle with trailing arms, coil springs, telescopic dampers
Type	Ford		
Block material	Cast iron	Steering	Rack and pinion
Head material	Cast iron	Tyres	185/70 × 14in
Cylinders	4	Wheels	Steel (cast alloy optional)
Cooling	Water	Rim width	7J × 14in
Bore and stroke	90.6 × 76.9mm		
Capacity	1993cc	*Brakes*	
Valves	Single overhead cam, 2 valves per cylinder	Type	Disc front and drum rear
		Brake size	9.74in (247mm) front, 9in (225mm) rear
Compression ratio	9.2:1		
Carburettor	Weber twin choke	*Dimensions*	
Max. power (DIN)	98bhp	Track, front	57.5in (1,460mm)
Max. torque	111lb ft at 3,500rpm	Track, rear	57.5in (1,460mm)
Fuel capacity	11.9gal (54ltr)	Wheelbase	102in (2,590mm)
		Overall length	175in (4,445mm)
Transmission		Overall width	68in (1,727mm)
Gearbox	Ford 4-speed and reverse	Overall height	51in (1,295mm)
Clutch	Diaphragm SLP	Unladen weight	2,183lb (990kg)
Internal Gearbox Ratios		*Performance*	
First	3.65:1	Top speed	110 mph (177km/h)
Second	1.97:1	0–60mph	8.5sec
Third	1.37:1		
Fourth	1:1		
Reverse	3.66:1		
Final drive	3.44:1		

build services for the GRS kit. Pit Stop, based in Maidstone, Kent and DBS Autocraft in Spalding, Lincolnshire were two of the biggest in this field, each building a number of cars for customers.

A year into production, over 100 cars had been made, most sold as super kits, and the order books were full. The production facilities in Maldon continued through 1985, but at the end of the year Bob managed to persuade the owners of a disused fire station building, situated at the side of the Witham factory yard and sharing the same side access as the factory, to sell. With the fences moved, this building provided much needed extra production space as well as a little additional outside storage. At this point the brothers terminated their lease on the Maldon premises and once again had all their production based at the one site, which made logistics a great deal easier. The new building was used for laminating and trimming excess material from the finished shells, while fabricating chassis and other in-house-made metal components were carried out in a separate building. Final assembly, painting and trimming were carried out in the main factory building at the rear of the showroom and office area.

G26 kits generally were only sold in the home market, but this example was exported to Malta. GINETTA OWNERS' CLUB

Like the GRS before it, the G26 was a large car, or at least large by the standards of their predecessors, and this in itself put pressure on space; bodies were built and stockpiled outside in the yard beside the factory. The volume of orders justified increasing production but there were constraints in some elements of the manufacturing process that made increasing volumes difficult, particularly the lamination of bodies.

Ginetta's sales and marketing at this time involved displays at kit car shows. Here is their stand at the Stoneleigh show in 1987. AUTHOR

One solution considered was to subcontract some of the laminating, and locally there was expertise in the boat-building industry. At one point a company was called in to quote for laminating bodies and the enthusiastic estimator came down to Witham to measure up a G26 and work out the quantities of resin and glass-fibre matting required for the job. He returned a few weeks later with his quotation; Bob glanced at it and responded by passing a copy of the latest G26 price list over his desk. The reality was that Ginetta were selling the bodies to their customers for less than this quote for making them. The set-up at Witham was extremely efficient and margins were always kept tight to keep the retail price attractive.

The G26 was featured widely in kit car magazines and Ginetta placed regular advertisements in these publications. This, along with frequent appearances at kit car shows throughout the country, was the main way they publicized the car. Now and again, however, other opportunities arose and one such was an invitation to provide a G26 to appear on the television programme *Top Gear.* At that time *Top Gear* was a serious motoring magazine programme presented by experienced motoring journalists (the tyre-smoking 'lads' mag' style of programme had yet to emerge). Ginetta supplied their demonstration car of the time, Q417OVL, and it fell to Frank Page to test the G26 in a feature that included a variety of kit cars. He was extremely complimentary, making it clear the G26 had nothing kit about it and implying that it was on a par with production cars from the major manufacturers. Such publicity was worth its weight in gold for a small company like Ginetta.

With the moulds in need of replacement, the opportunity was taken in 1986 to alter the rear bumper slightly to create the joint to the lower valance over the bumper rather than through the centre. This central split on the earlier cars wasn't a particularly good detail and the revision was worthwhile, as was a change to the top edge of the bootlid at the same time. This was designed to provide a route for the cabin air flow to exit without the risk of drawing in exhaust fumes back inside the car. By now, the brothers had been able to speed up body manufacture by taking on self-employed laminators during the quiet season in boat building and stockpiling shells for use a little later on. This enabled Ginetta to increase production to levels approaching those of the halcyon days of the G15.

The brothers had been asked if the Ford V6 engine could be fitted to the G26. The short answer was that the V6 engine would not fit under the curvy bonnet, although in practice people had managed to fit both the Ford V6 and Rover V8 in the G26 engine bay, although it was a technical challenge. The fact that the Ford Cortina was available with a 2.3-litre version of the V6 meant that such an installation would be very straightforward had there been suitable clearance. With this in mind, Ivor had for some time been keen to make a shorter-chassis, two-plus-two version of the G26, and so the decision was taken to develop this version with a revised front capable of housing the V6 engine.

THE GINETTA G28

The design of the G26, with a separate bodywork section from the bulkhead forward, lent itself to a simple revision, and a new front with a higher bonnet line was made that could accommodate the V6 engine. The new front featured a prominent bumper, with a small radiator air intake above and below, flanked by rectangular headlamps and flashing indicator lamps, while a large, forward-hinging bonnet topped it off. The chassis was a standard G26 unit with approximately 8in (200mm) removed from the centre section, necessitating trimming a similar amount from the body between the doors and rear wheel arches. This was accomplished by fitting smaller rear side windows sourced from the Ford Sierra XR4i, and by reducing the rake on the rear screen

The difference in profile between the G26 and the G28 are clearly evident from the drawing. The front panels can be switched between body styles, creating the G30 and G31 respectively. GINETTA CARS

and bootlid, giving the shape more of a box look in contrast to the fastback G26.

Shortening the chassis and corresponding underside of the body presented few practical problems, although of course the exhaust and handbrake cable needed to be shortened too, while the propshaft had to be shortened and rebalanced, but was made available on an exchange basis from Ginetta. Inside the car, the rear leg room was reduced and the rear seat was purpose-made to fit the reduced space available. A small triangle-section spoiler was fitted as standard to the rear edge of the bootlid, and this item also became available as an optional extra on the G26.

This prototype G28 was fitted by Ginetta with a 2.8-litre Ford V6 engine. GINETTA OWNERS' CLUB

GINETTA G28 AND G31 (1986–93)

Layout and chassis	Four-seater sports coupé with platform chassis	*Suspension and Steering*	
		Front	Twin wishbone, coil spring, telescopic dampers, anti-roll bar
Engine (customer choice – typical example)		Rear	Rigid axle with trailing arms, coil springs, telescopic dampers
Type	Ford		
Block material	Cast iron	Steering	Rack and pinion
Head material	Cast iron	Tyres	185/70 × 14in
Cylinders	4	Wheels	Steel (cast alloy optional)
Cooling	Water	Rim width	7J × 14in
Bore and stroke	90.6 × 76.9mm		
Capacity	1993cc	*Brakes*	
Valves	Single overhead cam, 2 valves per cylinder	Type	Disc front and drum rear
		Brake size	9.74in (247mm) front, 9in (225mm) rear
Compression ratio	9.2:1		
Carburettor	Weber twin choke	*Dimensions*	
Max. power (DIN)	98bhp	Track, front	57.5in (1,460mm)
Max. torque	111lb ft at 3,500rpm	Track, rear	57.5in (1,460mm)
Fuel capacity	11.9gal (54ltr)	Wheelbase	94in (2,388mm)
		Overall length	156in (3,962mm)
Transmission		Overall width	68in (1,726mm)
Gearbox	Ford 4-speed and reverse	Overall height	51in (1,295mm)
Clutch	Diaphragm SLP	Unladen weight	2,103lb (954kg)
Internal Gearbox Ratios		*Performance*	
First	3.65:1	Top speed	110mph (177km/h)
Second	1.97:1	0–60mph	8.5sec
Third	1.37:1		
Fourth	1:1		
Reverse	3.66:1		
Final drive	3.44 :1		

The prototype car was fitted with a 2.8-litre Ford V6 engine and was ready for display at the 1986 Motor Show alongside a G26 and another new model (of which more later). It is an irony that when a model isn't available lots of people enquire about it, but sometimes when it is there, interest seems to dwindle. Such was the case with the G28: the many people who had asked if the V6 engine could be fitted into the G26 did not emerge when Ginetta actually built a car that could accommodate this engine. Indeed, of the few G28 cars sold, several were fitted with the 2-litre, 4-cylinder Ford engine, customers buying the cars for their looks and not the increased engine bay dimensions.

The Ginetta G30 and G31

All was not lost, however. The fact that the different front sections of the G26 and G28 were fitted to exactly the same bulkhead panel meant that cleverly they were interchangeable, so the original G26 body could be fitted with the G28 front. This combination was known as the G30, while the G26 pop-up headlamp front fitted to the short chassis G28 body became the G31. This was a simple concept but it gave customers a choice. Some selected their model to suit their needs while others based their purchase on the overall look of the model. Perhaps the pick of the bunch in the looks

The bold front of the G28 was intended to allow fitment of the Ford V6 engine; however, this example, like some others, was fitted with the 2-litre ohc engine. AUTHOR

department was the G31, its sloping pop-up headlamp front end blending perfectly with the booted rear section in side profile, producing a smart GT look. The G30 also had a purposeful look about it, matching, as it did, the strong frontal appearance of the G28 with the fastback five-seater body; in fact, the G30 sold better than the original G28 model for which its front was designed.

The G30 and G31 kits started to be delivered to customers early in 1987, and from this point on, as orders were received for all four models, they were fed into the production schedule alongside one another. Ginetta continued to make this variety of models until 1991, by which time the focus of the factory was elsewhere and kit car production was no longer the company's priority. One final car was built in 1993 to special order, but the truth is that after 1988 there was a significant scaling-down of production on these models to make way for other new and more exciting developments.

There was very little development work done on these cars after their launch but towards the end on the range's life, a few chassis were built with bracketry to mount a Sierra independent rear suspension complete with differential unit. This improved the handling and ride comfort, and a few cars were sold with this configuration to special order. The

This G30 is fitted with a 2.3-litre V6 engine. AUTHOR

From this three-quarter rear view, the G30 is difficult to distinguish from the G26. These cars also made excellent towing vehicles. GINETTA OWNERS' CLUB

The stylish G31 could add a touch of class to any driveway – there was nothing 'kit' about these cars. GINETTA OWNERS' CLUB

The G31 proved effective in competition. This is Mick Mooring in his Cosworth-powered car. AUTHOR

PRICING

The prices differed for the four models although many elements of the price build-up were the same. The following is a breakdown of the offering to customers in 1988 along with the extras available.

Super kits: including doors, all glass, front and rear lights, fully painted, fully trimmed (excluding seats) and carpeted

G26	£2,959
G28	£3,055
G30	£2,988
G31	£3,018

Extras:
Galvanized chassis £99.50
Sunroof £100
Tinted screens £85
Tow attachment £47
Rear boot spoiler £39.50
7 × 14in steel wheels (set) £139.75
7 × 14in alloy wheels (set) £195
Seating kit £325
Five-speed gearbox bracket £19
The models could be purchased as a basic body/chassis unit although this was discouraged. As an example, a G26 was charged at £1,545 but items such as doors, lights and all the other items found on a super kit could be purchased individually . All the above prices were subject to VAT.

A G31 from the rear. There was ample luggage space in the large boot. GINETTA OWNERS' CLUB

brothers also experimented with revised front bodywork, and in 1989 one car was built in this form for factory evaluation but it remained a one-off and in factory ownership.

Production numbers for this range of four models make an interesting study. A total of 370 cars of all types were built, and of these 284 were G26s, while the G31 accounted for sixty-six cars. The G30 was the bestseller of the square-fronted cars with fourteen sold, but the G28 found just six purchasers. Clearly the bestseller was the original G26; this is partly accounted for by the fact that 160 cars were sold before the introduction of the other models, but despite this, it remained the better-selling version even after the others were available. In fact, even after the introduction of the other three models, it outsold their total production added together. This only served to emphasize that the G26 really had exploited a niche in the kit car market for a sporting machine that could accommodate the whole family.

THE GINETTA G27

Alongside the development of the G26 Ivor and Trevers had given thought to making the G4 Series 4 a little more of a race car. Once the major work on the G26 was complete, they took a Series 4 chassis and modified it to mount a Jaguar differential unit driving through shortened driveshafts to modified Jaguar hub-carriers located with twin trailing arms and coil spring damper units. At the front they made small alterations to enable the fitting of larger engines, such as the Rover V8. The bodywork remained the same as the Series 4 except for the option of a deep spoiler beneath the front bumper, which was either detachable or could be moulded in one piece together with the bonnet.

This project set out to be effectively a racing version of the G4 Series 4 and was at least partly driven by the desire of Trevers' son, Mark Walklett, to try his hand at motor racing. At the time there were kit car races up and down the country and despite being twenty years old, the original G4s had been very successful; this dismayed the organizers, who had intended the series to be for the modern breed of kit car. There were murmurings that the G4 might cease to be eligible for the series and so the new car, which might in another time have been christened the G4 Series 4R, was called the G27.

Launched in March 1985, the brochure called it the G27 2-Seater Competition Sports Car and emphasized the fact that it was designed for racing, stating:

The G27 at launch, with Ivor (left) and Mark Walklett. Note the G26 bodies behind awaiting dispatch. GINETTA CARS

GINETTA G27 (1985–2001)

Layout and chassis	Two-seater sports car with platform chassis	*Suspension and Steering*	
		Front	Twin wishbone, coil spring damper units, anti-roll bar
Engine (customer choice – typical example)		Rear	Rigid trailing arms and coil spring damper units
Type	Ford	Steering	Rack and pinion
Block material	Cast iron	Tyres	185/60 × 14in
Head material	Cast iron	Wheels	Cast alloy
Cylinders	4	Rim width	7J × 14in
Cooling	Water		
Bore and stroke	90.6 × 76.9mm	*Brakes*	
Capacity	1993cc	Type	Disc front and drum rear
Valves	Single overhead cam, 2 valves per cylinder	Brake size	9.6in (240mm) front, 10.5in (263mm) rear
Compression ratio	9.2:1		
Carburettor	Weber twin choke	*Dimensions*	
Max. power (DIN)	98bhp	Track, front	50.75in (1,289mm)
Max. torque	111lb ft at 3,500rpm	Track, rear	51in (1,295mm)
Fuel capacity	8.9gal (39ltr)	Wheelbase	90in (2,286mm)
Transmission		Overall length	142.5in (3,623mm)
Gearbox	Ford 4-speed and reverse	Overall width	56in (1,420mm)
Clutch	Diaphragm SLP	Overall height	37in (937mm) to top of windscreen
		Unladen weight	1,567lb(711kg)
Internal Gearbox Ratios		*Performance*	
First	3.65:1	Top speed	115mph (185km/h)
Second	1.97:1	0–60mph	7.5sec
Third	1.37:1		
Fourth	1:1		
Reverse	3.66:1		
Final drive	3.31:1		

> *The G27 is not aimed at the road market but for sprints – circuit racing – hill climbs etc. Although a strikingly quick road car it has its limitations when compared to the electric windows – super heaters – sound insulation – of some road cars of the 80s. We are content to let the purchaser decide on suitability.*

But despite this clear warning that it was not ideally suited to the road, when sales began most orders were received from customers who did wish to use the cars on the road. For sure, there were no creature comforts but the car was very usable as an everyday vehicle, and purchasers could see that. The G4 Series 4 remained available but once the G27 was listed, most purchased the latter.

As previously stated, apart from the range of Ford engines for which it was designed, the Series 4 G4 had restricted chassis space. This didn't stop several people fitting alternative engines, as diverse as the Sunbeam Rapier, Lotus Twin Cam, Alfa Sud, Lotus 907 and even the 6-cylinder Triumph Vitesse.

The G27, on the other hand, could accept larger units such as the Rover V8 and the Mazda rotary engine. This

The highly successful G27 race car of Mark Walklett fitted with a powerful Mazda engine. GINETTA OWNERS' CLUB

latter engine was admired by Trevers for its power and smoothness, and he and his son Mark planned to fit one of these groundbreaking rotary engines into a G27 being built up for Mark to race. Mark had convinced his father he had what it takes to be a fast and competitive driver and the plan was to enter a Mazda-powered G27 in the kit car series for Mark to drive.

The G4 Series 4 and G27 were on sale more or less throughout the eighties, but for most of that time they were totally overshadowed by the kit models of the GRS and G26 series cars, so the question has been asked why Ginetta carried on producing these cars in such small numbers when their efforts could just as effectively have been put into the other models. One possible answer is that these cars were closer to what the brothers thought of as a true Ginetta than what they were actually making in volume: the building of small, lightweight sports cars and racing cars was where their hearts lay. It is known that the facelifting of the G4 Series 4 with the pop-up light bonnet that also featured on the G27 was a last-minute addition to the Motor Fair stand in 1983 because they wanted another Ginetta on the stand alongside the G25, which otherwise would have displayed more GRS models than Ginettas.

The G27 was another kit with a complicated pricing structure, but, simplified, a fully assembled and painted body chassis unit with Ford engine mountings was available at £2,145 plus VAT. A further £650 added all braking infrastructure, steering column, headlamp mechanism and rear radius arms. For those wanting a limited amount of construction, £4,315 purchased the complete car less engine, gearbox, suspension and wheels, while £5,545 bought a complete car less engine and gearbox, although the purchaser needed to supply the Jaguar differential, discs, calipers and hub-carriers for factory fitment. There were few extras but a hood and, for racing, an approved roll-over bar were available.

Mark Walklett pushes the G27 Mazda hard preparing to lap another car during a Kit Car Series race. GINETTA OWNERS' CLUB

John Pease with his beautifully race-prepared G27, featuring many of the items prepared for the works car. JOHN PEASE

Many G27 owners used their road cars for sprints and hill-climb events, while Scot John Pease used his beautifully prepared car for circuit racing in the north of England. It was, however, the works car, driven by Mark Walklett, that left its stamp on the race circuits. Once the Mazda engine was delivering full power and had been made to run reliably, Mark won many races against worthy competitors and proved Ginetta's products were still a serious force in motor racing. A steady trickle of orders continued throughout the eighties, but the G27 would receive a new injection of life during the nineties, which will be detailed in following chapters.

THE GINETTA G29

Towards the end of 1985, Ginetta needed to source the Mazda rotary engine for their works G27 so Bob was in touch with Mazda's UK headquarters to negotiate supply of a suitably tuned unit. His call resulted in a visit from David Palmer, head of Mazda's public relations team, who surprised Bob by asking if Ginetta would be interested in making a Mazda-engined car to compete in the 1986 Thundersports race series. The competitors in these events drove some very powerful cars, not least the 5.7-litre Lolas that dominated the series, and the races were long with a driver change partway through.

Consulting with his brothers produced an enthusiastic response but with reservations over the amount of time available to make a suitable car. Palmer had suggested that fitting the rotary engine into a G22 would make an ideal car, but Ivor knew instinctively that the G22 chassis would not take the 260bhp and enormous torque produced by the Mazda engine without some modifications. If they were to meet this challenge, a new car would need to be made, but the lure of big league motor racing was too much for Trevers and Ivor, in particular, to resist.

The G29 Thundersports car was small by the standard of the competition but packed a punch with its Mazda engine. GINETTA OWNERS' CLUB

Bob dealt with the financing side of the arrangement and made an agreement that the costs of running the car, entry fees and travel would be through sponsorship and a Mazda rotary engine with the equivalent displacement of 2.4 litres and a Hewland FT200 gearbox would be made available, but the car would be down to Ginetta to supply, along with a team of mechanics. The driver line-up would be Palmer himself and the co-driver would be the experienced John Markey. It wasn't long before Palmer secured sponsorship from the cosmetics brand Hawaiian Tropic.

Within days of a deal being agreed in principle, Ivor had started work on the drawings, taking the G22 as the basis for his design; he made the chassis frame a longer wheelbase that could incorporate twin fuel tanks behind the seats and in front of the engine; it was square tube and incorporated a stiffening backbone section in sheet steel. Safety was another important consideration for Ivor. Speeds were high and in the event of an accident the risks were greater, so with this in mind he created a strong steel capsule around the driver area. For the bodywork, he took the G22 mouldings and increased them in length to clothe the new chassis and engine. Kevlar was used in parts for lightness and strength, and the centre tub was bonded to the chassis. Weighing in at just over 1,120lb (508kg), the new car was to be the Ginetta G29.

There was enormous pressure to have the car built and ready for the first race of the season. Despite having the G22 as a basis for the design, many areas went back to first principles and everything, right down to suspension and brakes, even fuel cells, had to be redesigned and parts sourced and fitted. The suspension featured Ginetta-made cast aluminium uprights, while the hubs, also of their own design, were quick-release centre-lock wheel nuts for fast tyre changes during the compulsory pit stops. Front suspension was twin wishbone, while the rear featured lower wishbones with lateral links and radius arms at the top; allowing full adjustment, outboard spring dampers were fitted. Trevers, Mark and Ivor worked long hours evening after evening, often supported by Bob and Doug, to get the car ready for the first race and all important publicity photos, featuring the Hawaiian Tropic promotional girls draped over the bodywork in their swimwear.

So pressured was the programme that the G29 was publicly announced at the end of March 1986 just days before the first Thundersports race of the season at Oulton Park over the Easter weekend. There had not even been time for testing and so the car arrived at the event totally untried; despite this, it showed promise and was running again at Brands Hatch a few days later. The car needed testing, however, and when it was finally taken to Snetterton for

This Thundersports race was supporting the British Grand Prix at Brands Hatch in 1986. Here we see a driver change pit stop for the G29: Doug and Bob Walklett are standing to the left of the standing driver, while Mark Walklett is one of the pit team and stands to the left of the seated driver. JOHN ROSE

Brands Hatch, September 1986: the G29 was fourth overall, driven by David Palmer and Phil Dowsett. GINETTA CARS

this purpose it was immediately clear that changing tyres to Avons would be an enormous improvement and, along with a new rear wing, it ran in this form throughout the rest of the season.

Although larger than the G22, the G29 was still small compared to most of the opposition but it was quick, and as it developed it was not too far behind the front runners even in early season races. Well-known racing driver Mark Hales teamed up with John Markey at one event when David Palmer was unavailable and the car came home in sixth place, but its finest hour came at Brands Hatch, when, again, one of the regular drivers was unable to race. In this instance it was Phil Dowsett who paired up with David Palmer and together they chalked up a fourth place for the team – the best result of the season.

Dowsett, who had made his name in Formula Ford and Formula Atlantic and would later race successfully in touring cars, had tested the G22 some years before and so taking on the G29 for a race was an interesting comparison. He later commented that the car was good to drive but needed better brakes to get the best out of it.

As it was, the season was coming to a close by this point, so it was too late for any more development, but it was clear that with further adjustments the G29 could have mounted a challenge against the Lolas that dominated the series. After the final Thundersports race of the season the one-off G29 was quietly put away and was never raced again.

The G29 leads some of its larger competition at Donnington. JOHN ROSE

CHAPTER NINE

NEW CAR, NEW PREMISES, NEW MANAGEMENT

The year 1986 had proved to be a whirlwind for the brothers, almost like the 1960s again. As we have seen, the G29 race car had taken a lot of their time and they had developed the short-chassis G26 variant, the G28. In truth the G29 had delayed the G28 launch quite some months. As they approached the 1986 Motor Show, the small Witham factory was buzzing, not just with the day-to-day production but readying the cars for the show stand. There was a white G26, a white G28 and another new car, the G32, also in white.

THE GINETTA G32

Amazingly, alongside the G29 programme and the G28 the Walkletts had found the time to completely revise the G25 Fiesta-based, mid-engined two-seater, and it was now ready for launch as the G32. On the run-up to the show, the announcement was made and the press released details – even the local television news picked up on it, with Bob interviewed and the new car featured on the early evening news bulletin.

What they had done was take the G25 and completely re-engineer it to answer some of the previous criticisms. This meant the car could no longer be built using parts from a Ford Fiesta; the redesign introduced many new, specially made parts and it would only be available as a component car of all new parts for home completion. The reason the car would require home completion was purely down to the fact that to sell a fully built car would require full type approval, something that would require a great deal of time and financial investment.

The G32 was a blend of Ford Fiesta and Escort parts. The front suspension featured Escort lower arms and anti-roll bar coupled to Fiesta hub-carriers and Ginetta's own top wishbone and spring damper units; while at the rear, Escort lower arms were anchored by Ginetta trailing arms, track control links and supporting Fiesta MacPherson struts and hub-carriers. Dual-circuit disc brakes were fitted all round, while the engine and gearbox were Ford's 1600cc CVH in either standard, injection or turbo form.

For the bodywork, the basic G25 shape remained, but now with a lower roof line. This meant the Fiesta door window frames had to be cut down to lower them and, although the Fiesta windscreen was retained, the rear window was now a special item. The Motor Show leaflet advised prices would be £6,795 for the standard 1600, £7,295 for the injection version and £8,595 for the turbo.

The first G32 as displayed at the 1986 Motor Show. Apart from its rear window slope and side air scoops, the production versions followed this design. GINETTA CARS

GINETTA G32 (1986–92)

Layout and chassis	Two-seater sports car with steel-tube chassis	*Suspension and Steering*	
		Front	Upper wishbone, lower track control arm, coil spring damper units, anti-roll bar
Engine			
Type	Ford	Rear	MacPherson strut with integral dampers, track control arms and radius rods
Block material	Cast iron		
Head material	Aluminium		
Cylinders	4	Steering	Rack and pinion
Cooling	Water	Tyres	185/60 × 14in (195/50 × 15in optional)
Bore and stroke	80 × 79.5mm (1.9i 83 × 88mm)	Wheels	Cast alloy
Capacity	1597cc (1.9i 1905cc)	Rim width	6J × 14 in (7J × 15in optional)
Valves	Single overhead cam, 2 valves per cylinder, hydraulic tappets	*Brakes*	
Compression ratio	9.5:1	Type	Disc front and rear
Carburettor	Fuel injection	Brake size	9.5in (241mm) front, 9.7in (246mm) rear
Max. power (DIN)	110bhp (1.9i 135bhp)		
Max. torque	102lb ft at 2,800rpm (1.9i 140lb ft at 3,500rpm)	*Dimensions*	
Fuel capacity	9.7gal (44ltr)	Track, front	55in (1,397mm)
		Track, rear	55in (1,397mm)
Transmission		Wheelbase	87in (2,210mm)
Gearbox	Ford 5-speed and reverse	Overall length	148in (3,760mm)
Clutch	Diaphragm single dry plate	Overall width	65in (1,651mm)
		Overall height	46in (1,168mm)
Internal Gearbox Ratios		Unladen weight	1,940lb (880kg)
First	3.15:1		
Second	1.9:1	*Performance*	
Third	1.28:1	Top speed	116mph (187km/h); 1.9i 127mph (204km/h)
Fourth	0.95:1		
Fifth	0.76:1	0–60mph	9.0sec (1.9i 7.8sec)
Reverse	3.62:1		
Final drive	3.82:1 (1.9i 4.27:1)		

Type Approval

Reaction to the G32 was very positive and, with sales of the kit models still strong, Ginetta started to consider perhaps getting the G32 type approved so it could be sold fully factory-built and ready to drive away. Bob and Ivor visited the Department of Transport offices in Bristol, the UK's approving body, and discussed the requirements and costs involved. In the fifteen years since the G15 and G21 had been approved there had been enormous changes and there were now twenty-six tests to be passed. Many were straightforward and, where parts used on other cars were being used by Ginetta, such as door locks, mirrors, lights and so on, the approvals were already in place; but other tests, such as heating and demisting, noise limits and the dreaded 30mph impact test at a cost of £10,000 alone, were more challenging.

It was daunting but Ivor thought it could be done. He

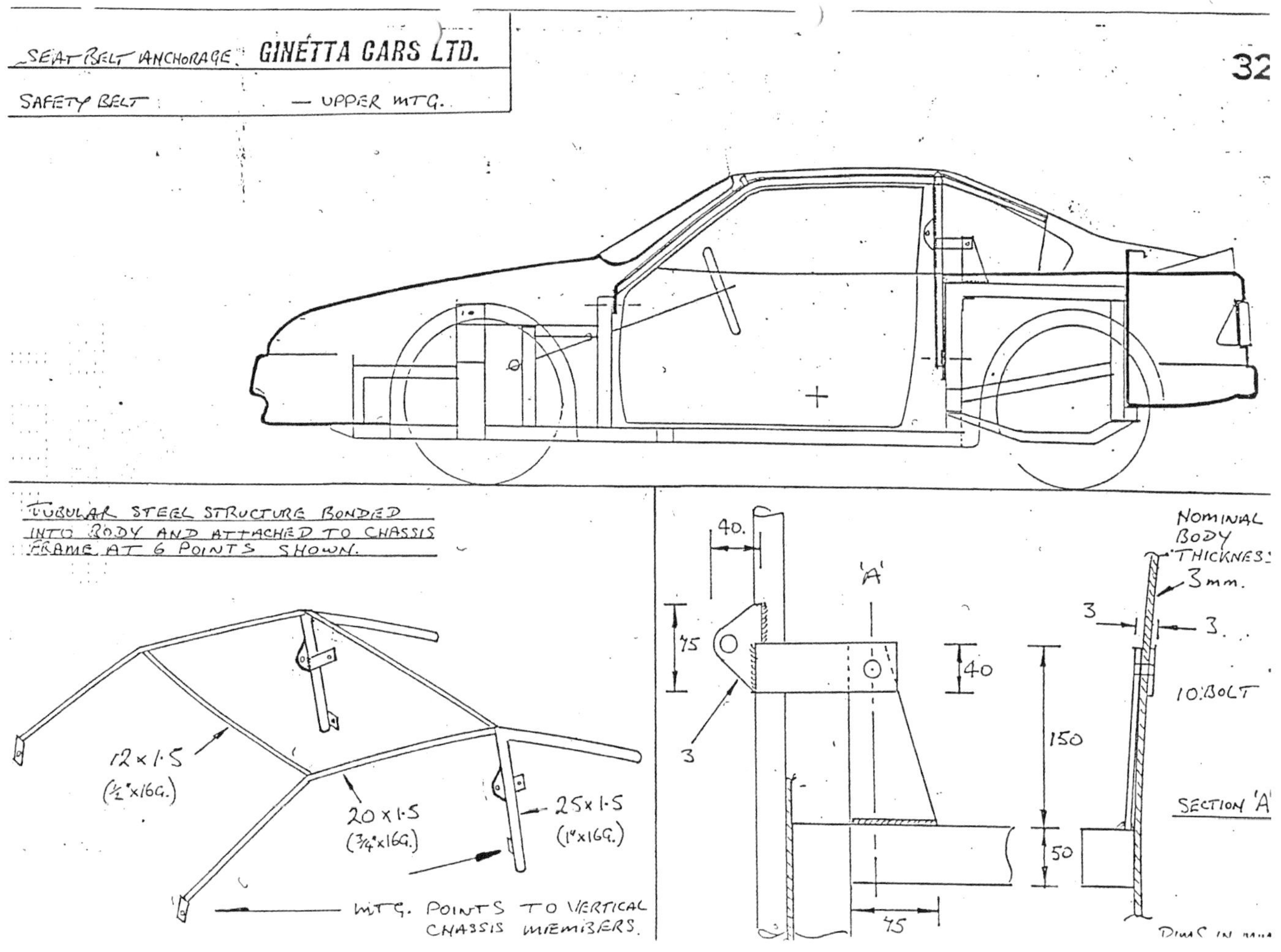

Safety was an important factor in the G32 design. This drawing shows the internal frame bonded into the cabin area and bolted to the chassis together with sturdy seat belt anchorages. GINETTA CARS

had already designed the G32 to meet many of the standards; others would need to be engineered into the car. A long-term Ginetta owner, Bill Piper, was a type approval legislation expert, and his services were called upon on a consultancy basis to help guide Ivor through the reams of documents that laid out the requirements, and also to witness some of the tests.

Slowly they worked through the process. Changes to the original design were few, but one major one concerned the rear window, which on the prototype was too steeply raked to pass; this was revised to make the window more vertical. Another change was that the side vents ducting air to the engine had to be deleted in favour of closed side panels – not helpful for an engine bay that was small and needed some airflow.

Another aspect of the approval process was conformity of production. All jigs, moulds and the manufacturing process had to be approved and were subject to occasional checks thereafter by the DoT. The brothers knew that the Witham factory wasn't up to the standards required even without the kit production that was in full swing. Again they found themselves at a crossroads. It was like history repeating: last time it was the G21 Ginetta couldn't produce, now it was the G32. This time, though, the brothers had the benefit of the Sudbury experience to fall back on and the same mistakes would not be made. They looked around Essex for an affordable factory but found nothing suitable, so Bob cast his net wider. It was suggested to him that there were very good opportunities in government development areas where incentives were offered to encourage employment into depressed areas. During the early eighties the property market in London and the southeast of England had boomed and it was not lost on the brothers that the site on which the Witham factory stood was worth a significant amount of money for redevelopment.

It wasn't long before the town of Scunthorpe came on their radar, and Bob's initial meetings with the council proved extremely positive. Not only could the company purchase a large factory at a reasonable cost complete with a vacant patch of land that could later be developed with another building as production increased, but the council offered accommodation for the brothers and workers prepared to relocate. There were subsidies on offer, too, which would make a substantial difference to costs over a period of time. The sale of Witham would finance this move and factory; it was a near perfect solution. The only downside was that both Bob and Ivor had young families rooted in Essex who couldn't really move north, while Trevers and Doug occupied the flats above Witham and would need to rehome themselves.

Move to Scunthorpe

By April 1988 the deal was done and a formal announcement was made on 3 May to local and national press in a formal setting with many local dignitaries present. For the authorities in Scunthorpe, the Ginetta deal was big, not because the company was huge or even a large employer, but simply because sports car manufacturing was big news and 'sexy' compared with more mundane businesses that might have been much larger. They capitalized on the move with grand advertisements in the local and national press and produced publicity material trumpeting Ginetta's arrival in the town with slogans like 'It's better for Ginetta in Scunthorpe'.

By June 1988 the move was in full swing. This time it was different from when they had moved to Sudbury sixteen years earlier. Then, many of the old moulds, out-of-date parts and other paraphernalia remained stored at Witham; this time it all had either to be moved to Scunthorpe or

THE SCUNTHORPE ENTERPRISE ZONE

By the 1980s the South Yorkshire and Humberside area was experiencing problems with the decline of heavy industries and the subsequent negative effect on the region's employment.

The government set up enterprise zones as a way of dealing with high levels of unemployment and dereliction in areas of similar decline, and announced that Scunthorpe would enjoy this status from 1983.

As well as improving infrastructure, the grants offered business start-ups and relocations to the area a combination of tax breaks, investment allowances and relaxed planning restrictions. Another benefit came in the supply of industrial and commercial land and buildings, some of which were purpose-built for relocating businesses.

The Scunthorpe Industrial Development and Enterprise Agency, the administrative organization, offered Ginetta a very attractive deal to relocate from Essex into a new purpose-built factory, coupled with other financial incentives: how could they not take the opportunity?

The Scunthorpe Enterprise Zone embraced Ginetta and used the business to promote the area to others thinking of relocation. Paper hats and badges were just two of the handouts they supplied as promotional material at motor shows. AUTHOR

The announcement of Ginetta's pending move to Scunthorpe was heralded in the press and on television: it was big news. Here Ivor and Bob Walklett pose with a new G32 at the official press announcement. GINETTA CARS

scrapped to clear the site. It was a big operation and disrupted production but Bob had costed this in and it was an accepted consequence of expanding the company. Among all the organized chaos some things had to continue uninterrupted, especially the G32 type approval process. The author remembers calling in at Witham one day when the factory was being stripped out and seeing a huge lorry in the yard being loaded with spare G21 bodies en route to Scunthorpe.

All the employees were engaged in the moving task, either at the Witham end or in Scunthorpe but in among this, with the building literally being pulled apart around him, he found Ivor working on a G32 to ensure they had another complete car following the imminent crash test of the first prototype.

Once Witham was cleared, all attention was on getting production under way at the new factory. Trevers and Ivor quickly set up the building to meet production needs and it wasn't long before the first G26 and G31 kits once again rolled out to their enthusiastic new owners. Bob, meanwhile, was setting up his office with new staff and stabilizing the operation to ensure normal business was resumed as soon as possible.

While several key staff members had uprooted and moved to Scunthorpe with the company, a lot of new people were taken on to replace those who preferred not to move north;

Moving an entire factory is a lot of work. Here spare G21 bodyshells are loaded up at Witham ready for the journey north to Scunthorpe. AUTHOR

The first production G32 and the second car part-built are loaded up at Witham en route to Scunthorpe. DUNCAN CAMPBELL

The G32 took a bashing during its crash test but the cabin remained sound. Here type approval expert and Ginetta owner Bill Piper (left) and Ivor Walklett (right) survey the remains following the successful test. GINETTA CARS

LEFT: **A proud moment for Bob Walklett as he stands in front of the new Scunthorpe factory in 1988.** GINETTA CARS

these people needed to be trained in the various tasks that were required and it all took time and resources. Aside from getting production under way as soon as possible, the company had to prepare for the next Motor Show in October, where they were planning a big announcement on the G32.

By now the crash test had been successfully completed and while the G32 took quite a bashing during the 30mph impact, the important elements remained intact, ensuring a pass to European standards. Only a small leakage of fuel simulation liquid, caused by the horn being pushed into the tank and puncturing it, stopped it passing the more stringent United States requirements; in practice, even with that pass, the car would have been unlikely to appeal in the US market, where larger cars with big engines are more popular. To ensure turbo-engined versions could be made if required, the car was weighted for the impact and brake tests to simulate the car in turbo form.

Although certain production conformity inspections were still to be passed at the time of the Motor Show, Ginetta were given permission to state the car had passed type approval standards and, as such, could sell complete drive-away cars to customers with the injection engine for a price of £10,995 including car tax and VAT. They also catalogued a more basic version with steel wheels and no front spot lamps for £500 less, but it is not thought any cars were ever sold to this specification. The show stand at Birmingham's National Exhibition Centre was very professional and featured three pre-production G32s finished in red, grey and pearlescent white, and firm orders were taken.

With the move to Scunthorpe and the lengthy approval process, Bob knew it would be some time before production could commence, and so invited potential customers as early as the spring of 1988 to express their serious interest in buying a car by paying a small £50 deposit. Bob never actually cashed these cheques, simply pinning them to the file; he knew that once the company took money from customers they would press for delivery of their car, something the company would not be able to do for some considerable time. However, by 1989 the factory was gearing up for full production, hoping to fill orders by late summer, the full type approval papers finally being issued on 6 April 1989. In fact, the first production G32 would not be delivered until November, three years after its public debut. By then it had to face up to competition from Toyota's restyled MR2, but Bob was confident that by keeping the price competitive they could undercut the MR2 sufficiently to keep attracting customers.

The first G32s to leave the factory were sold directly to customers, including this example, driven by the author for 200,000 miles. These were very usable cars. AUTHOR

While all this had been going on, Trevers had decided to look into the possibility of re-engineering the GRS into a four-door car. Frequently at shows people had expressed the view that they liked the GRS concept but they needed to have four doors.

THE GRS MARK 3

Rather than altering the Chrysler Hunter-based version which was now rather out of date and with donor cars getting harder to find, Trevers took the G26 Cortina-based chassis as the basis for a new Mark 3 version. This entirely new body featured the four steel doors from a Mark 4 or 5 Cortina and a rear hatch door from a Mark 3 Ford Escort estate car; the cabin, like the G26, used the entire interior from the donor Cortina while a one-piece tilt-forward bonnet gave the car a bold and purposeful look. As with the G26, the chassis accepted parts from a Mark 3, 4 or 5 Cortina, including the full range of engines, which this time also encompassed the V6 versions.

The Mark 3 was a large car but the old constrictions Ginetta had suffered at Witham were no longer an issue – if the orders came in, the cars could be built alongside other models in the new, spacious factory. Launched at the 1989 Newark Kit Car Show, the Mark 3 was priced at £1,695 for a basic unpainted body/chassis unit with new doors supplied at £500 a set and a tailgate at £245. Of course customers could supply their own doors and other parts but it was their

The Mark 3 GRS was a practical and solid vehicle, but perhaps its Ford doors were too recognizable to make it a success. GINETTA OWNERS' CLUB

From the rear, the Ford Escort-derived tailgate dominated the appearance of the Mark 3 GRS. GINETTA OWNERS' CLUB

choice how much work they wanted to do and how much they wanted done for them. The factory would paint the kit for a further £450, provide lighting for £154 and provide glass for £125, although door glass was not supplied. The interior trim kit was £342 and seats, with all matching trimming, £375. The galvanizing of the chassis frame was £135 if required. All these prices were exclusive of VAT.

In 1994, when reflecting on the GRS Mark 3, Trevers Walklett commented that it was a good car but the company didn't need it; this is clearly a truthful statement but it may not be the full story. It seems likely that despite people asking for a four-door GRS at kit car shows, the demand simply wasn't there and the orders didn't follow once the product was available. The original prototype, registered Q775PFE, was retained by the factory only until the end of the year, while one other car was built up at the factory in early 1990, but fitted with a Perkins diesel engine and sold to a local customer. These remained the only two cars built; both are thought to survive, although the diesel engine was later replaced by a very powerful petrol engine.

NEW DEVELOPMENTS

Despite the move to Scunthorpe and the workload this and type approving the G32 created, Ivor could still find the time to come up with new design ideas for his brothers to consider for future production. One such set of plans was for a very much more powerful Ginetta, expanding on the design principals of the G32. This model would have featured a

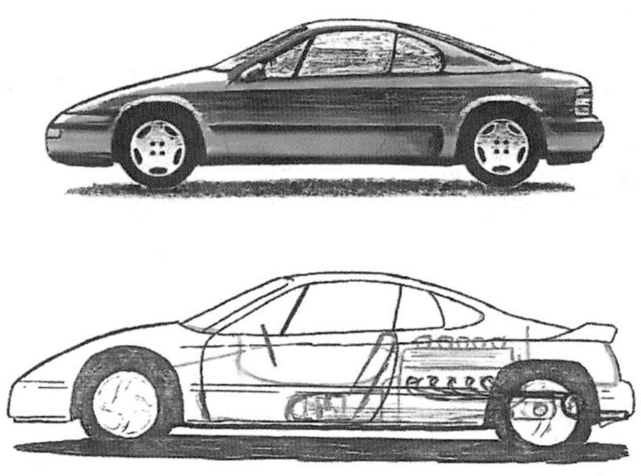

Ivor Walklett found the time to sketch this mid-engined Jaguar-powered coupé, but sadly it never got beyond the drawing board. IVOR WALKLETT

V12 Jaguar engine mid-mounted with the standard gearbox positioned between the two seats; from here the drive would have been carried through a transfer box similar to that found on four-wheel-drive cars, via a propshaft back past the engine, to a rear-mounted differential unit. Perhaps unsurprisingly this car never got beyond the drawing board – had it been built it would probably have been the G33 – but it still illustrates perfectly the breadth of ideas and lateral thinking that has marked Ivor out as one of the most prolific and innovative designers of his generation.

Exports to Japan

Larger production facilities also opened up other avenues for the company that they would previously not have been able to explore. During the eighties, the original G12 and G4 models had become sought-after as classics and their value rose accordingly. The market for these models was particularly strong in Japan, where Ginetta enjoyed a status on a level with Lotus, and Bob received enquiries from several Japanese businessmen, as well as UK-based car dealers, who were all interested in Ginetta building them new G12s for export to Japan.

The brothers decided to start making these cars again to special order. Work would be required on the tired moulds and a new chassis jig needed to be made, but the chance to make and sell these cars was seized, as the profits would be extremely good. The first car completed was ready for dispatch in July 1989, and others soon followed. The same people were asking Ginetta to restart making the original G4 as well, so Bob opened an order book for these models too. These cars were selling readily in Japan and it was clear that a whole new business stream had opened up.

With kit production still in full swing, the G32 production line being established and the new line of G12 cars now being made, the brothers agreed to make plans for erecting two new industrial buildings on the land they owned adjacent to the factory. These would be used for fibreglass laminating and chassis fabrication respectively, leaving the main factory for finishing and assembly.

GINETTA IS SOLD

It was against this backdrop of significant and stable expansion that one day the phone rang on Bob's desk. The caller was Martin Phaff. He explained that he was keen to meet with Bob to discuss his interest in purchasing the Ginetta business. This wasn't the first time Bob had received such unsolicited expressions of interest and he was quite dismissive, making it clear the business wasn't for sale. However Phaff is nothing if not tenacious and, phoning Bob again a few days later, asked to bring along his accountant from Cooper & Lybrand. This offer clearly had substance, and somewhat reluctantly Bob agreed to a meeting where Mike Modiri from Cooper & Lybrand outlined his clients' position. It was obvious to Bob that this was not an idle or half-baked attempt to buy Ginetta and he agreed to at least discuss the offer with his co-directing brothers.

While none of the four had any thoughts of selling or giving up the business, this offer could not be ignored: both Douglas and Trevers were already past state retirement age and Bob was approaching it. Perhaps accepting an offer that was on the table now would be preferable to waiting until age dictated they would have to sell and were maybe forced to accept a lesser sum of money. Indeed, Douglas had been hospitalized with a stroke on the run-up to the 1988 Motor Show and he had not enjoyed good health for some years. All in all, taking a good offer now did seem to make a lot of sense. From what has been written it seems that all four brothers were in agreement that to sell would be a sound choice and so negotiations began.

It soon emerged that Martin Phaff, who had recently sold a successful business to a PLC, had teamed up with Mike Modiri to make the purchase, which would be largely financed by banks as well as Yorkshire Venture Capital. This was in stark contrast to the way the brothers had run the business. They had always ensured that it was their own money that was on the line – indeed on the day of the sale, Bob paid all outstanding creditors in full, so the slate was clean for the new management coming in. For Ivor the sale had come too early. Still only in his mid-fifties, he had much more to offer and as a result he retained a partial financial interest in the business and continued as a technical director.

The business changed hands officially on 7 November 1989. Trevers also agreed to stay on for six months as a consultant to ensure a smooth transition of the production facilities to the new management, but for Bob and Douglas it was the end of thirty-one years at the helm of Ginetta. Bob would enjoy a long retirement and died while this book was in preparation, at the age of ninety-one, but for Doug retirement was sadly short, and he passed away in the autumn of 1992, just three years after the business was sold.

Under new management, this is G32 production at Scunthorpe in April 1990. GINETTA OWNERS' CLUB

NEW MANAGEMENT, NEW IDEAS

The new management team saw Martin Phaff installed as managing director running the business and Mike Modiri as director and company secretary, while Ivor Walklett took care of technical matters, including the design of new models. Martin also brought in Stuart Hobson, an engineer who had past experience with both Jaguar and Austin Rover, to run the factory.

New management invariably has different ideas to previous regimes and in the case of Ginetta, Martin was keen to expand G32 production and increase the sales of the heritage models to Japan, as the level of profit was very attractive. All this would be done at the expense of kit production, which he was keen to phase out, despite being cautioned against it by Bob Walklett on his departure and by Ivor, who both knew this was bread-and-butter income. Ginetta immediately stopped advertising kits and attending kit car shows and from the beginning of 1990, only special orders were taken.

One of the first tasks on taking over the company for Martin Phaff was to hand over the first production G32 to its new owner in a grand unveiling complete with champagne. Again, this was in contrast to previous first deliveries in the Walklett era, which would pass unnoticed, even the purchaser in many cases not knowing that they were recipient of the first production car.

In terms of model line-up, Martin Phaff also had new ideas. He was keen to produce convertible versions of the G32 to broaden its sales appeal and to make an all-new model that he termed a 'big boy's car' or, in other words, a powerful, large-engined sports car. Ivor was immediately set to work

Cars quickly started being supplied through the dealer network from 1990. This was a typical offering from the Sports Car Centre in Worcestershire, but with price increases, buyers proved hard to find. DAVID DOOLAN

Publicity was an important part of Martin Phaff's policy. Here, from left to right, Mike Modiri, Jack Davis (a UK dealer), Martin Phaff and the Scunthorpe mayor celebrate the signing of a contract to supply G32s to Singapore dealer Christopher Sim, seated. GINETTA OWNERS' CLUB

designing these new cars. With the G32 back orders now being delivered there was a need to keep the order book full and so Martin toured the country looking to set up a dealer network. Each new dealer was expected to take two cars, one to demonstrate and one for stock, and it didn't stop there: once the UK network was in place, dealerships were set up in Europe and the Far East.

On 1 January 1990 the price of the G32 was increased by £2,000 to £12,995, although this price did include a galvanized chassis and colour-coded door mirrors as standard. It was a big increase, and probably necessary to fund the dealer profit margins, but it would throw the G32 into the MR2 price bracket and would in due time have the effect of blunting sales.

THE GINETTA G32 CONVERTIBLE

Meanwhile, work was under way building the first G32 convertible; this involved the removal of the roof, the provision of an additional engine cover and, of course, the new soft top. Clever design detailing meant the seat belt anchorages remained the same as on the coupé and this ensured the type approval wasn't affected. Mechanically, the car was the same as the coupé with the exception of additional chassis bracing along the sill sections, which intruded into the interior of the car. A thermostatically switched extract fan mounted in the rear wheel arch was also added to pull hot air from the engine compartment; this was necessary as there was even less natural engine bay ventilation than in the coupé.

The convertible made its public debut at the 1990 Motor Show, billed as the only British mid-engined convertible on the market, with deliveries getting under way soon after. There was criticism of the convertible from some prospective purchasers who felt the level of engine noise was high, particularly with the hood erected. In the coupé the engine is well insulated unless the sunroof is open, but on the convertible there is less to break the sound waves.

The G32 convertible was a new take on the G32 instigated by new MD Martin Phaff.
GINETTA OWNERS' CLUB

A number of convertibles were exported to Italy, where no doubt their owners could enjoy the Mediterranean sun. GINETTA OWNERS' CLUB

A turbo version of the G32 specially prepared by Collins Performance Engineering was exhibited at the 1990 Motor Show. DAVID BAKER

Contrasting exterior and interior colours were a popular choice with convertible purchasers. Note also the MM wheels. DAVID DOOLAN

A high percentage of G32s were fitted with the Mark 2 Fiesta dashboard, as can be seen from the interior of this coupé.
AUTHOR

Publicity in magazine articles for the G32 was good, and a full road test was also carried out by *Autocar* on 6 March 1990. Unfortunately the demonstration car that was supplied, G609MKY, had not been properly inspected before being released for test and suffered a number of faults, not least a difficult gearchange (not the G32's strongest feature even when properly adjusted) and as a result the magazine was far from complimentary; this was another setback and lesson learnt for the new management.

In anticipation of production being increased, the workforce was expanded and reached some fifty souls by the summer of 1990; however, one insider commented to the author that despite the additional hands the productivity didn't increase correspondingly. The country was now facing another recessionary period and it was a hard fact that the G32 wasn't selling in the numbers anticipated. As the Walklett brothers had discovered previously, dealers didn't all sell in volume and, after they had taken a few cars, reordering didn't necessarily follow. In London, dealer Barouche Motor Sport sold quite a number of cars and several overseas dealers also did well. Three of the first convertibles made were dispatched to an Italian dealership, but disaster struck when en route to Italy the hoods were ripped off in exceptionally windy conditions; some minor revisions to the hood design were made in the wake of this.

Alongside the new convertible on the 1990 Motor Show stand sat a racing version of the G32, specially built up and tuned by Collins Performance Engineering in Cheshire. This very carefully built car was said to produce around 260bhp from its highly tuned, turbocharged engine. It featured a lightweight body and included a roof-mounted intercooler reminiscent of the Ford RS 200 rally car; it was subsequently used for a few seasons mainly for sprints but never showed really promising results.

One other car was fitted with a standard Ford 1.6 Turbo engine delivering 133bhp, which was offered at £15,850. This car was a road version externally indistinguishable from a standard G32 coupé, and in truth the turbo offered little more in performance than the 1.9-litre version of the G32 that had been catalogued from early 1990 as a £1,605 option.

By September 1990 the price had increased again to £13,700 for the coupé, while the new convertible was launched at £14,600. Cars originally featured 14in diameter Performance multi-spoke alloy wheels but later on MM eight-spoke alloys were fitted to 1.6-litre models, while the range-topping 1.9-litre versions came with slightly wider 15in-diameter MM eight-spoke alloy wheels fitted with lower-profile tyres.

Extras offered were metallic or mica paint finishes, leather seats and door inserts, electric wing mirrors and Wilton carpets. There was also a list of dealer-fitted options, which included electric windows, sunroof, walnut interior trim, alarm and radio/cassette player.

By early 1991 the writing was on the wall for the G32. Sales had dropped significantly. Small revisions – fitting a Ford Fiesta Mark 3 dashboard in place of the Mark 2 version and later replacing the mechanical fuel injection with electronic – did nothing to revive its fortunes.

In October that year the price was listed at £16,800 for the coupé and £18,168 for the convertible; many of the extras were now standard, including a sunroof, electric windows and central locking, but this price was unrealistic and after this there were no sales, apart from one car built for the dealer in Singapore. This car, built as late as 1993, is worthy of particular note due to it being fitted with a 1800cc version of Ford's twin ohc Zetec engine. The Zetec is the engine the G32 should always have had, giving the level of performance and flexibility the chassis deserved, and in later years many owners have retrofitted these engines in anything from 1600 to 2000cc form into their cars.

Rather like with the G21, the promise of the G32 was never truly realized, held back as it was by a combination of being too slow to the market, price increases that made it uncompetitive and a global recession. In the end, just ninety-seven coupés were built along with sixteen convertibles.

Several owners have used their G32 in competition, and Vince Hawtree, seen here, has been a devotee from the early days of the model. DUNCAN CAMPBELL

GINETTA G32 EXPORTS

Belgium	1
Cyprus	1
Guernsey	3
Italy	13
Singapore	12
Sweden	3

This convertible is fitted with the Mark 3 Fiesta dashboard, introduced towards the end of G32 production. DAVID DOOLAN

CHAPTER TEN

TROUBLED TIMES

As the new management at Ginetta bedded in, one of the bright spots was the sales of the older models to Japan. By the summer of 1990 they were building both G4 and G12 cars for Japan and a significant customer had now emerged in the Wary House Company, run by entrepreneur Tamotsu Maeda. Initially orders for Japan had been in ones and twos but the Wary House Company changed that by ordering significant batches of cars, particularly G4s, with agreements to take further cars over the next two years.

Mike Modiri realized this could help the company finances not just because of the income these orders would generate, but because interest rates in Japan at the time for a loan were around 10.5 per cent whereas in the UK they were a crippling 17.5 per cent. Ginetta was saddled with a huge level of debt and by transferring the loans to Japan they could be paid directly in Japanese yen from the sales of cars; at the same time this would remove the uncertainty caused by exchange rate fluctuations when converting yen to pounds stirling when bringing the money back into the UK. It was a win-win situation, and an article in the *Daily Mail* newspaper at the time suggested Ginetta would save £90,000 a year in interest payments alone.

Meanwhile, work was progressing apace on the new 'big boy's' Ginetta desired by Martin Phaff. Ivor had designed the chassis, and a prototype was under way at the Scunthorpe factory. With Trevers no longer associated with Ginetta and back in Essex, Ivor teamed up with Mark Walklett, Trevers' son, to create the new bodywork. It was Mark who took a G4 Series 4/G27 bodyshell and reworked it into a dramatic new model that would be known as the Ginetta G33.

Martin Phaff stands with the now large workforce at Scunthorpe. The model range is now split between the G32 and G33, with the heritage G12 also being promoted strongly.
GINETTA CARS

THE GINETTA G33

The appearance of the G33 harked right back to the G4 of thirty years earlier – the flowing curves gave the car a retro look yet it was totally clean and modern in its overall appearance. The bonnet featured pop-up headlamps, while the doors were smooth with no handles, only discreet push buttons to allow access. The windscreen was taken directly from the 1968 G16 model and featured cut-off top corners – distinctive although not entirely practical – but the crowning glory of the design was the twin head fairings, reminiscent of sports racing cars from the 1950s. These head fairings were a major talking point, and indeed the idea was taken up quickly after the car's launch by other designers for their new shapes. Mark had done an outstanding job with the G33, meeting the brief for a car that not only was powerful but also looked powerful: a true muscle car.

The chassis frame was developed from the G27 and featured twin-wishbone front suspension complete with coil spring damper units, while at the rear the Ford Sierra Cosworth-derived differential powered independently sprung rear hub-carriers restrained by transverse arms and trailing links. Anti-roll bars were fitted front and rear, as were disc brakes. The power unit was the by now popular Rover V8,

GINETTA G33 (1990–8)

Layout and chassis	Two-seater sports car with tubular steel chassis
Engine	
Type	Rover
Block material	Aluminium
Head material	Aluminium
Cylinders	V8
Cooling	Water
Bore and stroke	94 × 71.1mm
Capacity	3947cc
Valves	2 valves per cylinder
Compression ratio	10.5:1
Carburettor	Fuel injection
Max. power (DIN)	198bhp
Max. torque	220lb ft at 3,500rpm
Fuel capacity	9gal (41ltr)
Transmission	
Gearbox	Rover 5-speed and reverse
Clutch	Diaphragm
Internal Gearbox Ratios	
First	3.32:1
Second	2.13:1
Third	1.40:1
Fourth	1:1
Fifth	0.78:1
Reverse	3.429:1
Final drive	3.14:1
Suspension and Steering	
Front	Twin wishbone, coil spring damper units, anti-roll bar
Rear	Rigid differential, with lower wishbones, fixed-length half shafts, trailing arms, coil spring damper units
Steering	Rack and pinion
Tyres	205/50 × 15in
Wheels	Cast alloy
Rim width	7J × 15in
Brakes	
Type	Disc front and rear
Brake size	12in (304mm) front, 10.5in (263mm) rear
Dimensions	
Track, front	54.5in (1,382mm)
Track, rear	54.6in (1,387mm)
Wheelbase	87.5in (2,225mm)
Overall length	151in (3,832mm)
Overall width	64in (1,626mm)
Overall height	41in (1,041mm) to top of hood
Unladen weight	1,927lb (874kg)
Performance	
Top speed	145mph (233km/h)
0–60mph	5.3sec

The curvy lines of the G33 developed by Mark Walklett were an instant success. DAVID DOOLAN

coupled to its five-speed gearbox. Inside, the G33 was basic but neatly trimmed and offered a sufficient level of refinement for what was after all a raw sports machine. The final finishing touch saw the car standing on a set of deeply dished Fondmetal alloy road wheels. The road presence of the G33 was indisputably outstanding.

The new car was ready just in time for display on the company's stand at the 1990 Motor Show; that year, as we have seen, also saw the launch of the G32 convertible exhibited alongside the standard G32 coupé and the turbo racing version, but it is fair to say that despite such a dazzling array of cars the G33 stole the show for Ginetta. After the show, the pressure was on to get the new model ready for production. The prototype was fitted with a 3.5-litre Rover V8 engine but the production versions were to be equipped with the 3.9-litre fuel injection unit and the launch price was set at £17,800.

There was, however, one major issue with the G33, and that was its size. Basing the prototype on the G27 meant that developing the product would be quicker but conventional wisdom dictated that from the point of view of interior comfort, road footprint and its presence as a muscle car, it should be bigger. As a result, the production cars were made larger – quite significantly larger, in fact, with approximately 3in (75mm) added to the wheelbase and 4in (100mm) to the track with correspondingly larger body dimensions. The pressure to deliver the first cars meant that type approval would have to wait and, although designed to meet the standards, complete cars were supplied to dealers without the engine and gearbox fitted; these components were supplied separately.

The G33 drew on the lines of the G4 and G27, but the whole car was larger dimensionally, giving it more road presence. MEL HEADLEY

Crash test results for the G33 were very good – relatively little damage was done, considering the 30mph impact. DUNCAN CAMPBELL

The first car was delivered in May 1991 to dealer MacDonald Racing based in County Durham. MacDonald had the idea of tuning a standard G33 to a whole new level, not that most people felt more power was needed with a 0–60mph time of just 5 seconds. MacDonald tuned the engine from the standard 198bhp to a massive 320bhp by removing the fuel injection and fitting in its place four twin-choke DRLA 40 Dellorto carburettors, a hot Crane camshaft, gas-flowed heads and tubular exhaust manifolds; he also stiffened up the chassis around the front suspension. The cars modified by MacDonald Racing were named the G33 Rapide and were priced at an additional £2,000 over the standard car, which had risen in price to £19,965 by October 1991. There were few extras listed, but leather seats and door inserts along with a colour-matched dashboard and console cost £595, while a metallic or mica paint finish was an additional £415.

The export market was important to Martin Phaff, and across Europe dealers were keen to get their hands on a car. There was a problem in certain markets, however, as the Rover V8 didn't meet the emission standards required, and in these cases the Ford Cosworth 2-litre turbo engine was fitted when requested. Soon a catalytic converter was made available for the Rover version at an additional £1,670. G33 production quickly settled to between one and two cars a week and the demand was encouraging. Its closest rival was probably the TVR V8 S but the G33 undercut this in price by several thousand pounds. *Autocar* magazine published a report, having driven the prototype, and followed this up with a full road test of the production version. There is no doubt they enjoyed the car, opening their test by saying 'few cars provide as much driving pleasure as Ginetta's sensual, thundering roadster', but there was criticism too, particularly of the hood, which, due to the cut-off windscreen corners, tended to obstruct vision and wasn't fully waterproof. With the top down, however, on a dry summer's day and with the backdrop of its low thunderous exhaust note, the G33 offered a driver nothing but pleasure.

It was also subject of a test on the BBC television series *Top Gear* by racing driver Tiff Needell, who drove it around

MacDonald Racing developed the G33 Rapide, a more powerful version; note the 'Rapide' lettering on the lower front wing. GINETTA OWNERS' CLUB

With the hood erected, visibility was restricted on the G33. DAVID DOOLAN

Cadwell Park circuit and clearly enjoyed the experience, commenting variously, 'not only does the G33 look right – it sounds right', 'a delight to drive' and 'sheer motoring satisfaction and enjoyment' – praise indeed, but again the hood came in for comment.

Things then, seemed to be going well for Ginetta – but were they? Those close to Ginetta started wondering if all was well; one surprise was that the spare land to the side of the Scunthorpe factory, earmarked by the Walklett brothers for the two additional factory units that never materialized due to the company sale, was sold off. Then in 1992 there were more surprises, when Mike Modiri left the business and there was a formal announcement that Ginetta had sold the rights to the ownership of the Ginetta G4 and G12 models to the Japanese Wary House Company. This move astonished many, particularly when it was realized that the sale included the use of the Ginetta name and badge on these cars. The income netted by this sale was, however, considerable, being in the region of £275,000 and the deal stipulated that the manufacture of the cars would continue to be carried out by Ginetta in Scunthorpe for at least the next three years. The sale of the rights to certain models later became a theme, as in the next few years the rights to both the G16 and GRS were sold too.

Mark Walklett had also left the business, and in late 1990 he and his father Trevers formed a new Essex-based company – DARE UK (Design and Research Engineering). Ivor Walklett was also a director although he continued in his role of technical director at Ginetta.

Martin Phaff sits proudly with the G33 and G12 on the run-up to the 1991 Motor Show. GINETTA CARS

Martin Phaff, now the main decision-maker at Ginetta, was keen to develop the G33 theme further and broaden its appeal. To this end he put the wheels in motion for a facelift of the car, which would also include chassis modification.

The Ginetta G33 SC

The bodywork was altered at the front by removing the pop-up headlamps and substituting them for a modern light unit from a Mazda, which was expertly contoured into the smooth bonnet. At the rear, the back panel was changed completely by rounding, fitting larger tail lamps and altering the bootlid to turn down the back of the car between the lights; and finally a louvred underpanel was incorporated. The chassis was lengthened by 2in (50mm) and some small changes were made at the front to stiffen it up and improve the geometry. The bodywork changes were carried out by Ginetta employees David Sewell and Jerry Clarke, and in their honour the revised car was called the G33 SC.

Their efforts were well received, although, while the frontal appearance was universally liked, the rear end treatment was less successful. One other important feature of the redesign was the windscreen, which was more conventional and lost its cut-off corners, making the hood a better fit and answering previous criticisms. The interior also came in for attention and became more luxurious than the G33, in keeping with Martin's ideas for making the G33 concept more of a comfortable cruiser and less of a seat-of-the-pants roadster. The plan was to have the revised G33 SC launched at the forthcoming Motor Show at Birmingham's NEC in October 1992 alongside the standard G33 and a new 'Club' version, fitted with a 1.8-litre Ford Zetec engine.

IN RECEIVERSHIP

However, a few weeks before the start of the show at the end of September, the unthinkable happened. The mounting debt had become unsustainable and, when one of the major component suppliers saw unpaid invoices mounting, they decided to call in the debt; the banks, concerned about the debt in yen against the fluctuating pound, would no longer extend credit. Ginetta was declared insolvent and the official receivers moved in to liquidate the company. Ginetta fans worldwide were horrified. Less than three years after the sale of the company it had come to this awful end – would Ginetta go the same way as most of their contemporaries and cease to exist as a business?

It was perhaps fortunate that the receiver saw in Ginetta a worthwhile business. There were orders for the G33 on the books, the new G33 SC and of course the manufacturing agreement for the Wary House Company. On taking over control, he ordered that cars currently in production should be completed and hoped to sell the business as a going concern; he also decided that, as it was already paid

The G33 SC was introduced at the 1992 Motor Show but a cloud hung over the company, which was under the stewardship of the official receiver.

TOM KENNY

The rear appearance of the G33 SC was significantly different from the G33 as this photograph shows; the car was eventually broken up. DUNCAN CAMPBELL

for, the company stand at the Motor Show should go ahead as planned. At the show the following G33 variants were offered: the 1.8-litre Club at £16,965; the V8 with 3.9 and 4.5 injection options at £19,975 and £23,575 respectively; the 2-litre Cosworth-powered version at £25,955; and the G33 SC in both 3.9 and 4.5 injection form at £23,625 and £27,225 respectively. The option of the 4.5-litre modified Rover V8 engine featured the specialist-made unit engineered by TVR for their models of the period and gave the Ginetta a lot of extra punch.

A company in liquidation displaying cars at the Motor Show is unusual and, unsurprisingly, people were reluctant to place orders, but their presence did show potential buyers of the company that there was still life in the business. Several concerns expressed interest in buying the business, including, allegedly, the Lamborghini Company; even the remaining Walklett brothers looked at it, but in the end it was Martin Phaff, never really leaving the side of the receiver, who eventually pulled together a financial package that enabled the remains of the business to be released back under his control.

RESCUE PACKAGE

The package involved several dealers who were persuaded to invest in the future of the company. The new business consortium taking over from the receiver comprised Martin Phaff and his wife Hilary, Ingemur Engstrom and Benny Smets, respectively the Swedish and Belgian dealers, and David Tearle, a UK-based dealer from Corby; all were now directors of the new company.

The deal did not include the ownership of the Scunthorpe factory and so this was retained and sold separately by the receiver, so the new Ginetta company needed to find premises in which to continue manufacturing. A giant parts sale was organized, attended by various people, including Owners' Club members, which helped both clear the factory and bring in some much-needed finance. Meanwhile, most employees had either left or been laid off, but Martin persuaded some key people to return, including Duncan Campbell and David Baines. Knowledge and continuity were an important element in getting production back to a reasonable level.

Even more important were orders, and it was quickly decided that the best way to generate these was to return to kit car production. This meant less investment in costly major components, such as engines and gearboxes, which was helpful to a business lacking working capital. While still under the Scunthorpe roof during the summer of 1993, the last few factory-built G33s were completed and the company started offering the G33 in component form less engine and gearbox. A painted body/chassis unit complete with windscreen and lights was offered at £6,298, while suspension, steering, brakes, propshaft, fuel system, electrical components, wheels and tyres, interior trim and weather protection could all be specified, adding an additional £5,290 to the price. This package did find a few buyers, but the main driver to get the business back up onto its feet was a surprise to some: Ginetta reverted to selling old favourite, the G27.

The G27 was relaunched by Martin Phaff as the G27 GRS. GINETTA CARS

The G27 had not really been offered for sale since the new management had taken over in 1989, but now Martin Phaff announced that it would be sold as a kit once more and for the first time with a live rear axle. Effectively this was a G4 Series 4 renamed G27, as of course the rights to the G4 name had been sold. As the factory possessed a crate full of Hillman Hunter rear axles left over from G21 production, the new model was launched early in 1993 as the G27 GRS, the last part of the name being a nod to the Hunter-based model once in the Ginetta line-up.

Apart from the car having a live rear axle with trailing arms and Panhard rod the 'new' car was as previously offered, and pricing was competitive at £2,185 for an unassembled body/chassis unit, or £2,945 assembled and £3,935 assembled and painted. From then on the buyer could choose from a wide range of extras spanning everything from electrics, instruments, lighting and brakes to suspension, wheels and tyres, weather equipment – even a jack and key fob were on the options list. It was surprising in a way that the G27 should be chosen as the main model to put Ginetta back on the map after the disastrous liquidation as it had never been a big seller by the standards of some other models, but clearly Martin Phaff saw a future in it and put a big effort into sales. As it turned out, his efforts soon started to pay off.

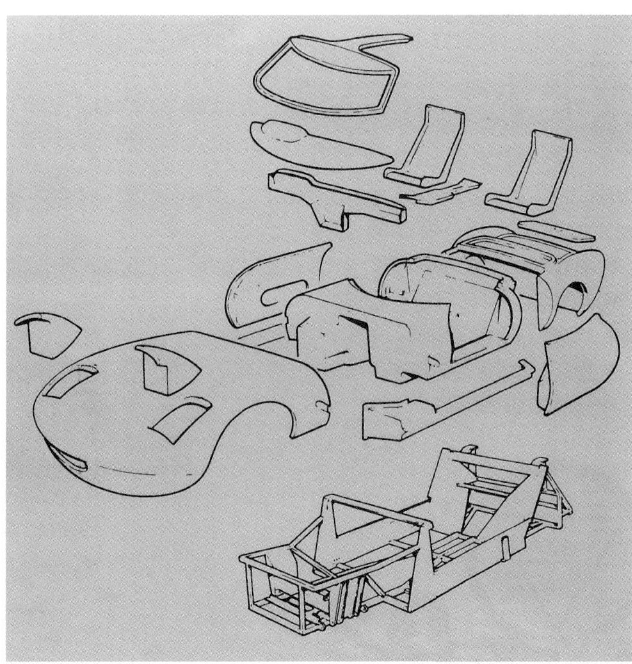

An exploded view of the G27 body and chassis. GINETTA CARS

G4 and G33 models in production at the Ginetta factory in Rotherham, South Yorkshire in 1993. DUNCAN CAMPBELL

At this time an approach from the USA to supply G33's for fitment of Oldsmobile Quad 4 engines was seriously discussed. A senior Oldsmobile executive, John Rock, had a hand in this behind the scenes. It was hoped the car would be known as the Rocket 44 reviving an iconic Oldsmobile name from the past, but in the end a lack of finance at Ginetta and proper upfront funding from Oldsmobile ensured no further progress.

By the end of 1993 the company were established in an industrial unit on the Eastwood Trading Estate in Rotherham, South Yorkshire and Scunthorpe was far behind them. Ginetta was a small operation again and things had changed in many ways. Rather than building all Ginetta parts in house, the company now established fabrication agreements with local firms, and the chassis and many metal components were made near Scunthorpe by a company run by former Ginetta employee David Sewell, while the bodies were laminated by a company near Doncaster. These major parts were brought together and assembled at Rotherham ready for dispatch to the customer.

Following the collapse of the original Ginetta business, the Wary House Company had severed its ties with Martin Phaff. There had been issues over quality and some of the components being used just before the receiver was called in, and in the aftermath part-completed cars saw little progress. With customers back in Japan demanding their new cars, Maeda faced a problem. As a result, he and his UK-based colleague and co-director, Kumiko English, approached DARE UK, run by the Walklett family, to assist. They were operating in a small way from some outbuildings on land adjacent to Trevers' home in Essex and agreed to

The DARE factory in West Mersea, Essex. The first G12 and G4 cars destined for Japan are just being built. DARE UK

From the left, Tamotsu Maeda, Ivor Walklett, Kumiko English and Trevers Walklett standing outside the Ginetta showroom in Tokyo, Japan. IVOR WALKLETT

help finish off the cars already part-built. Having completed this task, Maeda was keen that they should take over full production, but they were initially reluctant to get involved with manufacturing cars again.

While they were considering their position, Ivor Walklett happened to be driving through West Mersea, near his home, when he saw a factory unit for sale and stopped for a closer look. Tucked in behind a row of domestic houses was a single-storey factory of good size that would make a perfect facility to build cars. As a result DARE made a proposal to the Wary House Company: if their new customers would be prepared to wait up to a year for their cars, DARE would set up a manufacturing plant, remake the jigs and moulds to a modern high standard, thereby ensuring quality of product, and supply the cars on an exclusive manufacturing agreement. The deal was agreed, and from the end of 1994 DARE-built Ginetta G4s and G12s started leaving the West Mersea factory destined for Japan. Numbers rapidly increased and for a time in the mid-nineties DARE were making as many, if not more, cars than Ginetta themselves.

Immediately after the refinancing of the Ginetta business, the new Swedish director, Ingemur Engstrom, was keen to rework the G33 with a high Volvo content to the running gear. His idea was to instal the 2-litre turbo engine and M90 five-speed gearbox in place of the Rover, into a modified version of the G33 SC. The G33 SC itself had not progressed as a model: followings its 1992 Motor Show appearance, the prototype was returned to the factory and eventually broken up, because its chassis had been lengthened quickly to build the show car by cutting and shutting a standard G33 chassis. However, there were several hybrid G33s subsequently built for the Belgian market with the longer G33 SC chassis frames and SC bonnet and windscreen but still retaining the standard G33 rear bodywork; these special versions were mainly fitted with the 1800cc Ford Zetec engine. G33 production drifted on until 1995 before the last car was made; total production is thought to have been ninety-six cars across all variations.

GINETTA G33 EXPORTS

Belgium	7
France	2
Germany	14
Holland	2
Norway	1
Singapore	2
Sweden	7
Switzerland	4

THE GINETTA G34

Engstrom's vision for the next Ginetta took shape quite rapidly following positive talks with Volvo in Sweden. He was put in touch with a former director of Volvo, Bengt Lidnialm, now retired but still with good contacts in the business. Lid-

This G34 prototype featured right-hand steering. Note the large bonnet bulge to clear the Volvo engine. P. G. JOHANSSON

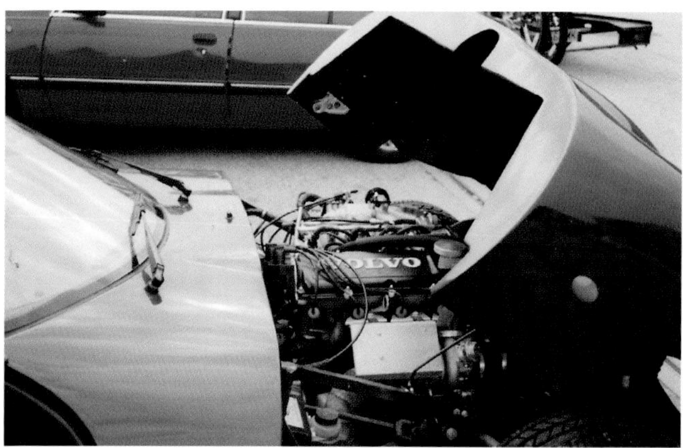

The Volvo engine dominates the G34 engine bay. MARK SMITH

nialm also had use of a former Volvo plant at Arvika, close to Gothenburg, and it was there, not Rotherham, that the new prototype started to take shape.

The chassis was the longer G33 SC variant, further lengthened by another 3in (75mm), with engine mountings and other minor changes to instal the Volvo unit, but at the rear the chassis was modified and the independent rear suspension omitted and replaced with the entire rear sub-frame and axle from a Volvo 960. The bodywork was basically once again the SC front and windscreen with the standard G33 rear end but the additional axle width necessitated the widening of the rear body. While this axle clearly increased the Volvo content of the car, it was questionable whether it was a good move in terms of the car's handling. The result was a rear track width significantly more than the front, and 'scoops' in the body sides behind the B posts were introduced to disguise the widened bodywork. The other visual change was the addition of a large square bulge on the bonnet top to give suitable clearance for the high Volvo engine.

The importance of the links with Volvo should not be underestimated: through Lidnialm and with the support of the Swedish government, Volvo offered unlimited resources in supporting the type approval process, emission testing

The G34 interior owed much to its predecessor, the G33. P. G. JOHANSSON

GINETTA G34 (1995–8)

Layout and chassis	Two-seater sports car with tubular steel chassis	*Suspension and Steering*	
		Front	Twin wishbone, coil spring with adjustable damper units, anti-roll bar
Engine		Rear	Rigid axle, trailing arms, coil spring with adjustable damper units
Type	Volvo B200FT		
Block material	Iron	Steering	Rack and pinion
Head material	Aluminium	Tyres	195/50 × 15in front, 205/50 × 15in rear
Cylinders	4		
Cooling	Water	Wheels	Cast alloy
Bore and stroke	88.9 × 80mm	Rim width	7J × 15in
Capacity	1986cc		
Valves	Single overhead camshaft, 2 valves per cylinder	*Brakes*	
		Type	Disc front and rear
Compression ratio	8.5:1	Brake size	11in (280mm) front, 10.5in (268mm) rear
Carburettor	Fuel injection and turbo		
Max. power (DIN)	165bhp (G34R 228bhp)		
Max. torque	169lb ft at 2,900rpm (G34R 250lb ft at 2,600rpm)	*Dimensions*	
		Track, front	54.5in (1,386mm)
Fuel capacity	9gal (41ltr)	Track, rear	58.5in (1,488mm)
		Wheelbase	90.5in (2,295mm)
Transmission		Overall length	156in (3,965mm)
Gearbox	Volvo 5-speed and reverse	Overall width	69.5in (1,760mm)
Clutch	Single dry plate	Overall height	41in (1,041mm) to top of hood
		Unladen weight	1,786lb (810kg)
Internal Gearbox Ratios			
First	3.54:1	*Performance*	
Second	2.05:1	Top speed	148mph (238km/h); G34R 162mph (261km/h)
Third	1.38:1		
Fourth	1:1	0–60mph	5.9sec (G34R 5.5sec)
Fifth	0.81:1		
Reverse	3:1		
Final drive	3.73:1 limited slip		

and test track time, all at no cost. Engstrom was keen to use the 2-litre turbo engine, the more powerful version developing 165bhp, as in several European countries there were tax breaks for cars under 2000cc and in the lightweight car it could still reach 60mph in 5.9 seconds.

Back in England, Martin Phaff was less convinced, and in time it became clear that Engstrom and Ginetta would part company. At the end of 1994, Engstrom duly left Ginetta and ceased to be a director, taking the right to use the G33 models with him along with an agreement that Ginetta would sell the new car in the UK. The car was known in Sweden as GIN 1. The reason for this strange name is that in Swedish the word for 'one' is written and pronounced 'etta', so anyone reading GIN 1 would say 'Ginetta'. It was an unusual arrangement but in Sweden it was all action, with a new company set up, GIN 1 CAR AB, and new managing director, Irigolf Elmhammar, while Engstrom remained as a technical director. Two prototypes were built and, on 12 June 1995, full European type approval was signed off in Stockholm.

The G34 lines echo the G33. Note the air vents on the rear wings disguising the greater width of the Volvo axle. P. G. JOHANSSON

The appearance of the G34 gives the effect of it being lower and wider than the G33 – to some extent this is an illusion. DAN LEKANDER

Only two G34s found their way to the UK. This was the second of the two, fitted with the more powerful Volvo engine. GINETTA OWNERS' CLUB

In the meantime a prototype had been sent to Ginetta in England for evaluation and despite reservations on the rear axle geometry and its effect on the ultimate handling, the car started to be marketed. The G34 was offered as a drive-away model for £23,998, equipped with leather trim, heated seats and alloy wheels with an emphasis on the car being made with 'Swedish engineering quality'.

Around six cars were made up to the end of 1995, one of which was sent to Ginetta in the UK, but getting ready for serious production seemed to take a long time and a factory move to Alvdalen in the north of Sweden took place before full production really began at the start of 1997. Martin Phaff's reservations on its ability to sell well in his home market were justified and, as far as we know, only two cars found buyers in the UK, despite new options including a 230bhp version of the Volvo engine. The cars made with the more powerful engine were dubbed G34R in Sweden. Curiously, once full production started in Sweden, the model was rebranded in the UK as the Ginetta G40, and a brochure was issued proclaiming the 'G40' as the model to celebrate forty years of Ginetta cars, an anniversary that was still actually a year away.

But sales weren't going well even in Sweden. The company had hoped to build at least fifty cars in the first year, but in fact fewer than half that number were sold, most going to buyers in Sweden although a few found their way to Switzerland and Norway. The end for the G34 (aka the G40) was imminent, and the last car was built in early 1998 before the factory doors closed for good, with just twenty-one cars built in total. Martin Phaff investigated the purchase of bankrupt stock but unsurprisingly did not pursue the opportunity.

THE GINETTA G27 RACE CARS

Martin Phaff always had good new ideas for publicizing the Ginetta name and boosting sales, and in 1995, following conversations with various racing experts, had the idea of a race series exclusively for the G27 model. His idea was for customers to buy a car made at the factory specifically to compete in the race series. All race cars would be identical.

The G27 was now in what has become known as Series 3 form. The original G27, as designed in the 1980s with independent rear suspension, was now known as the Series 1, while the Series 2 was the initial solid rear axle version of

The Series 3 G27 was the first without the T-bar windscreen support and featured indicators to the side of the radiator. AUTHOR

the G27. In an effort to make production of the cars quicker and more economical, the Series 3 appeared in 1994 from new moulds, the main body moulded in one piece rather than separate bolt-together parts. The front indicator lights moved down to a new position next to the radiator air intake and the head fairings seen on the G33 also now found their way onto G27s as well.

At the same time the windscreen was part of the main tub and no longer featured the built-in T-bar, the roll-over bar being deleted as well. The initial Series 3 cars still featured the Triumph-derived front suspension, but for the race series cars a number of specific changes were made.

The new race series cars featured the same Series 3-type bodies but were equipped with a full four-point roll-over safety cage. The suspension came in for some attention too: at the rear, the normal bolt-on bracketry to the axle casing was fully welded, while at the front the Triumph suspension was replaced with fabricated wishbones and Ford Sierra hub-carriers.

The prototype was tested at Mallory Park in late 1995 and, with the 1996 race season and new Ginetta Championship set to get under way in a few months, work to build the new identical cars was frantic at the Ginetta factory, which was now located in Amos Road, Sheffield.

Martin Phaff found plenty of enthusiasts keen to get involved with the race series and order cars. The factory was a hive of activity, and around fourteen cars were ready to contest the first races of the season, with more joining the grids as the year progressed.

In Series 3 form, the G27 featured much more of a one-piece bodyshell, making the cars easier to manufacture and easier to build. AUTHOR

G27 cars were now made at Sheffield in Yorkshire. Moving partially completed cars with a forklift was a long-established method at Ginetta; here employee and Ginetta expert Duncan Campbell moves the first G27 race car, still incomplete, in August 1995. DUNCAN CAMBELL

The G27 race car, now with full roll protection, undergoing its first test at Mallory Park. All race series cars would be identical to this. DUNCAN CAMPBELL

The first G27 race car outside the Sheffield factory. The roll-over structure was yet to be finalized. DUNCAN CAMPBELL

The championship continued over a number of seasons and another clever marketing and publicity idea was to invite celebrity drivers, including pop music and television stars, to take part in various rounds in the factory car. Certain rounds of the championship were run in conjunction with a celebrity challenge and parts of one race were broadcast on television showing motoring pundit Vicki Butler-Henderson racing a G27.

Martin Phaff's idea for the one-make G27 race series was a big success and started to turn Ginetta's fortunes. Here we see typical close racing in the championship. GINETTA OWNERS' CLUB

THE 1999 PENTEL G27 CHAMPIONSHIP RACE CAR SPECIFICATION

Body:	Two-seater open-top sports car in lightweight GRP. Gel-coat finish in red, yellow, green, blue or white	Differential:	Axle with a 3.89:1 ratio was installed and free (no limited slip)
Chassis:	Jig-formed tubular-steel chassis with full roll cage	Front suspension:	Double wishbone, coil spring adjustable dampers
Engine:	All fitted with identical sealed 1800cc Ford Zetec (high power) units giving 150bhp on twin Weber carburettors and mapped ignition; a wet sump was obligatory	Rear Suspension:	Twin trailing arms each side, Panhard rod, coil spring adjustable dampers.
		Brakes:	260mm-diameter front discs, 225mm rear drums
		Wheels and tyres:	7J × 15in alloy or steel wheels all fitted with 195/50 × 15in Bridgestone tyres
Gearbox:	Five-speed straight cut	Weight:	600kg

The first season, 1996, saw Nigel Reubens crowned as champion, an achievement he repeated the following season. The race series not only raised Ginetta's profile, but gave a boost to general road car sales as well. The policy was for the G27 to be subject to gradual improvement, and items such as the rear axle progressed from the Hillman Hunter item to a Morris Ital unit and then to a Ford Escort, while at the front the Sierra set-up pioneered on the race car became standard on the road version too. In addition, an independent rear suspension based on the Sierra set-up was also offered as an alternative.

More publicity came when a G27 was loaned to the BBC for the filming of a drama series, *All Quiet on the Preston Front*, first aired in 1994; this car featured regularly in the series, driven by a main character. Despite all this, the company did struggle for working capital and at least two new directors, Christopher Trippett and Angus Brown, joined the board during the mid-nineties, bringing with them much-needed finance, although they didn't stay with the company long.

On top of all this, the legislation governing the standards of motor vehicles was constantly changing and Ginetta needed to keep ahead of this. An important change was the introduction of single vehicle approval (SVA), which meant that cars could be approved for registering and use on the road without the need for type approval. This was good news in many ways for Ginetta, but with it came certain standards that Ginetta needed to incorporate into the G27 in order for the cars to pass these tests.

The G27 interior. AUTHOR

Series 4 G27 now with headlamps under plastic shields. GINETTA OWNERS' CLUB

As a result, a Series 4 G27 was introduced in January 1998, which was distinguished by the fact it no longer featured the pop-up headlamps; these were replaced by conventional lamps usually mounted behind plastic covers, and the tail section of the car now featured a small air spoiler on its rear extremity. Over time, the main engines fitted to the G27 by kit builders had continued to be the Ford 1600 X-flow and 1600 or 2000cc Pinto units, but increasingly it was the Ford Zetec, usually in 1800 or 2000cc form, that proved the engine of choice, although the Ford Cosworth and 2-litre Vauxhall Astra engines also appeared occasionally in finished cars.

Ginetta were now quoting a guide price of around £6,500 to build a G27 kit from second-hand refurbished parts and in the region of £10,980 for a factory-built example to a fairly basic specification; but the times were changing. The days of people buying kits to use on the road as everyday cars were passing, as modern mass-produced cars became ever more sophisticated. This highlighted the basic nature of cars like the G27, but for fun they were still a winner every time, and buyers increasingly were building their cars for occasional weekend use or for track days. This made Martin Phaff consider a change of direction for the next new Ginetta. The G27 continued in production until 2001, by which time approximately 200 cars had been built over a sixteen-year period. In February 2005 the jigs and moulds for the G27 were sold to Kent-based GKD Sports Cars Ltd, who reworked them and produced a new model known as the GKD Evolution based on the G27.

The G27 engine bay could house a variety of engines – in this case the Ford 1600 X-flow. AUTHOR

Mark Walkett drives the DARE G4 to another victory in the H.R. Owen Championship. DARE UK

The number of Ginettas in Japan quickly expanded. Here is a grid full of G4 and G12 cars at the Ebisu Circuit, with visiting Mark Walklett on pole position. DARE UK

Meanwhile DARE in Essex were continuing to build G4 and G12 models for the Japanese market and Mark Walklett had picked up his racing again, competing very successfully in a DARE-built G4 in the 750 Motor Club Roadsports Championship – at one point he won overall six times in succession.

By now DARE were engaged in building their own cars – the DARE DZ and TG models – but their core work was still G4 production. The Japanese market had slowed considerably by 1998 and, in agreement with rights owner Tamotsu Maeda, they began offering cars on the home market as well. A regular flow of customers were found, mainly for the G4, predominantly for use as road cars; the extensive development undertaken by DARE ensured cars were consistently

Not a usual sight at the pumps – a road-going DARE G12. DARE UK

built to a high standard and they were also engineered to meet the requirements of SVA.

This meant that DARE offered turn-key G4s with a variety of engines for those that could afford the experience. On-the-road prices ranged from £25,407 for a 1700cc X-flow-engined car to £28,580 for a Zetec 1800-powered car. G12s were also available on the home market, but not officially for road use, at £43,032, which included the Cosworth YAC engine also specified for Japanese export sales. The G4 and G12 were also available less engine and gearbox for £15,980 and £25,850 respectively.

Trevers Walklett became ill in 1999 but his work ethic never slowed and he was working hard at DARE only weeks before his death in early 2000. His skills and determination over more than five decades would be sorely missed, and his contribution to the Ginetta marque had been incalculable.

A further development to the G4 – to answer critics who said the cockpit was too small – was a long-wheelbase version, 3in (75mm) longer, and a new hardtop, which detached above the windscreen, leaving a curved screen in place; previously, of course, the G4 hardtop had included the windscreen as part of the one-piece moulding.

Revisions to the windscreen were made to enable a hard and soft top to be fitted to the G4. DARE UK

With the hardtop fitted, the joint above the screen can be clearly seen. DARE UK

DARE have continued to build G4 and G12 models to the present day. The business is still run by Ivor and Mark Walklett, who have been joined by Ivor's son Tom, now also a driving force in the business. Cars are still built to order although, due to legislation in different markets, the majority of production tends to be for competition machines.

Martin Phaff at Ginetta had come up with another new model, which was officially launched at the Birmingham International Motor Show in 2000. As mentioned above, it followed a new path, designed to meet the needs of customers who were looking for a very basic high-performance car, suitable for weekend fun and track days.

The G20: a basic car designed for pure fun. GINETTA CARS

THE GINETTA G20

Named the G20, it flew in the face of tradition by using a previously allocated G number, although it's not clear why. The beauty of the G20 was its simplicity. The body was made from just two basic mouldings – the bonnet and the main shell, which also incorporated much of the interior, including the dashboard; the instruments were centrally mounted, meaning cars could be sold either for left- or right-hand drive configuration. No doors or bootlid were fitted: only a small curved Perspex windscreen deflected the breeze. The chassis, derived from the G27, featured sheet steel panels to form the footwells and an alloy-clad transmission tunnel; the frame was made higher at the sides, offering good side

The G20 interior was simple and could be fitted with either left- or right-hand steering. GINETTA OWNERS' CLUB

The G20 makes a fun road car. AUTHOR

BELOW: **A G20 championship race car outside the Sheffield factory displaying its chassis and Zetec engine and strong roll-over protection.** DUNCAN CAMPBELL

GINETTA G20 (2000–09)

Layout and chassis	Two-seater sports car with space-frame chassis	*Suspension and Steering*	
		Front	Twin wishbone, coil spring damper units, anti-roll bar
Engine		Rear	Twin wishbone, coil spring damper units
Type	Ford	Steering	Rack and pinion
Block material	Cast iron	Tyres	195/50 × 15in
Head material	Aluminium	Wheels	Cast alloy
Cylinders	4	Rim width	6J × 15in
Cooling	Water		
Bore and stroke	80.6 × 88mm	*Brakes*	
Capacity	1796cc	Type	Disc front and drum rear
Valves	Twin overhead cam, 4 valves per cylinder	Brake size	9in (225mm) front, 10in (250mm) rear
Compression ratio	10:1		
Carburettor	Fuel injection	*Dimensions*	
Max. power (DIN)	138bhp	Track, front	50.75in (1,289mm)
Max. torque	135lb ft at 4,800rpm	Track, rear	51in (1,295mm)
Fuel capacity	8.9gal (39ltr)	Wheelbase	84in (2,134mm)
		Overall length	145in (3,690mm)
Transmission		Overall width	60in (1,524mm)
Gearbox	Ford 5-speed and reverse	Overall height	n/a
Clutch	Diaphragm SLP	Unladen weight	1,455lb (660kg)
Internal Gearbox Ratios		*Performance*	
First	3.65:1	Top speed	126mph (203km/h)
Second	1.97:1	0–60mph	6.4sec
Third	1.37:1		
Fourth	1:1		
Fifth	0.82:1		
Reverse	3.66:1		
Final drive	3.89:1		

impact protection, and an integral roll-over bar was also included. The chassis featured twin wishbone front suspension and alloy hub-carriers, while the rear suspension was all independent and Ford-derived.

The genius of the G20 lay in the fact that, compared to the G27, for example, it was very inexpensive to make, which meant that the product could be offered at a very competitive price but still make a very good profit. In fact, it was stated that a kit could be built using second-hand parts for as little as £5,500, while a new car fully built and fitted with a new 1800cc Ford Zetec engine could be had for £12,999.

G20 sales took off quite well and, as well as road cars, the company quickly developed a racing version complete with a full roll cage to protect the driver, and lightweight panels without headlamps. The G27 Challenge race series was replaced by a new G20 Cup, which started in 2002 running alongside the G27s; the latter were gradually phased out, leaving a G20-only series. Like the G27 before them, all the cars were identical. The G20s had 1800cc Ford Zetec engines that ran on fuel injection and Pectel engine control units (ECU); the five-speed gearbox was matched to a 3.62:1 limited slip differential; everything was sealed and all cars ran on 7J × 15in Vectar alloy wheels with Dunlop R195/55/15 tyres. The whole specification was designed to enable competitive racing on a relatively low budget and it seemed to work.

The following year, 2003, Martin Phaff came up with yet another idea that was groundbreaking in racing: he offered young competitors the chance to race on circuits, wheel to wheel, in their own championship. Drivers had to be under seventeen to compete but at least fourteen. It was a master stroke, and there was no shortage of budding teenage drivers willing to take up the challenge, many indulged by wealthy parents. This generated more new car sales, as the cars raced in what became known as Ginetta Juniors were different to the G20 Cup cars in that they were fitted with a hardtop. It must be said that the G20 Junior cars were rather crude in that the bodies were pure G20 with a moulded top incorporating a conventional windscreen and rear window, but the simple Perspex glazed door mouldings were hinged from the windscreen pillars. It was important, of course, to ensure the young and inexperienced drivers were completely safe while they raced, hence the closed bodywork, but additionally the engines were downgraded to a 1400cc version of the Ford Zetec. At least one G20 coupé road car was built, though, and fitted with a Ford 2.5-litre Duratec engine; with custom leather interior, it was quite a car.

The G20 Junior Championship was another great success and this and the G20 Cup continued for a number of seasons. Sales of G20 road cars, Cup cars and Junior cars kept the company busy through the next few years until another unexpected event occurred.

Martin Phaff had the brilliant idea of a race series for fourteen- to sixteen-year-olds: the G20 Junior race series was a huge success. Here they queue up for scrutineering at Brands Hatch. Note the hardtops and crude doors. AUTHOR

CHAPTER ELEVEN

THE LNT GROUP TAKES THE REINS

In 2004 TVR Cars made headlines when its long-standing owner, Peter Wheeler, sold the company to a young Russian, Nikolay Smolensky. Behind the scenes there had been at least one other party interested in the company: a self-made multi-millionaire Yorkshire businessman, Lawrence Tomlinson, who shrewdly stepped aside when Smolensky allegedly offered £15 million for TVR.

But Tomlinson wasn't done with the idea of owning a sports car manufacturing concern. He had first experienced motor racing by competing in the G27 Challenge for a

This is the current state-of-the-art car manufacturing facility at Garforth, Leeds – Ginetta has come a long way. GINETTA CARS

The first all-new Ginetta following the LNT takeover, the G50 was available as both a road car and a race car; most were made for the latter purpose. GINETTA OWNERS' CLUB

season and totally enjoyed the experience. As a result, he tried his hand at other categories of the sport, and cars and racing quickly became an important part of his life. In the wake of his unsuccessful attempt to buy TVR, he approached Martin Phaff to buy Ginetta, and the business formally changed hands in December 2005.

Having grown a hugely successful care home business, Tomlinson later established the LNT Group as part of his rise in the world of business and in due course added a racing team to the portfolio. In 2006 LNT entered a Panoz Esperante GTLM into the GT2 category at the Le Mans 24 Hours race, driven by Lawrence Tomlinson him-self and co-driven by Tom Kimber-Smith and Richard Dean. It won, an achievement of which Tomlinson is justifiably very proud.

Tomlinson saw in Ginetta the perfect opportunity to take a marque with a rich racing heritage and a back catalogue second only to Lotus and grow it once again to produce hundreds of cars a year. The purchase allowed for Martin Phaff to stay on for three years but Tomlinson had every intention of transforming Ginetta into a modern, highly efficient business fit for the twenty-first century. Work began on a new headquarters building for the LNT Group at Garforth, on the outskirts of Leeds, almost immediately, and at its heart is a large car assembly area and stores fit for the very best in specialist car manufacture.

The new building was opened in December 2007 by Formula 1 world champion Damon Hill. Forty-three years earlier, Hill's father, Graham, had briefly tested Chris Webb's G4 for *Practical Motorist* magazine, and that actual car was by now part of Lawrence Tomlinson's personal collection of historic Ginettas. Furthermore, Damon Hill's son Josh was successfully racing in the Ginetta Juniors challenge at the time, so it would be hard to think of a more fitting personality to formally open the next chapter in the Ginetta story. Among the invited guests that day was Ivor Walklett, the man who started it all fifty years earlier, no doubt proud that Ginetta was being given the profile and investment it so richly deserved.

Since Lawrence Tomlinson took over Ginetta, new models have come thick and fast. First was the G50, a 3.5-litre V6-engined racer that was available as a road car for a time. A one-off electric version was also built and for publicity and charity it became the first sports car and electric car to be driven from England to France through the service tunnels of the Channel Tunnel, its driver none other than the great two- and four-wheel world champion, the late John Surtees.

Then came the G40, a modern replacement for the G20, again a racer but also available for road use. The purchase of the rights to a highly regarded sports car called the Farbio saw the model reworked and rebranded as the Ginetta G60, the first Ginetta supercar.

In motor racing Ginetta have continued to make their mark. The original Juniors Challenge has continued, now with the G40, and a 'staircase' from there has been developed where drivers can progress up though different Ginetta classes. In 2010, a Ginetta Zytec, driven by Nigel Mansell and his sons Greg and Leo, raced at Le Mans, and the company is planning a comeback in 2018 with a brand new LMP 1 car, which at the time of writing is under detailed development. Other pure racing machines developed by Ginetta include the G55 and G57.

There is no doubt the Ginetta name, in racing at least, is at a level never seen before and is being steered by the LNT Group to even greater heights. The older models are still just as popular on the road and track. During the Walklett era, the factory catered for spares and repairs; since then, help has been available from a variety of sources. In Lancashire, Ginpart, run by David Holroyd, provided high-quality restorations and spares for a number of years. In Suffolk, Spadge Hopkins set up Cottage Classics, later known as Ginetta Heritage, providing a complete range of services, but this has also now ceased trading. DARE UK provide a comprehensive service for the G4 and G12 models and can help with some parts and services for other models, while Road and Track, based in Newark, Nottinghamshire, is run by Ian Higgins, who has many years' experience in racing Ginettas and their preparation.

The G40 was announced in 2010, a dual-purpose machine for road and racing, including a revised Junior race series. AUTHOR

Billed as one of the fastest track day machines on the market, the G57, with 6.3-litre Chevrolet V8 power, is something special. CLIVE BERRY

The G60 was Ginetta's first step into the world of super cars. GINETTA CARS

Ginetta builds predominantly racing cars today. This is the highly successful G55. CLIVE BERRY

In December 2007, former Formula 1 world champion driver Damon Hill opened the new LNT headquarters near Leeds. Hill (on the left) stands next to three men who between them had shaped Ginetta's destiny for fifty years: Lawrence Tomlinson, Martin Phaff and Ivor Walklett. Now, ten years later, Tomlinson continues to push the Ginetta name to even greater heights. AUTHOR

Since Ginetta passed into the hands of LNT they openly admit to not having the knowledge or capacity to carry out work on the older models. However, following concerns expressed by the Ginetta Owners' Club over several years, in 2016 Lawrence Tomlinson generously passed all available moulds to the club for safe keeping and to ensure body panels can be supplied for repairs or replacement should the need arise for owners of older cars.

Since 1958, Ginetta cars have been a continuous and important part of the UK specialist car industry, certainly not the largest or most high-profile specialist car maker, but an immensely influential one that has always punched well above its weight. During the sixty years since the first production Ginetta appeared it has seen literally hundreds of car makers come and go, some much larger than Ginetta has ever been, and now it sits with just a few – most notably Morgan and Lotus – that maintain the tradition of building cars for the enthusiast to enjoy which stand out from the crowd and offer true performance motoring, whether it be on road or track, at an affordable price.

Long may the Ginetta marque continue to thrive.

INDEX